Laboratory Manual for

Introductory Soils

Tenth Edition

Ray R. Weil

Professor of Soil Science
Department of Environmental Science and Technology
University of Maryland
College Park, Md.

Kendall Hunt
publishing company

Front cover: Author's photo of a tropical Alfisol in the Uluguru mountains of Tanzania showing the interface of soil horizons and above and below ground worlds.

Back cover: Author's photo of a shovelful of topsoil in a farm field in Maryland managed with no-tillage and multi-species cover crops.

All photos and illustrations within this manual by Ray Weil, unless otherwise noted.

Kendall Hunt
publishing company

www.kendallhunt.com
Send all inquiries to:
4050 Westmark Drive
Dubuque, IA 52004-1840

Table of Contents

Acknowledgments   *iv*

Preface   *v*

About the Author   *vi*

General Objectives of this Study of Soil Science   *vii*

Soil Science Lab Safety Guidelines   *viii*

Suggested Schedule of Laboratory Exercises   *ix*

Exercises

1   Chemical Weathering of Plant Nutrients in Rocks and Minerals   1

2   Parent Materials for Soils: Rock and Minerals   5

3   Some Field Skills: Texture "By Feel" and Color by Munsell Charts   25

4   Using a Pit to Study the Soil Profile   35

5   Use of Soil Survey Information in Land Planning   47

6   Getting to Know a Catena in the Field   61

7   Soil Texture: Mechanical Analysis of Particle Size   69

8   Soil Density, Porosity and Structural Stability   81

9   Investigating Capillary Rise   89

10   Effect of Soil Composition on Percolation and Retention of Water   99

11   Using a Tensiometer to Monitor Soil Moisture Status   107

12   Effect of Cations on Flocculation   119

13   Cation Exchange Properties of Soil   125

14   Soil Acidity and Alkalinity (pH)   137

15   Microbial Activity Related to Decomposition and Nitrogen Transformation   145

16   Buried Slide for Observation of Soil Microorganisms   157

17   Determination of Soil Organic Matter Content   163

18   Active Fraction Carbon and Soil Health   173

19   Movement of Phosphorus and Nitrogen in the Soil   181

20   Test for Plant-Available Soil Phosphorus   187

21   Simulated Wetland Soil Mesocosms (Winogradsky Columns)   193

Appendices

A   Obtaining a Representative Soil Sample for Analysis   205

B   Water Needed to Bring Soil to 60% Saturation for Aerobic Incubation   207

C   Water Holding Capacity Based on Soil Texture   209

D   Determination of Soil Moisture Content   211

E   Using Moles and Moles of Change   213

F   Using a Spectrophotometer   215

G   Soil Characterization Project   217

Acknowledgments

In large measure my inspiration for writing this manual began with my experience as a graduate teaching assistant under the late Professor Wybe Kroontje at Virginia Tech. He instilled in everyone around him a tremendous enthusiasm for the teaching of soil science. A large debt of gratitude is also owed to my graduate teaching assistants at the University of Maryland for their dedication to giving our students a quality lab experience and for their many practical suggestions for improving the lab manual. The continued evolution of this lab manual has greatly benefited by the many creative ideas and enthusiastic responses of thousands of students in ENST 200, my introductory course in soil science. Exercise 21 on wetland soil mesocosms was developed with the assistance of University of Maryland soils lecturer, Eni Baballari. Finally, since the Covid-19 pandemic forced students to try to get a soil science lab experience online and at home for several semesters, students and instructors, alike, have gained a renewed appreciation for the great value of in-person, hands-on experiences in learning about soils.

--R. Weil

Preface

The exercises in this manual are designed to encourage the quantitative investigation of soil properties, as well as to give you a "feel" for what soils are and how they behave. You will have opportunities to see, touch and manipulate soil in the lab and in the field. This should help you develop a more in-depth understanding of the soil system than could be conveyed by lectures and readings alone.

Some of these exercises are really demonstrations of important soil science concepts. Experimental conditions are set up to study the effect of various factors on certain soil properties. It is hoped that "seeing is believing" and that these exercises will reinforce principles learned in lecture.

In a number of the exercises, particular soil properties are investigated and quantified using a variety of physical and chemical techniques. One advantage of performing these analyses yourself is that the process should lead you to a better appreciation of the meanings and limitations of data from similar analyses discussed in lectures and textbooks.

A unifying thread throughout the lab manual is the repeated use of your own soil which you should sample carefully and thoughtfully at the start of the course. By the end of the course you will have built up a substantial body of information about the soil you sampled. The lab work will therefore be most meaningful to you if you make an effort in the beginning to obtain your soil sample from a place with which you interact and in which you have a real interest – e.g. your home garden, your uncle's farm, your research site, or your parent's back yard. Wherever it's from, be sure that you sample a *natural, mineral soil* – not an artificial soil mix.

Another thing you can do to help your lab experience have meaning is to pay careful attention to the "Comments" column that is adjacent to the "Procedures" in each exercise. This format is intended to explain the "why" of what you are doing, as you are doing it. In their haste to complete a lab activity, students often fall into the trap of carrying out the procedural steps in cookbook fashion without stopping to consider *why* they are doing each step and *what it means.* You will be amazed at how much more meaningful each exercise can become if you constantly ask yourself (or better, yet, ask your lab partner) *why am I doing this step* and *what does it mean?*

In addition to providing "hands on" lessons in important soil science concepts, many of the techniques and approaches employed throughout these exercises will introduce you to some of the basics of scientific instrumentation and the scientific method of investigation. The skills you will learn include:

- *Acquisition and use of online soil survey information*
- *Performance of chemical titrations*
- *Use and calibration of electronic measuring instruments, e.g. pH meter and spectrophotometer.*
- *Creation and use of standard curves*
- *Ability to estimate soil texture by "feel"*
- *Facility with general laboratory procedures*
- *Sharing and interpreting data with colleagues and classmates*
- *Presentation of analytical results in graphic and tabular form*
- *Recognition and description of soil properties in the field*

In summary, to get your money's worth out of soil science lab, remember to read ahead, carry out procedures with care and precision, read and think about the comments accompanying each step, and always try to relate what you are doing to soil processes that take place in the real world.

Enjoy!

About the Author

 Ray Weil is Professor of Soil Science at the University of Maryland, College Park and Adjunct Senior Research Scholar, Earth Institute at Columbia University, New York. Before coming to Maryland, he earned a BS at Michigan State University, served in Ethiopia as a US Peace Corps Volunteer, earned a MS degree at Purdue University, managed a 500-acre organic farm in North Carolina and earned a Ph.D. in Soil Science at Virginia Tech. He is a leader in researching and promoting the adoption of sustainable agricultural systems in both industrial and developing countries. His research focuses on organic matter management for enhanced soil quality and nutrient cycling for water quality and sustainability. Ray teaches undergraduate and graduate courses, including the Fundamentals of Soil Science course for which this Lab Manual was developed.

In addition to numerous scientific papers, Ray's books include *Soil Organic Matter in Sustainable Agriculture*, which he co-edited with Fred Magdoff, and the most widely used textbook in soil science, *The Nature and Properties of Soils,* which he has authored or coauthored 1995. He is a Fellow of both the Soil Science Society of America and the American Society of Agronomy and twice been awarded a Fulbright Fellowship to support his work in developing countries.

One hallmark of his professional work is the integration of his teaching and research programs so that each one benefits from the other. His research program combines three interrelated areas: 1) Organic Matter Management for Soil Quality; 2) Sustainable Cropping Systems; and 3) Soil Management for Improved Nutrient Cycling and Water Quality. His soil quality program has achieved international recognition for its innovative efforts to develop a soil quality index and methods for the rapid, routine assessment of soil quality indicators, including aggregation, soil microbial biomass and a fraction of soil organic carbon called POXC (permanganate oxidizable carbon). The latter is a leading soil health indicator used by scientists around the word. His research probes fundamental relationships between soil organic matter management and soil ecological functions. His research on nutrient cycling in agroecosystems has focused on nitrogen, phosphorus and sulfur. In addition to studying the interaction between crop management and soil quality, Weil has worked to develop new soil management practices, especially new cover crop systems, with the potential to improve profitability and reduce environmental impacts while helping to mitigate and adapt to climate change.

Ray lives with his wife, Trish, in Hyattsville, Maryland. He enjoys gardening, mountain climbing, backpacking, and commuting by bicycle from his home to the University of Maryland in nearby College Park.

General Objectives of this Study of Soil Science

The soil is the perfect system to study as an introduction to the natural sciences. It is in the soil that the worlds of water, rock and living things all come together. The study of soil science encompasses and integrates many basic concepts and principles from the fields of physics, chemistry, geology and biology. For example, such phenomena as the physics of capillary water movement, the chemical equilibrium of cation exchange and the growth responses of soil microorganisms are fundamental to an understanding of what the soil is and how it works.

The laboratory component of the course provides you the opportunity to carry out scientific observations using tools as simple as your eyes and fingers and as sophisticated as pH meters and spectrophotometers. Some skill in laboratory technique will be developed and your powers of observations and reasoning will be sharpened in relating physical and chemical measurements to the properties and function of a complex natural system.

Ideally, the laboratory exercises in this manual will be carried out concurrently with a broader study of soil science theory and principles from lectures, textbook readings, etc. Although each exercise is introduced with enough background information to make it meaningful, you will generally derive maximum benefit from the hands-on experiments if you have studied the basic theoretical aspects of the phenomenon beforehand.

The study of soils is far more than merely the opportunity to integrate a variety of natural science concepts. Soils play a central role in the ecology of natural and managed systems, so knowledge of soils has a wide range of practical applications, many of which are discussed in this course. Used as part of a comprehensive survey of soil science, this manual can enhance your professional capabilities in such diverse fields as horticulture, agronomy, forestry, architecture, resource planning, geology, botany, and real-estate.

A basic knowledge of soil is invaluable in understanding and dealing effectively with such current issues as climate change, world food production, ecosystem pollution, community development, farmland and recreational land management and preservation, and land use planning in general. Of course, any enterprise involving the production of plants, whether these are native trees and shrubs, crops, forages, or ornamentals, requires a working knowledge of the soil system. Your personal life can be enriched in ways such as more knowledgeable home gardening and landscaping, buying a home without a wet basement, sagging foundation, or failing septic system, and a deeper appreciation of the diversity and beauty in natural environments as you travel around the country and the world.

Soil Science Lab Safety Guidelines

1. **Wait for the instructor** to arrive before beginning a lab.
2. Tie back long hair and neckties. Avoid wearing long dangly jewelry/clothes on lab days.
3. Do **not** bring food or drink to the lab.
4. Report any injury or problem to instructor immediately.
5. Be sure you know the location of the **safety shower, first aid kit, chemical spill kit, sharps disposal box** and **fire extinguisher.**
6. Wash and wipe lab bench with sponge before leaving. Be sure gas and water are off.
7. Carefully clean up broken glass or chemical spills. DISCARD BROKEN GLASS IN SHARPS DISPOSAL BOX. ASK INSTRUCTOR HOW TO CLEAN A CHEMICAL SPILL.
8. Read the label *twice* before using any chemical in a bottle.
9. Never contaminate the contents of a bottle by putting reagents back in it.
10. Never throw solid waste in sink. When washing soil from containers use a bucket to catch muddy water. Soil particles settle to the bottom of the bucket thereby avoiding clogged drains.
11. In some labs we will create waste which must be disposed of carefully. Please follow directions to avoid polluting our environment!
12. Never use flammable liquids (i.e. alcohol) near a flame.
13. When heating a test tube, never point the mouth of the tube toward yourself or anyone else. Some chemicals eject violently when they start to boil.
14. Never pick up hot objects with your hands. After heating glassware or crucibles place the item on a wire gauze to cool.
15. To dilute acid, pour acid slowly into the water with stirring. Never add water to a concentrated acid.
16. Any chemical spilled on the skin should be washed off immediately and the area held under running water for several minutes. NOTIFY INSTRUCTOR IMMEDIATELY.
17. Never taste any chemical.
18. Never inhale gaseous fumes. If you are to determine the odor of a gas, gently fan a small amount of the vapor toward your nose with your hand.
19. If any chemical gets into your eyes, flush with water for at least 15 minutes. TELL YOUR INSTRUCTOR IMMEDIATELY.
20. In case of FIRE, notify instructor immediately. TURN OFF HEAT SOURCE, if you can.
21. If clothing catches fire, use a fire blanket or safety shower.
22. Mercury vapor is invisible but toxic. A broken thermometer that releases mercury should be reported immediately to instructor.
23. In case of skin burn, notify instructor. Minor skin burns should be immediately placed under cold running tap water and left there for 5-10 minutes
24. ALWAYS WEAR PROTECTIVE GLOVES AND GOGGLES WHEN ASKED TO DO SO.
25. DO NOT FORCE a glass tube through a stopper, the glass may break and stab you.
26. Never place chemicals directly on a balance pan. Use a beaker, or weighing paper.
27. Never pipette by mouth; use a pipetting device instead.

FOLLOW THESE GUIDELINES AND ENJOY A SAFE PRODUCTIVE LAB!

Suggested Schedule of Laboratory Exercises
For 15 Three Hour Lab Periods

WEEK	EXERCISE #	EXERCISE TITLE
1	1	Chemical Weathering of Plant Nutrients in Rocks and Minerals
		and
	2	Parent Materials For Soils: Rock and Minerals
2	3	Some Field Skills: Texture "By Feel" and Color by Munsell Charts
3	4	Using a Pit to Study the Soil Profile
4	5	Use of Soil Survey Information in Land Planning
		and
	21	Simulated Wetland Soil Mesocosms (Winogradsky Columns) - set up
5	7	Soil Texture: Mechanical Analysis of Particle Size
6	8	Soil Density, Porosity and Structural Stability
7	6	Getting to Know a Catena in the Field
8	10	Effect of Soil Composition on Percolation and Retention of Water
		and
	9	Investigating Capillary Rise
9	12	Effect of Cations on Flocculation
	16	Buried Slide for Observation of Soil Microorganisms (set up)
10	13	Cation Exchange Properties of Soil
		and
	15	Microbial Activity Related to Decomposition and Nitrogen Transformation (set up)
11	14	Soil Acidity and Alkalinity (pH)
12	16	Buried Slide for Observation of Soil Microorganisms
		and
	21	Simulated Wetland Soil Mesocosms (Winogradsky Columns) - takedown
13	15	Microbial Activity Related to Decomposition and Nitrogen Transformation (determine CO_2 and nitrate produced)
14	17	Determination of Soil Organic Matter Content (one method)
		or
	18	Active Carbon and Soil Health
15	19	Behavior of Phosphorus and Nitrogen in the Soil
		or
	20	Test for Plant-Available Phosphorus in Soil

Exercise 1

Chemical Weathering of Plant Nutrients in Rocks and Minerals

OBJECTIVES

After completing this exercise, you should be able to . . .

1. Qualitatively describe the effects of particle size, temperature, and acidity on the rate of mineral weathering.
2. Relate the experimental conditions used to conditions found in nature during mineral weathering.
3. Explain how the rate of "weathering" was determined in this exercise.

INTRODUCTION

The fertility of a soil is based on its ability to supply plant nutrients in the form of dissolved ions of Ca, Mg, K, P, Fe, etc. which the plant can take up and assimilate. Under natural conditions these ions are released into solution by the gradual decomposition of the crystal structures of minerals in the soil. Calcium, for example, is not available for plant uptake so long as it remains a part of calcite, dolomite, feldspar, or other mineral structures. However, when these minerals break down by hydrolysis, carbonation, or other weathering processes, free Ca^{2+} ions are released into solution and can be used by plants. In this exercise we will demonstrate the release of Ca^{2+} from dolomitic rock in a model of mineral weathering. We will examine the influence of 1) particle size (which is a function of *physical weathering*), 2) temperature (a function of *climate*) and 3) acidity of the solution (a function of vegetation, climate, and parent material of soils). Compared to ambient weathering, the conditions imposed in the lab will be rather extreme in order to allow the reactions to take place in minutes rather than months and years.

MATERIALS

- dolomitic limestone gravel (3-6 mm diam.)*
- fine limestone powder (passes 80 mesh sieve)*
- 0.005 M solution of HCl
- CO_2-free distilled water (CO_2 removed under vacuum and kept out using an ascarite trap on the carboy)
- 4 filter funnels, filter papers and a rack
- 1 M NH₄OH solution in dropper bottle
- Saturated ammonium oxalate solution in dropper bottle

- 1 glass stirring rod
- 1 burner
- 1 test tube rack
- 4 - 250 ml beakers
- 1 ring stand with asbestos pad
- 5 test tubes

---

* Ca-Feldspar (anorthite) can be substituted for limestone. In either case the gravel should be washed clean of surface powder before using. The fine powder should be ground from the gravel so it will have the same make-up.

1

PROCEDURE	COMMENTS

1. Obtain 4 clean 250 ml beakers. Rinse with distilled water. Label them A, B, C and D, respectively. Add 1 g of limestone gravel to beakers A and C. Add 1 g of limestone powder to beakers B and D.

Tap water is not suitable. It comes from groundwater or streams that likely contain relatively large amounts of Ca^{2+} due to the same processes we are demonstrating in this exercise. See Figure 1.1 for set up.

2. To beakers A, B and C add 100 ml of 0.005 M HCl, each. Stir A and B occasionally for 20 minutes.

Beakers A and B differ with respect to the particle size of the limestone they contain. See Figure 1.1.

3. To beaker D, add 100 ml of distilled water. Stir the contents of beaker D occasionally for 20 minutes.

Beakers B and D differ with respect to the acidity of the solution. See Figure 1.1.

4. Place beaker C on the ring stand, light the burner and boil gently for 20 minutes.

Beakers A and C differ with respect to temperature. See Figure 1.1.

5. Set up 4 filter funnels fitted with filter paper. After the 20-minute period filter the solutions in beakers A-D and catch the filtrate in *clean* test tubes labeled A-D, respectively. When test tubes are ¼ full discard the remaining solution. Be sure that each tube has an equal volume of filtrate in it (estimate by "eye").

Allow Beaker C to cool; filter it last.
Allow suspensions to settle before filtering.

6. To a fifth test tube labeled E, add distilled water to ¼ full.

This will serve as a control or check on the "background" level of Ca^{2+}.

7. To each test tube, add 5 drops of 1 M NH₄OH solution and then 5 drops of saturated ammonium oxalate and swirl. Compare the amounts of white precipitate formed.

The ammonium oxalate reacts with the Ca^{2+} to form a white precipitate of calcium oxalate. The amount of Ca^{2+} present can be estimated by the amount of precipitate formed. The Ca^{2+} participating in this reaction is that which has been "weathered" from the limestone.

8. Rank tubes A-E according to the relative amount of precipitate formed. This may be done by swirling the tubes and then holding them in a vertical position against the printed lines in Table 1.1, noting the relative visibility of the lines through each suspension. Record results in Table 1.1.

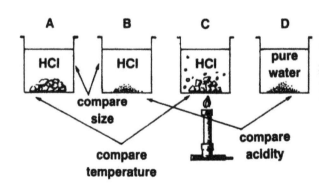

Figure 1. 1 Diagram of experimental set up.

Date _____   Name _____

Section _____   I.D. No. _____

Exercise 1

FACTORS AFFECTING THE RELEASE OF PLANT NUTRIENTS BY MINERAL WEATHERING

Table 1.1   Conditions Affecting Calcium Release from Minerals.

Tube Label	Experimental Conditions: particle size, temperature, and acidity	Relative amount of Ca^{2+} released (On a scale of 1=low to 5=high)	Appearance of suspension (Relative cloudiness)
A			
B			
C			
D			
E			

Answer these questions to help in understanding what you have observed.

1. To prepare for this exercise, your instructor ground pieces of limestone into a fine powder. Give an example of natural forces or agents that would result in this same type of weathering.

    _____

    _____

    _____

2. In this exercise, you used a burner to heat the limestone in a beaker. What environmental or geographic condition was this meant to simulate?

    _____

    _____

3. By comparing the calcium in the filtrate from beakers B and D, you observed the effect that even a very dilute acid solution has on how fast limestone dissolves. What are three sources of acidity that help limestone dissolve and form soils in nature?

_____

_____

_____

4. **BONUS QUESTION:** If the CO_2 had been boiled out of the distilled water used in this exercise, would the difference between tubes B and D have been greater or less? Explain.

_____

_____

_____

_____

_____

Summarize three conclusions you can draw from the results of this exercise:

1. _____

2. _____

3. _____

Exercise 2
Parent Materials for Soils: Rock and Minerals

OBJECTIVES

After completing this week's lab, you should be able to...

1. Differentiate between a "rock" and a "mineral".
2. Recognize the minerals listed in Table 2.6.
3. Use the properties of crystal form, streak, color, cleavage, fracture, hardness and specific gravity to identify mineral specimens.
4. Describe the variety and appearance of minerals as they occur in soil material.
5. Name, describe and recognize the 3 types of rocks and 4 examples of each type (listed in Table 2.7)
6. Associate the minerals in Table 2.6 with the essential plant nutrients they contain.
7. Give three examples of the influence of parent materials on soil properties and development as seen in soil monoliths.

INTRODUCTION

It has been said that soil is merely a rock on its way to the sea. Because soil is rock transformed, the study of rocks is a necessary interface between geology and soil science. Certain soil properties, especially texture and natural fertility, are more or less inherited from properties of the rocks from which the soil formed. The nature of the rock is, in turn, largely influenced by the minerals of which it is composed.

Aside from developing an appreciation of the fascinating diversity and beauty of rocks and minerals, this exercise is designed to help you achieve the basic skills and knowledge needed to identify some of the rocks and minerals you are likely to encounter in the field. If you are able to recognize them, the rocks and minerals you find in road-cuts, excavation, out crops or in the soil can give you valuable clues to the geologic history, the nature of the soils and the kinds of management problems you are likely to encounter in the area. Some examples:

- The shiny flakes of mica in a Coastal Plain soil tell you that this material was deposited here after being washed from the Piedmont Plateau where many of the crystalline rocks are rich in micas.
- Limestone outcrops indicate to you that the soils are likely to have a good nutrient holding capacity and natural fertility, but that ground water supplies may be easily contaminated in the area.
- Pyrite crystals in coal mining spoil warn you that reclamation efforts may face serious problems with acid mine drainage and extreme soil acidity.

5

BACKGROUND INFORMATION ON MINERALS

What is a mineral? It is a *naturally* occurring inorganic substance of *fairly definite chemical composition* whose constituent atoms are arranged in a regular pattern so as to produce a crystalline form. Minerals differ from one another with respect to their elemental composition, their susceptibility to chemical and physical weathering and their physical appearance. By the time you have completed this lab and studied the specimens several times, you will probably recognize many of the minerals "on sight". However, there are a number of specific characteristics useful in identifying minerals: these are discussed below. For a given mineral certain characteristics will be more helpful than others. The most useful characteristics of some common soil forming minerals are given in this chapter for your reference. Several general characteristics by which minerals are identified are discussed below. Observe these for yourself using the specimens in the mineral display boxes.

SOME PHYSICAL PROPERTIES OF MINERALS

1. **Luster**
   The appearance of a mineral in reflected light is called its luster. The different lusters are difficult to describe, but their names are quite suggestive. Examine the minerals listed below as examples.
   Metallic luster: Few soil minerals have a metallic luster. This appears like a shiny metal and the powdered mineral (streak) is generally lighter in color than the intact specimen. Pyrite provides a good example of a mineral with a metallic luster.
   Non-metallic luster: Most soil minerals have one or another of the following non-metallic lusters.
   Vitreous: glassy….e.g. quartz.
   Pearly: iridescent appearance of a pearl…e.g. gypsum
   Greasy: oily appearing…e.g. serpentine

2. **Hardness**
   The hardness of a mineral refers to its resistance to being scratched.[1] A mineral's hardness is measured by comparing it to materials of known hardness. That is, a mineral is harder than, say, glass if it can scratch a piece of glass but cannot itself be scratched by glass. Two useful lists of materials for determining hardness are given here:

Moh's Scale of Hardness

1. Talc	6. Orthoclase
2. Gypsum	7. Quartz
3. Calcite	8. Topaz
4. Fluorite	9. Corundum
5. Apatite	10. Diamond

Hardness of Some Common Materials

Fingernail	~2
Copper penny	3.0
Hardened steel file	5.0
Window glass	5.5
Steel nail or knife blade	6.5
Porcelain plate	7.0

---

[1] The hardness of a rock is often more related to how tightly the individual mineral crystals are bound together.

Try using the above materials to determine the hardness of minerals. Will calcite scratch your finger nail? Can orthoclase scratch glass?

3. **Streak**

   When a mineral is scratched across an unglazed porcelain plate it leaves a trail of fine powder called its "streak." The color of the streak is an identifying characteristic for many minerals. For example, the streak of hematite is a rusty red. Limonite may appear similar to hematite but has a yellow-brown streak. Orthoclase leaves a white streak, though specimens may be red or pink in color. Minerals of hardness greater than 7 are harder than porcelain and so will not leave a streak.

4. **Color**

   While the color of a mineral can be helpful in identification, it is not as reliable as some of the other characteristics of minerals. Small impurities or surface stains may result in a wide range of colors for different specimens of essentially the same mineral. Thus quartz may be white, pink, gray or translucent while orthoclase maybe white, pink or red. However, it is often useful to distinguish between light colored (white, pink, gray) and dark colored (black, dark green) minerals in classifying rocks (see Figure 2.2). Also color is a fairly reliable diagnostic characteristic of several minerals, e.g. sulphur (canary yellow), olivine (light green) or pyrite (brass-yellow).

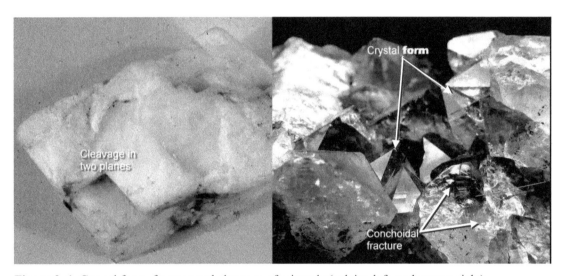

Figure 2. 1 Crystal form, fracture and cleavage of minerals (calcite, left, and quartz, right).

5. **Cleavage**

   A mineral with good cleavage tends to break or "cleave" along smooth surfaces at definite angles. Cleavage occurs along the planes of weakness between layers of atoms in the crystal structure. Mica has a perfect cleavage in one direction resulting in its tendency to form thin sheets. Feldspars cleave in two directions forming rhombohedra shapes. The angle and type of cleavage is a diagnostic characteristic for many minerals. Cleavage in two or more directions is usually best observed as small "stair-step" like edges on a specimen. A hand lens (10X) may help in observing these cleavages. The smooth external surfaces of an intact crystal should *not* be confused with cleavage (see Figure 2.1). Also, not all minerals cleave when a force is applied. Instead, many exhibit some kind of uneven break or *fracture*.

6. Fracture

Those minerals which do not have good cleavage may display one of the following types of fracture when chipped or broken.

Fracture	Mineral
Conchoidal,,..........	quartz (see Figure 2.1)
Fibrous, splintery....	pyrolusite
Uneven................	talc

7. Specific Gravity

The specific gravity (s.g.) of a mineral is the ratio of its weight (mass) to that of an equal volume of water. Pick up a piece of magnetite (s.g. 5.2) in one hand and a similarly sized piece of quartz or serpentine (s.g. 2.65) in the other. It should become clear that some minerals are "heavier" than others. Most silicate minerals in soils have a s.g. of 2.5 to 3.0. Some of the heavy metal-containing minerals have specific gravities greater than 6 or 7.

8. Effervescence

Carbonate minerals release bubbles of CO_2 when treated with a drop of 10% HCl (or household vinegar). This "fizzing" reaction is diagnostic for calcite.

9. Other Diagnostic Characteristics

Some minerals have a peculiar *taste* (e.g., halite), *feel* (e.g., talc) or *smell* (e.g., pyrite). *Crystal forms* are diagnostic for many minerals, but intact crystals are not commonly found in soil and rock samples in the field.

Table 2.1 describes the characteristics of some of the more important soil forming minerals. For each mineral, those characteristics most useful in identifying the mineral have been printed in bold type. Pay particular attention to these. Also study the "other comments" column as the information given there helps relate the minerals to their role in soils.

In Table 2.2 several important primary minerals are listed along with secondary minerals and soluble compounds that result when they break down during the weathering process. The soluble compounds may be taken up by plant roots, absorbed on soil surfaces or flushed out of the soil into the groundwater.

Table 2.1 Some Characteristics of Some Minerals Important in Soils

Mineral	Chemical Composition	Hard-ness	Spec. Grav.	Streak	Cleavage or Fracture	Luster	Color	Other comments
					SILICATES			
Quartz	SiO_2	7	2.65	--	**Conchoidal fracture**	Vitreous	Color-less, White	Found widely in soils, often 50-90% of the sand & silt fractions of soils. About 20-30% in granitic rocks. Very resistant to weathering. Often form prismatic crystals with hexagonal pyramid tips.
Feldspar Group Orthoclase & Microcline	$KAlSi_3O_8$	**6**	2.6	**White**	**Good in two directions about 90°**	Vitreous	**Flesh pink** gray Micro-cline if deep green	Very common in soils & acidic igneous rocks. In soils mostly sand and silt sized. Important source of K for plants.
Plagioclase	$Na(AlSi_3O_8)$ To $Ca(Al_2Si_2O_{10})$	**6**	2.6-2.7	**Color-less**	**Good in two directions 94°**	Vitreous to pearly	Color less, white, red, gray	Plagioclase feldspars form a series from the Na type (albite) to the Ca type (anorthite). All have striations on the basal cleavage plane.
Mica Group Muscovite	$KAl_2Si_3O_{10})$ $(OH)_{10}$	2-2.5	2.7-3.1	Color-less	**Good in 1 direction giving thin flexible, elastic "folia" or sheets**	Vitreous to pearly	Color-less to light yellow	Micas are common in soils weathered from crystalline rocks such as those in the Eastern Piedmont region. Muscovite and biotite are common in granites, gneiss, and schists. Muscovite is very resistant to weathering & is common in sand fractions as well as in clays.
Biotite	$K(Mg, Fe)_3$ $(AlSiO_3O_{10})$ $(OH)_2$	2.5-3	2.8-3.2	Color-less	**Folia as above**	Pearly to vitreous	**Black brown, dark green**	
Chlorite	$(Mg, Fe)_5(Al, Fe)_2Si_3$ $O_{10}(OH)_8$	2-2.5	2.6-3.3	Color-less	**Folia as above, but inelastic**	Vitreous to pearly	**Green**	Chlorite is a secondary mineral often in clay fractions
Glauconite	Similar to biotite	--	2.8-3.2	--	Occurs as **soft pellets**	--	**Green to olive**	Glauconite is found as "pellets" or greensand in marine deposits. It is an excellent source of K for plants.
Olivine	$(Mg, Fe)_2SiO_4$	6.5-7	3.3-3.4	Pale green to white if any	**Conchoidal fracture**	Vitreous	**Olive to grayish green or brown**	Usually found as **granular masses.** Common mainly in basic rocks (gabbro basalt). Relatively easily weathered.
Amphiboles (Hornblende)	Complex ferromagnesian silicate with Ca, Na, Mg, Fe, and Al	5-6	3.2	Color-less	**Prismatic at 56°** and 124°	Vitreous or silky	**Black or dark green**	Common in **igneous and metamorphic rocks. Crystals are like long prisms.**

9

Table 2.1 Some Characteristics of Some Minerals Important in Soils (continued).

Mineral	Chemical Composition	Hard-ness	Spec. Grav.	Streak	Cleavage or Fracture	Luster	Color	Other comments
Pyroxenes (Augite)	Complex ferromagnesian silicate with Ca, Na Mg, Fe, Al and Si	5-6	3.2	Greenish gray	**Prismatic at nearly 90° splintery surface**	Vitreous	**Dark green to black**	Common in igneous and metamorphic rocks. Distinguished from hornblende by its cleavage and short, **stubby crystals**.
Serpentine	$Mg_6(Si_4O_{10})(OH)_8$	2-5	2.2-2.65	Color-less	Conchoidal fracture often fibrous crystals	**Greasy**	**Variegated greens**	Common mineral often occurring as a weathering product of olivine, hornblende or Augite. Rich source of Mg for plants. Soils formed from serpentine rocks may even have harmful levels of Mg.

Clay minerals: These are predominately in the clay size fraction in soils (<0.002 mm) and cannot be identified megascopically. They are extremely important in soils (see exercises 4 and 8). The principal silicate clay minerals are kaolinite, illite (a hydrous mica), montmorillonite (a smectite) and chlorite.

					OXIDES			
Hematite	Fe_2O_3	5.5	5.26	**Dusky Red**	Uneven fracture	Metallic if crystal-line	Black to reddish brown	Important as iron ore. In soils iron oxides occur primarily as amorphous coatings on other soil particles, but some crystalline hematite can occur in sand & silt fractions. Partially responsible for bright red and brown soil colors
"Limonite" (Goethite)	Fe O (OH) nH_2O	5.0-5.5	3.6-4.0	**Yellow brown**	--	--	Dark brown to black	Goethite is the principal "limonite mineral" in soils being abundant in oxisols, ironstone and Bs horizons
Magnetite	Fe_eO_4	6	5.18	**Black**	Some octahedral parting	Metallic	**Iron-black**	An accessory mineral in many basic igneous and metamorphic rocks. In soils it occurs mostly as sand sized particles. Magnetite exhibits strong magnetism. Often as streaks of black sand on ocean beaches.
Rutile	TiO_2	6-6.5	4.2	Pale brown	Uneven fracture	**Hard, brilliant luster**	**Red**	Occurs commonly in soils, often appearing as gem-like red sand grains. On beaches it may be found as streaks of red sand.

Table 2.1 Some Characteristics of Some Minerals Important in Soils (continued).

Mineral	Chemical Composition	Hard-ness	Spec. Grav.	Streak	Cleavage or Fracture	Luster	Color	Other comments
SULFUR BEARING MINERALS								
Gypsum	$CaSO_4 \cdot 2H_2O$	**2.0**	2.32	Color-less	Good cleavage in one direction, fibrous fracture and uneven fracture in 2 other directions	**Vitreous, pearly or silky**	Colorless white or gray	Common in soils of arid regions, both as crystals & as a cementing agent in indurated soil horizons. Because it is soft & relatively soluble, it has been weathered out of humid region soils. It occurs in sedimentary rocks. In ground form it is used as a soil amendment to reclaim sodic soils & as a calcium fertilizer.
Pyrite	FeS_2	**6-6.5**	5.0	**Green to brown-ish black**	Uneven fracture	**Metallic**	**Brass yellow**	Pyrite, sometimes called "fool's gold" occurs in all three types of rocks but its significance to soils is greatest when it occurs in sedimentary rocks or in clays associated with coal seams. When exposed to air by excavation it is responsible for much acid mine drainage.
CARBONATES								
Calcite	$CaCO_3$	**3**	2.7	Color-less	Perfect in 3 directions 75° -- **forms rhombo-hedra**	Vitreous	**White colorless** or some tint	Occurs in many rocks, especially forms of limestone, marble and cave formations. In arid regions it accumulates soil Ck horizons. Finely powdered, it is known as lime & is used to correct soil acidity. Calcite effervesces freely with dilute, cold HCl.
Dolomite	$Ca\,Mg\,(CO_3)_2$	3.5-4	2.85	Color-less	Perfect in 3 directions 73°	Vitreous	**Pink, flesh, white**	Occurs mainly in dolomitic limestone & marble. Dolomite effervesces only slightly with dilute cold HCl, but its powder effervesces freely. May occur as rhombohedral crystals with curved crystal faces.
PHOSPHATES								
Apatite	$3Ca_3(PO_4)_2$ $Ca(F, Cl)_2$	5	3.15-3.2	White	Conchoidal fracture, poor cleavage in 1 direction	**Vitreous**	Usually **green, may be brown** or red	Apatite is the only common soil mineral containing phosphorous. It occurs in all types of rocks. In rich deposits it is the "rock phosphate" from which P-fertilizers are manufactured.

Table 2.2 Weathering Products of Common Minerals.

Primary Mineral	Secondary Minerals Formed	Soluble Compounds Released
Quartz	----------	SiO_2
Orthoclase Feldspars	Clay minerals Muscovite	K_2CO_3 SiO_2
Muscovite	Vermiculite, Other clays	SiO_2 K_2CO_3
Augite and Hornblende	Clay minerals Limonite	SiO_2 $CaH_2(CO_3)_2$ $MgH_2(CO_3)_2$ $FeH_2(CO_3)_2$
Olivine	Serpentine, Limonite	SiO_2 $MgH_2(CO_3)_2$ $FeH_2(CO_3)_2$
Pyrite	Limonite	$FeSO_4$ H_2SO_4

BACKGROUND INFORMATION ON ROCKS

A rock can be defined as an aggregate of minerals of different kinds in varying proportions. A rock also has specific characteristics that permit identification in the field and laboratory.

The classification of rocks is based on 1) the manner in which they are formed in nature, 2) their mineralogy and 3) their texture. They are further classified on the basis of stratification, chemical composition, and geologic age. The three main types of rocks are *igneous, sedimentary, and metamorphic* (Table 2.3).

Table 2.3 Types of Rocks.

Igneous	Sedimentary	Metamorphic
Formed by cooling and consolidation of a once hot and fluid mass of magma (liquid rock).	Formed from weathered rocks (soils), by direct precipitation or from precipitation by organisms.	Previously formed rocks altered chemically and physically by heat and pressure.
Visible crystals may or may not be present	Stratification or layering	Crystals may be banded
No stratification	No crystals (except possibly in precipitates)	Distorted crystals
No banding		Laminations or Foliations
No lamination		

1. **Igneous**

These rocks are formed by the cooling and consolidation of a once hot and fluid mass of rock material called magma.

Igneous rocks are classified on the basis of (1) texture or grain size and (2) mineralogical composition. The texture of igneous rocks is related to rate and mode of cooling of the magma; the slower the magma cools, the larger the crystals will grow and the coarser the texture will be.

Figure 2.2 shows how igneous rocks are classified by mineral composition and texture. For example, granite is a coarse textured rock (easily visible crystal grains) which is, by volume, about 1/3 orthoclase and 1/3 quartz, with the remaining 1/3 made up of plagioclase and dark colored ferromagnesian minerals (biotite and hornblende). Granite appears, therefore, as a light colored rock (white or pink) with scattered specks of dark colored minerals. A rock with about the same mineral composition, but with a fine grained texture (crystals not easily visible size) would be a *rhyolite*.

Shown on the right hand portion of the chart, *gabbro* and *basalt* are dark colored rocks of coarse and fine grained texture, respectively. *Syenite*, on the extreme left, is a light colored rock similar to granite but virtually devoid of quartz.

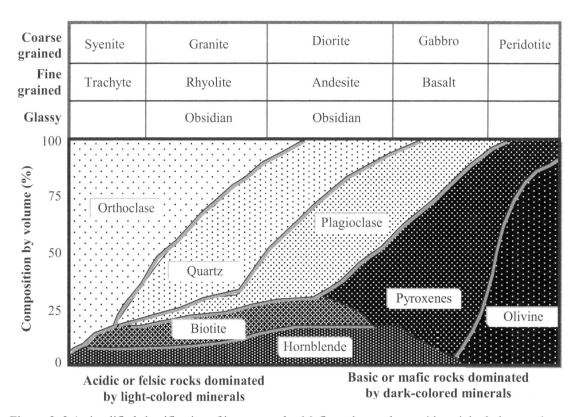

Figure 2. 2 A simplified classification of igneous rocks. Mafic rocks are those with mainly dark mnerals with iron and magnesium. Mafic rocks release alkalinity when weathered. Felsic rocks and light colored and acidic.

2. Sedimentary

Materials forming these rocks were derived from the weathering of previously existing rock masses. In addition to mechanically deposited rock detritus, sedimentary rocks also include substances precipitated directly from an aqueous solution or those in which organisms have been active in extracting materials from solution. Stratification is an important characteristic of sedimentary rocks. Listed below are the major sedimentary rocks with their diagnostic properties.

Table 2.4 A Key to Sedimentary Rocks

Texture				
Fine		Coarse	Very Coarse	
With CaCO$_3$	Without CaCO$_3$		Rounded	Angular
Limestone	**Shale**	**Sandstone**	**Conglomerate**	**Brecia**

Sandstone is a sedimentary rock composed of particles that range in size from 2 to 0.05 mm in diameter. Quartz is such a common mineral in this size fraction that quartz and sandstone are considered synonymous. However, other minerals may also occur in this range and thus make up a high percentage of the mineral composition of some sandstone; for example, the green sandstones of Maryland are made up primarily of the mineral glauconite. The cementing materials for sandstone are usually calcite or quartz, although other carbonates, iron oxides, gypsum, opal and other substances are sometimes found.

Shales are fine-grained sedimentary rocks made up of silts and clays and with a thinly laminated structure. Most shales are gray, but they may be white, red, green or black.

Limestone is a rock with a composition of calcium carbonate. Otherwise, this kind of rock can vary widely in color, texture, origin and their association with other rocks. Limestone is a very common rock and soils formed from these rocks are usually considered good for agricultural purposes.

Conglomerate is a rock consisting of consolidated gravels (> 2 mm diameter). Conglomerate nearly always originates in aqueous environments such as old stream channels.

3. Metamorphic

Due to high temperature and pressures, these rocks have undergone some chemical or physical changes subsequent to their original formation. Banding, laminating and mineralogical changes take place during metamorphism (Figure 2.3). The resulting banded appearance is not to be confused with the layering of sedimentary rocks.

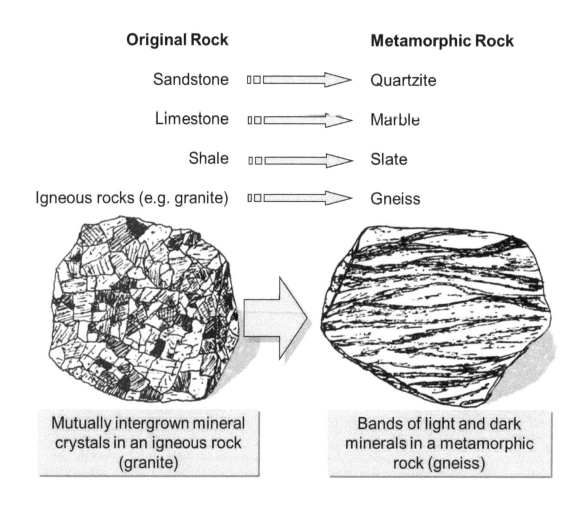

Figure 2.3 Comparative appearance of igneous and metamorphic rocks.

Table 2.5 Key to Metamorphic Rocks

Name	Structure	Texture	Mineralogy	Remarks
A. Foliate (rocks that break into sheet like layers)				
Gneiss	Color banding and/or foliation and/or lineation—little or no tendency to cleave along bands	Coarse, medium, fine granular	Quartz, feldspar, and micas common; hornblende-pyroxene; metacrysts	Composition, banding; coarse laminations; common rock forming minerals; weathers like granite.
Schist	Finely foliated, cleaves along foliation to form rough surface with grains or flakes clearly visible	Similar to gneiss	Micas predominant; schist named for most common mineral, e.g., chlorite schist, talc schist	Very common metamorphic rock; weathers more rapidly than gneiss.
Phyllite	Finely foliated; splits easily with flakes barely visible on surfaces	Aphanitic to fine granular	Clay minerals not visible; mica noticeable	Commonly has silky sheen; may be crumpled badly.
Slate	Finely foliated; splits in thin planes; "slaty" cleavage"—smooth surface	Similar to phyllite	Minerals seldom visible	Extremely smooth cleavage surfaces; used for roofing and blackboards; weathers slowly.
B. Non-foliate (rocks that do not break into sheet like layers)				
Quartzite	Massive	Coarse to fine; equi-granular	Predominately quartz	Brittle; breaks through grains; vitreous; weathers very slowly.
Marble	Massive; some streaky foliated	Coarse to fine; rarely aphanitic	Calcite, dolomite, serpentines (verd antique)	Used as building stone, monuments, ornaments and statuary.

KEY TO THE ROCKS

A.   Mineral crystals easily visible by naked eye.

    1.   minerals in bands or layers………..………….gneiss
              (metamorphic)   schist
                                              phyllite

    2.   minerals intergrown in random pattern………….igneous
              a. light colored mineral dominant, and
                  light in weight……………………………..granitic
              b. dark colored mineral dominant and
                  heavy in weight………….…………. ……..gabbro
                                      coarse mafic

B.   Minerals crystals not easily visible by naked eye.

    1.   glassy appearance………………………….obsidian

    2.   stony appearance
              a.   tends to split into layers
                     smooth to fingernail…………………….shale
                                 slate

              b.   cannot be split into layers

                      i.   fizzes freely in acid…………….calcitic limestone
                                       or marble

                      ii.   fizzes slightly in acid
                               or freely if powdered…………..dolomitic
                                       limestone

                      iii.   does not fizz in acid
                             gritty feel to fingernail………….sandstone

Materials

- set of labeled hand specimens of minerals including all those listed in Table 2.6
- set of labeled hand specimens of rock including all those listed in Table 2.7
- hand lens (10x)
- 10% HCl in dropper bottle
- streak plate
- small window glass
- steel nail
- copper penny
- dissecting microscope with top lighted stage
- washed, iron-free sand fractions from representative soils, mounted on microscope slides
- soil monoliths that show evidence of parent material[2].

---

[2] Detailed information on how to make a soil monolith can be found in these papers: Haddad, N., R. Lawrie, and S. Eldridge. 2009. Improved method of making soil monoliths using an acrylic bonding agent and proline auger Geoderma151:395-400 and Barahona, E., and A. Iriarte. 1999. A method for the collection of soil monoliths from stony and gravelly soils. Geoderma 87:305-310.

PROCEDURES	COMMENTS

PROCEDURES

1. Skim through the background information before coming to the lab.

2. Using the specimens suggested, observe the eight characteristics used in identifying minerals.

3. In lab, examine the set of mineral specimens and fill out Table 2.6 using the information given in this manual as well as your own observations. Use the streak plates, materials to scratch-test for hardness (penny, fingernail, glass, etc.), HCl solution, etc

4 Examine the sets of rock specimens and fill out Table 2.7 again, combining the information in this manual with your own . observations.

5. Using a binocular dissecting microscope, examine two slides ("a" and "b") of sand grains taken from various soils. If possible, light the slides from below *and* above. Use a rule or special eye piece to view a mm scale. Sketch a few representative grains from each slide and answer the questions on page 23.

6. Examine the soil monoliths on display. In particular try to discern the influence of the various parent materials on soil profile properties. Fill in Table 2.8 with your observations. Note the geographic locations and the various types of parent materials represented. Try to include as much detail as possible in your profile sketches for Table 2.8. Draw the horizon boundaries where these are indicated on the monoliths.

COMMENTS

You will be expected to be able to identify mineral and rock specimens, so study their diagnostic characteristics until you feel enough familiarity to recognize the minerals should you see other specimens.
The mineral and rock specimens will be available in the lab for you to study over the next few weeks. Try to list, in column 4, a couple features of each mineral that distinguish it from other, similar-appearing minerals.

Look for evidence of the mineral properties you studied in relation to the hand samples. Color, cleavage, fracture, crystal form, luster, etc. Realize that these properties may be much more difficult to discern on the tiny, weathered sand grains.

Look for similarities and differences between the soil in the upper horizons and the parent material in and below the C horizon with regard to colors, structure, texture, etc. Also look for differences in soil depth or stoniness which might relate to rates of weathering of the parent material.

Date_____   Name_____

Section_____   I.D. No. _____

EXERCISE 2
Minerals, Rocks, and Parent Materials

Table 2.6 Some Minerals Important in Soils

Mineral Name	Elements Contained	Common in What Rocks	Identifying Characteristics
Quartz			
Orthoclase			
Plagioclase			
Muscovite			
Biotite			
Calcite			
Dolomite			
Apatite			
Olivine			
Hornblende			
Serpentine			
Hematite			
Limonite			
Pyrite			
Gypsum			

Table 2.7 Some Rocks Important in Soil Formation

Rock Name	Dominant Minerals	Rock Type	Texture	Identifying Characteristics
Syenite				
Granite				
Rhyolite				
Gabbro				
Basalt				
Obsidian				
Gneiss				
Phyllite				
Schist				
Marble				
Slate				
Shale				
Sandstone				
Limestone (Calcitic)				
Limestone (Dolomitic)				
Conglomerate				

Date _____   Name _____

Section _____   I.D. No. _____

EXERCISE 2
OBSERVATION OF SAND FRACTIONS FROM VARIOUS SOILS

1. What size are the sand grains? Estimate the largest and smallest diameters in mm.

    Slide a. _____   Slide b. _____

2. Are all grains individual minerals or are some of the grains actually aggregates of several minerals (i.e. "little rocks")? What size grains consist of a single mineral? Several minerals?

    Slide a. _____   Slide b. _____

3. What are the dominant minerals present? Indicate which properties helped you identify them. [Are they dark or light? Are the shapes platy, blocky, circular or elongated? Can you see fractures or cleavage? Are the surfaces scratched?]

    Slide a._____

    Slide b._____

4. Indicate any evidence that the sand grain have been weathered (changed) physically and / or chemically since they broke away from their parent rock.

    Slide a._____

    Slide b._____

5. Sketch the shape of three sand grains from each slide. Draw a scale bar showing 1.0 and 0.5 mm. In the space provided, indicate the soil from which the sand was obtained.

    a. ◯   b. ◯

Soil: _____   Soil:_____

Table 2.8 Examination of Soil Monoliths

Profile #1.

Soil Series:_____

_____

Parent material:_____

_____

Geographic Location: _____

_____

Describe what you can see that suggests the relation
between the soil and its parent material:

_____

_____

_____

Profile #1

Horizon symbol	Color of soil	Sketch	Depth (cm)
			0
			30
			60
			90
			120

Profile #2.

Soil Series:_____

_____

Parent material:_____

_____

Geographic Location: _____

_____

Describe what you can see that suggests the relation
between the soil and its parent material:

_____

_____

_____

Profile #2

Horizon symbol	Color of soil	Sketch	Depth (cm)
			0
			30
			60
			90
			120

Exercise 03
Some Field Skills:
Texture "By Feel" and Color by Munsell Charts

OBJECTIVES

After completing this exercise, you should be able to . . .

1. Describe the feel of sand, silt and clay.
2. Properly moisten and manipulate soil samples to determine texture by feel.
3. Determine the texture of a soil sample "by feel."
4. Explain the use of Munsell® color notation and what a symbol such as "5 YR 4/2" means.
5. Determine the Munsell® color notation and name for a soil sample using the Munsell® color charts in the proper way.

INTRODUCTION

The ability to estimate a soil's textural class out in the field is one of the most useful skills you will develop in this course. Soil surveyors, conservationists, farmers, homeowners and planners all have occasion to require information about soil texture because this basic property is related to many useful soil properties such as water holding capacity, responsiveness to lime and fertilizers, permeability and workability. All that is needed to determine soil texture in the field with reasonable accuracy is your hands, some water and *some experience*.

In this exercise you will first feel the 3 soil *separates* (sand, silt, and clay) in relatively pure form. Then you will moisten and manipulate samples of soil to "get the feel" of the various *textural classes* (mixtures of the 3 separates in proportions defined by the textural triangle (Figure 7.3 in this lab manual). You will practice moistening soil to a putty like consistency and following a logical sequence of manipulations to on soils of known textural class to determine if the soil is a loam, a silt loam or a clay loam, etc. Small balls of these "putty-like" soils will then be compared to one another and placed in the appropriate circles on the attached "Worksheet." These same balls will also be used for practice in determining the *Munsell® color designations* of soils. Soil color, while not generally of practical importance in itself, is one of the most obvious properties by which soils differ from one another. Accurate color descriptions are important in the field characterization of soils. Also soil colors and patterns of color often are indicative of such soil properties as drainage, organic matter content, mineralogy and profile development.

"Soil colors are most conveniently measured by comparison with a color chart. The collection of charts generally used with soils is a modified version of the collection appearing in the Munsell® Book of Color and includes only that portion needed for soils, about one-fifth of the entire range found in the complete edition.

"The arrangement is by the three simple variables that combine to describe all colors and are known in the Munsell® system as Hue, Value, and Chroma.

"The Hue notation of a color indicates its relation to Red, Yellow, Green, Blue and Purple; the Value notation indicates its lightness; and the Chroma notation indicates its strength (or departure from a neutral of the same lightness).

"The nomenclature for soil color consists of two complementary systems: (1) color names, and (2) the Munsell® notation of color. Neither of these alone is adequate for all purposes. The color names are employed in all descriptions for publication and for general use. The Munsell notation is used to supplement the color names wherever greater precision is needed. Bizarre names like 'rusty brown,' 'mouse gray,' 'lemon yellow,' and 'chocolate brown' should never be used.

"The soil color names and their limits are given in the diagrams which appear opposite each chart. In using the color charts, first select the page representing the hue closest to that of the soil. For value and chroma, accurate comparison is obtained by holding the soil sample directly behind the apertures separating the closest matching color chips. It should be evident which colors the sample lies between, and which is the closest match."[1]

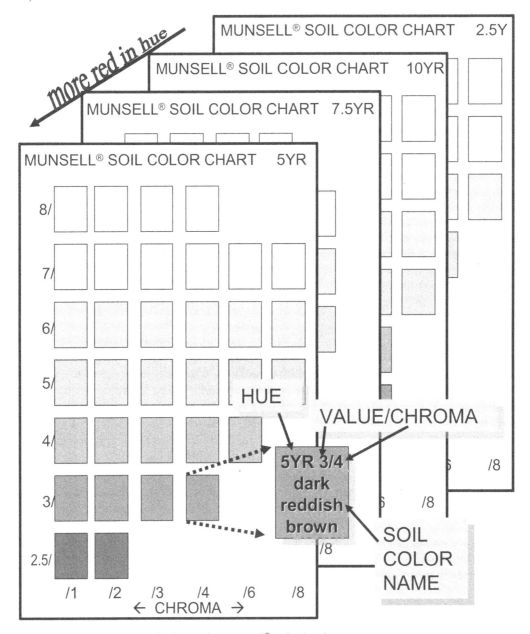

Figure 3.1 Arrangement of color in the Munsell® color book.

---

[1] Quoted in part from U.S. Dept. Agriculture Handbook 18 – Soil Survey Manual.

MATERIALS

- samples of soil separates (i.e., sand, silt, clay)
- samples of soils of various textures (as many as possible of the 10 textural classes in Figure 3.4)
- plastic teaspoons to scoop out samples if the soils are dried and ground.
- Munsell® color charts
- wash bottles with water
- towels to clean hands and bench

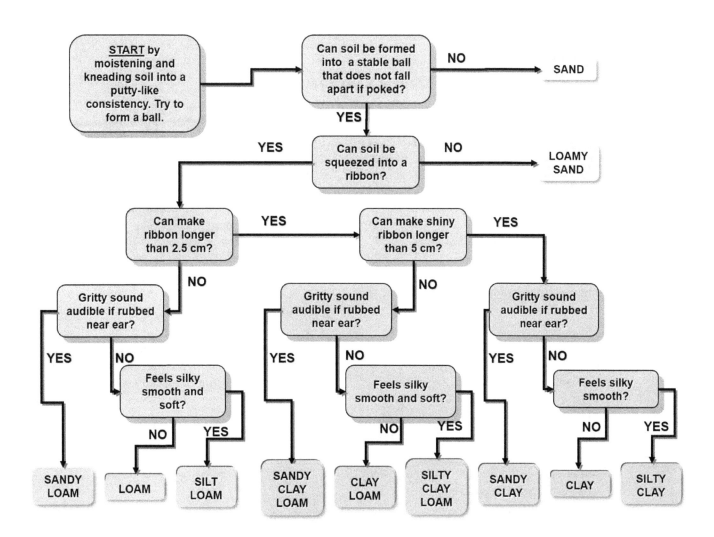

Figure 3.2 Flow chart for determining textural class by the "feel" method. The chart is highly simplified and should be used in conjunction with the procedures on pages 28-30 and the worksheet on page 33. Silt, a rare texture class, is not included here.

PROCEDURE

Individual Soil Separates

1. With a moistened forefinger tip, touch the clay sample in the container labeled "Bentonite clay" so that some of the clay sticks to you fingertip.

2. Rub this clay, in the moist state, between your forefinger and thumb. Describe the "feel" of the material in Table 3.1.

3. Wash your fingers. Then repeat steps 1 and 2, but using first silt, and then sand.

Soils of Known Textural Class

4. Place about 1 teaspoonful of soil into the palm of your hand. If it is dry, moisten it gradually with water from a squeeze bottle, manipulating the soil between each small addition of water until the state of maximum plasticity is reached and the soil is uniformly moist and pliable like putty.

   While manipulating the soil to make a putty, take note of the degree to which the sample feels sticky, smooth, firm (offers resistance to manipulation) or gritty.

5. Try to form the soil into a ball. If a stable ball will not form, but instead it falls apart if you poke it with your finger, the soil is a **sand.** *If* you *can* form a stable ball, go to step 6.

6. Try to form a ribbon from the soil by squeezing it out between your thumb and forefinger (Figure 3.3). If you cannot form even a short ribbon, and the soil is very gritty, you have a **loamy sand**. *If* you *can* form a ribbon, go to step 7.

COMMENTS

Bentonite is a very sticky clay in the smectite family of high activity clays. Kaolinite, a low activity clay, would feel less sticky than this.

Be sure to rub long enough and with enough moisture so that any small clumps in the material break down and the material feels smooth.

After kneading the soil in your palm it should become like moist, pliable putty, but not so moist as to show free water on the soil surface. Soil in this condition should not stick to a smooth surface such as a spatula.

This step is very important as texture can be estimated properly only when the soil is in a moist putty-like state. In the field this state is usually easy to achieve as the soil may be already uniformly moist. Still, a squeeze bottle of water is a necessary piece of equipment for field texturing.

A sand or loamy sand will not form a ball, even when moist. In addition, a sand will not leave a film of soil on your hands. A sandy loam will form a ball that crumbles easily.

28

7. Make sure the soil is still moist enough to be like putty. Form as long a ribbon as you can. Also note the characteristics discussed in the right column.

a. If the ribbon breaks off when less than 2.5 cm (1 inch) long, your soil is in one of the *loam* textural classes. **Go to step 8.**

b. If the ribbon breaks off when between 2.5 cm and 5 cm (1 to 2 inches) long, your soil is in one of the *clay loam* textural classes. **Go to step 8**.

c. If you can make the ribbon more than 5 cm (2 inches) long, your soil is in one of the *clay* textural classes. **Go to step 8.**

8. This step will allow you to add the modifier "sandy" or "silt(y)" in front of the *loam, clay loam* or *clay* tier (Figure 3.4) you identified from step 7. Squeeze and rub your putty-like soil near your ear.

a. If a grinding noise is audible, you probably need to add "sandy" in the front of the soil textural class name.

b. If there is no grinding noise and the soil feels silky smooth and soft, you should add "silt" or "silty" to the front of the soil textural class name.

c. If the soil is slightly gritty and only slightly smooth and no grinding is heard, then you do not need to add any modifier to the front of the textural class name.

As you finished with each "known" soil, roll your moist soil into a small ball and place it in the appropriate circle on the worksheet. Save for color determination. Wash your hands.

9. A more precise estimation of the percentage of sand can made by breaking off a pea-size clump of soil. Wet this "pea" of soil in the palm of your hand and rub it around with your finger to make a slurry. The sand grains will stand our clearly from the silt and clay slurry.

10. Repeat steps 4-9 for each of the "known" soils provided by your instructor. Then, once every circle on the worksheet is filled, compare the feel of the different textural classes by again manipulating each briefly in sequence.

To help decide whether the soil is in the clays, clay loams or loams (See Figure 3.4) note the following:

- how shiny the moist surface becomes when smeared by your thumb; clays will be shiny, loams will be smooth or rough,, but not shiny.

- the malleability as well as length of the ribbon formed; and

- the firmness or resistance to deformation when molded, the order of firmness being: clay > clay loams > loams.

Note that these steps are summarized in the flow chart (Figure 3.2)

Figure 3.3 Ribboning a clay soil.

This procedure is particularly useful to determine the sand content of a fine textured soil. While estimating the content of sand, silt, and clay, try to mentally locate your sample on the textural triangle (Figure 3.3).

Practice is the key to developing skill in "texturing by feel." When dealing with soils high in organic matter (tends to feel "silty") or of different types of clay minerals you may have to "re-calibrate" your fingers.

Soil of Unknown Texture

11. Repeat steps 4-9 for each of the soils, washing your hands between samples.

12. Record, in Table 3.2, the textural class and approximate percentage of sand, silt, and clay for each of the unknowns.

If you are including your own soil, record the textural class in Table G2 in Appendix G.

Estimate the percentage from the textural triangle (Figure 3.2)

Munsell Color Designations

13. Re-read the part of the chapter introduction dealing with soil color, *especially the last paragraph.*

Be sure you understand the Munsell notation, as described in Figure 3.1. You will use moist soils so your Munsell notations should be followed by the word "moist". Since you are using the soil "balls" from the previous section, the soil color recorded will be considered to be the "rubbed" color, which may differ from the color of an undisturbed soil clod.

14. Determine the Munsell color *notation* and the color *name* for each of the small balls of moist soil on your "worksheet." Record this information in the spaces provided.

PLEASE KEEP THE COLOR CHIPS CLEAN! Use with *clean hands* and do *not* place soil in *front* of the color page. Place it behind the page and look through holes.

15. Determine the color notation and name for each of the three unknowns. Record in Table 3.2.

An example of a complete color notation would be: "reddish brown (5YR 3/4, moist)." If you have included your own soil, record its complete designation in Table G2.

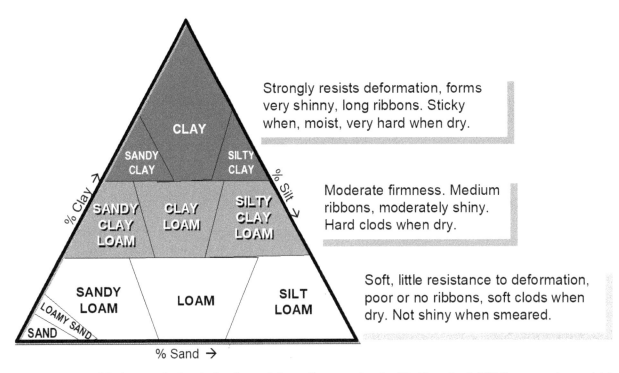

Figure 3.4 Modified textural triangle for determining soil texture by the "feel" method. "Silt" texture class, which is rare in nature, is not included. (Adapted from *Soils Laboratory Exercise Source Book*. Am. Soc. of Agron. 1971.)

Date _____   Name _____

Section _____   I.D. No. _____

Exercise 3
Some Field Skills: Texture "By Feel"
and Color Charts

Table 3.1 Characterization of soil separates – sand, silt and clay.

Relatively pure "soil separates"	What does it look like?	Describe how it feels
Sand		
Silt		
Clay		

Table 3.2 Results for soils of unknown texture and color provided by your instructor.

Soil ID	Munsell Color Notation	Munsell color name	Textural class	Estimated percentage		
				Sand	Silt	Clay
A						
B						
C						

Date _____   Name _____

Section _____   I.D. No. _____

WORKSHEET for EXERCISE 3

Clay (c)
very shiny ribbons > 5 cm
slight to no grittiness,
very sticky, plastic,
very firm when moist,
hard when dry
*color: _____

Silty Clay (sic)
very shiny ribbons > 5 cm
very smooth,
very sticky, plastic,
firm when moist,
hard when dry
color: _____

Sandy Clay (sc)
shiny ribbons > 5 cm
very gritty, sticky,
plastic,
firm (moist), hard (dry)
color: _____

Clay Loam (cl)
shiny ribbons 2 - 5 cm
slightly gritty,
moderately plastic and sticky,
firm (moist), or slightly hard
to hard (dry)
color: _____

Sandy Clay Loam (scl)
slightly shiny ribbons 2 - 5 cm
very gritty, sticky,
moderately plastic, friable to
firm when moist, slightly
hard when dry
color: _____

Silty Clay Loam (sicl)
shiny ribbons 2 - 5 cm
moderately plastic,
friable to firm (moist),
slightly hard (dry)
color: _____

Loam (l)
dull, poorly formed ribbon,
not sticky or plastic,
gritty,
friable (moist), soft (dry)
color: _____

Silt Loam (sil)
velvety,
dull, poorly formed ribbon,
slightly plastic and sticky,
forms stable ball,
friable (moist), soft (dry)
color: _____

Sandy Loam (sl)
v. gritty, dull,
poorly formed ribbon,
may be formed into stable
ball,
non-plastic, non-sticky,
v. friable (moist), soft (dry)
color: _____

Loamy Sand (ls)
very gritty,
no ribbons,
no stable ball, leaves only
slight film on hands,
loose consistence,
non-plastic, non-sticky
color: _____

*NOTE: Color is *not* generally indicative of texture. The color is to be noted in this worksheet solely for the purpose of practicing the use of the Munsell color charts. Also note that these colors are the "rubbed" soil colors which may differ from the colors of an undisturbed soil clod. Also not that "Sand" and "Silt" texture classes, which are very rare in natural soils, are not included.

Exercise 4
Using a Pit to Study the Soil Profile

OBJECTIVES

After completing this field trip, you should be able to . . .

1. Recognize several landscape positions common in your geographic area.
2. Describe the main horizons of the soils examined.
3. Distinguish horizon boundaries on the face of a soil pit by changes in observable soil properties.
4. Describe a soil profile in terms of the horizons present, their boundaries, texture, color and structure.
5. Recognize and explain soil management practices and other features seen in the field.

INTRODUCTION

Soils are natural bodies in landscapes. Soil material we analyze in the laboratory is, therefore, no more "a soil" than a water sample is "a river." To fully appreciate the nature of a soil, it is necessary to go to the field and study it as a part of the landscape in which it is found. This exercise will be conducted in the field in order to introduce you to the soil as a natural body.

Learning how to study and describe a soil profile in the field has many practical benefits. Application of soil fertility or soil engineering to the management of land often requires the ability to recognize different types of soil in the field. This skill allows one to gain some idea of what kinds of soils one must deal with and where the different types of soils are located. The ability to distinguish and accurately describe soil profile features is also a prerequisite to understanding of the processes of soil formation, past and present.

Much may be inferred about a soil by its surface features, vegetative cover, and landscape position, however soils exist and function in three dimensions, not just two. A complete understanding of soil relationships and functions therefore requires a careful examination and a detailed description of the soil profile. The profile, or vertical cross section, may be studied in several ways. The best way to study a soil in detail is by digging a soil pit. Such a pit is generally about 2 meters deep (or down to the parent material or hard rock), 2 meters long and 1 meter wide, and may be dug (by hand shovel or by back-hoe). The pit should be oriented so that one clean face is directly lit by sunlight. Road cuts or other excavations may be conveniently used, however some excavation is necessary to expose fresh soil material along the vertical face. A second method of studying soils in three dimensions enlists a soil auger, either screw or bucket type. The auger can be worked into the ground in stages to bring up samples of soil material from incremental depths from the surface on down. In this exercise you will study soil profiles exposed in soil pits. In Exercise 6, "Getting to Know a Catena" you will have a chance to try the soil auger approach.

At least two soil pits should be examined in considerable detail. The characteristics of these soil profiles should reflect the influences of the five soil forming factors: organisms (including man), topography, climate, parent material, and time. All five of the soil forming factors should be discussed in relation to the soils studied, even though two or three of these factors are likely to differ very much between two nearby soils.

In order to efficiently describe all of the soil properties called for in this exercise, it is advisable that you first master the techniques of determining texture by feel and using Munsell color books (see

Exercise #3), that you learn to use a pH kit (Exercise #14), and that you become familiar with common rocks and minerals (Exercise #2). You will also need to familiarize yourself with the nomenclature and definitions of the master soil horizons (O, A, E, B, C, R) and the small letter designations used to distinguish particular types of soil horizon properties commonly found in your region (Table 4.1). The more you have studied about the soil profile, the more meaningful will be your field experience in this exercise.

One final word of advice: *Do wear clothing and footwear appropriate for the weather and for really "getting into" soils!*

MATERIALS

- 1 or 2 soil pits large enough for 5-6 people to enter at one time. A pit deeper than 1.2 m (4 ft) should be shored up for safety.
- soil auger (bucket type)
- tiling spade
- trowel or large knife
- golf ball tees
- pH testing kit
- water in squeeze bottle (to moisten soil)
- 10% HCl in dropper bottle (to test for free carbonates)

- Munsell color book
- plastic bags for soil samples
- 6-place metal muffin baking tin
- 10× magnifying hand lens
- tape measure (6 feet or 2 meters long)
- abney level
- tear sheet from this lab manual chapter (preferably with clip board)
- pencil or waterproof pen

PROCEDURE

Description of Soil Pits

The soil profile description forms accompanying this exercise can serve as a guide to organize your observations. The outline below may assist in you profile investigation, but there is not precise, step-by-step procedure for examining and describing soils in the field. Each site is different and presents unique puzzles and challenges. So, ask questions, observe closely, and get your hands dirty (actually, you should try to keep your *writing hand clean*).

Figure 4.1 illustrates the different types of soil structure you might encounter. You can sometimes see these structures in the profile, but more often you will have to gently break apart the soil to see how it breaks down. The shapes of structural units will usually be most visible if the soil is relatively dry.

Figure 4.2 can serve as a guide to designating horizons in the soil profiles. This is a very generalized picture and no one soil is likely to have all of the horizons shown. If the O and A horizons, and occasionally part of the B horizons, have been mixed by cultivation, the uppermost horizon is designated Ap (p for plowed).

Some Profile Investigation Guidelines:
1. Take care to avoid trampling or piling excavated soil near the profile observation side of the pit.
2. Evaluate the slope, vegetation, parent material, managment and other characteristics of the site and record your notes in the spaces provided.
3. Clean off a pit face that is receiving direct sunlight. This is accomplished, using a large knife or similar implement, by carefully picking out small chunks of soil. Start at the top of the profile, and work your way down, cleaning a narrow (20 to 50 cm wide) panel of the pit wall. Once you have picked a horizon, do not further disturb it until the entire profile has been cleaned, as the falling soil and debris obscures the horizons below.

4. Once the profile is cleaned try to identify the location of major horizon boundaries.
    a. First look for changes on color.
    b. Second, press your knife horizontally into the soil every few cm from the top to the bottom of the profile. Differences in the ease of penetration can signal changes in soil texture, structure and density (be aware, however, that these may be somewhat obscured by variations in soil water content).
5. Mark your estimate of the horizon boundary locations with a knife scratch or by insert golf tees.
6. With your palm held under the knife to catch pieces of soil pried loose, collect a handful of soil from each of the zones that you suspect may be different horizons. Lay these soil samples down on a clean paper side by side in sequential order and label the sample with the depth form which it came.
    a. Using the methods from Exercise #3 perform the texture by feel determination on the samples.
    b. Subtle difference in color can be more readily seen by holding small pieces of soil from two horizons side by side.
7. On the pit face, use a magnifying glass to observe soil pores, channels and roots and record the presence and abundance of these features.
8. Look for redoximorphic features, salt accumulations, carbonates, and other features that are probable under the circumstances. Record these in the soil profile forms.

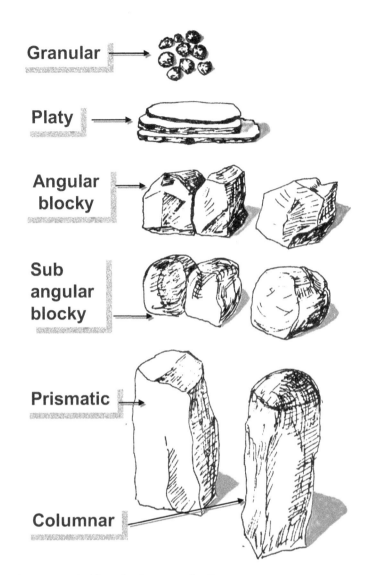

Figure 4. 1 Guide to basic types of soil structure.

37

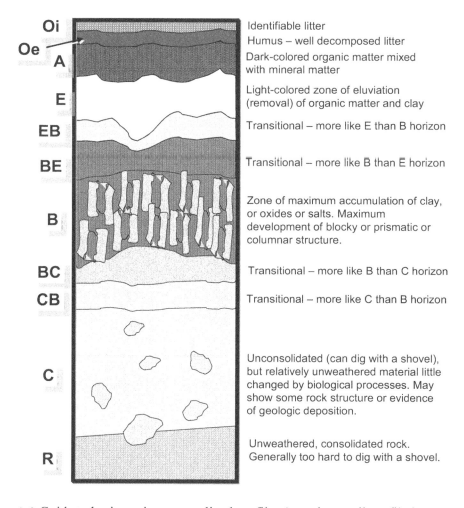

Oi — Identifiable litter
Oe — Humus – well decomposed litter
A — Dark-colored organic matter mixed with mineral matter
E — Light-colored zone of eluviation (removal) of organic matter and clay
EB — Transitional – more like E than B horizon
BE — Transitional – more like B than E horizon
B — Zone of maximum accumulation of clay, or oxides or salts. Maximum development of blocky or prismatic or columnar structure.
BC — Transitional – more like B than C horizon
CB — Transitional – more like C than B horizon
C — Unconsolidated (can dig with a shovel), but relatively unweathered material little changed by biological processes. May show some rock structure or evidence of geologic deposition.
R — Unweathered, consolidated rock. Generally too hard to dig with a shovel.

Figure 4. 2 Guide to horizons in a generalized profile. Any given soil profile is likely to include some, but not all of these possible horizons. Note: for certain very wet soils, L (liminic sediments) and W (water) horizons can also occur.

Table 4. 1 Small letters Used to Designate Subordinate Distinctions Within Master Horizons

	Description of horizon characteristic		Description of horizon characteristic
a	Organic matter, highly decomposed	m	Cementation or induration
b	Buried soil horizon	n	Accumulation of sodium
c	Concretions or nodules	o	Accumulation of Fe and Al oxides
d	Dense unconsolidated materials	p	Plowing or other disturbance
e	Organic matter, intermediate decomposition	q	Accumulation of silica
f	Frozen soil	r	Weathered or soft bedrock
g	Strong gleying (mottling)	s	Illuvial accumulation of OM and oxides
h	Illuvial accumulation of organic matter	ss	Slickensides
i	Organic matter, slightly decomposed	t	Accumulation of silicate clays
j	Jarosite	v	Plinthite (high iron, red material)
jj	Cryoturbation (frost churning)	x	Fragipan (high bulk density, brittle)
k	Accumulation of carbonates	y	Accumulation of gypsum
kk	>50% soil pores plugged with fine pedogenic carbonates	z	Accumulation of soluble salts

Date _____   Name _____

Section _____   I.D. No. _____

Exercise 4
Using a Pit to Study the Soil Profile

Site Locations
(sketch a map)

Notes on Vegetation

Physiographic Region and Landscape Position

Notes on Land Use

Soil Management Practices

Soil Description Techniques Used

Date _____ Name _____

Section _____ I.D. No. _____

SOIL PROFILE DESCRIPTION –Exercise 4

Location _____ Soil Classification

Site No _____ Order _____ Great Group _____ Series _____

Depth	Horizon	Textural Class[1]	Structure			Munsell Color		Consistence[2]	pH	Boundary[3]	Comments[4]
			Strength[5]	Size[6]	Shape[7]	Dry	Moist				

[1] SL=sandy loam, LS=loamy sand, L=loam, CL=clay loam, SiL=silt loam, SCL=sandy clay loam
[2] plastic, nonplastic, sticky, non-sticky, loose, friable, firm, hard, etc.
[3] a=abrupt, c=clear, g=gradual, d=diffuse and w=wavy, s=smooth, i=irregular
[4] mottles (iron depletions or concentrations), clay skins, roots, pans, carbonates, concretions, etc.
[5] weak, moderate, strong expression of structure
[6] fine, medium, coarse
[7] granular, platy, subangular blocky, angular blocky, columnar, prismatic

PROFILES PROPERTIES (CIRCLE APPROPRIATE VALUES)

Drainage[1]........................	very poorly	poorly	somewhat poorly	moderately well		well	excessively
Moisture Availability[2].........	v. low	low	medium	high			
Infiltration Rate[3]	low	medium	high				
Permeability Rate[4]	low	medium	high				
Surface Runoff[5]	low	medium	high				
Depth to hard rock (cm)	0 25	50	75 100	125	150	175	200

Parent Material	(√) Type	Specific Comments
	( ) residuum	rock: _____
	( ) alluvium	texture: _____
	( ) coastal plain sediments	age: _____
	( ) colluvium	
	( ) loess	
	( ) glacial till	
	( ) other	

SITE CHARACTERISTICS

Vegetation/Land Use:

Slope (%)	0-2 2-5 5-10 10-15 10-30 > 30	
Position	(√) Position	Comments
	( ) Summit	
in	( ) Shoulder	
	( ) Backslope	
	( ) Footslope	
Landscape	( ) Depression	
	( ) Flood Plain	
	( ) Terrace	

PROFILE SKETCH

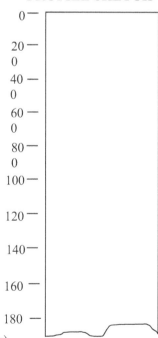

[1] Based on soil colors and depth to redoximorphic features (e.g. gray mottles).
[2] See "Guide to Estimating Moisture Availability by Soil Texture," Appendix C.
[3] Based on surface texture and structure.
[4] Based on texture and structure of least permeable horizon.
[5] Based on slope, infiltration, and permeability.

Date _____ Name _____

Section _____ I.D. No. _____

SOIL PROFILE DESCRIPTION – Exercise 4

Location _____ Soil Classification

Site No _____ Order _____ Great Group _____ Series _____

Depth	Horizon	Textural Class[1]	Structure			Munsell Color		Consistence[2]	pH	Boundary[3]	Comments[4]
			Strength[5]	Size[6]	Shape[7]	Dry	Moist				

[1] SL=sandy loam, LS=loamy sand, L=loam, CL=clay loam, SiL=silt loam, SCL=sandy clay loam
[2] plastic, nonplastic, sticky, non-sticky, loose, friable, firm, hard, etc.
[3] a=abrupt, c=clear, g=gradual, d=diffuse and w=wavy, s=smooth, i=irregular
[4] mottles (iron depletions or concentrations), clay skins, roots, pans, carbonates, concretions, etc.
[5] weak, moderate, strong expression of structure
[6] fine, medium, coarse
[7] granular, platy, subangular blocky, angular blocky, columnar, prismatic

43

PROFILES PROPERTIES (CIRCLE APPROPRIATE VALUES)

Drainage[1]......................	very poorly	poorly	somewhat poorly	moderately well	well	excessively
Moisture Availability[2]........	v. low	low	medium	high		
Infiltration Rate[3]	low	medium	high			
Permeability Rate[4]	low	medium	high			
Surface Runoff[5]	low	medium	high			
Depth to hard rock (cm)	0 25 50 75 100 125 150 175 200					

Parent Material	(√) Type	Specific Comments
	( ) residuum ( ) alluvium ( ) coastal plain sediments ( ) colluvium ( ) loess ( ) glacial till ( ) other	rock: _____ texture: _____ age: _____

SITE CHARACTERISTICS

Vegetation/Land Use:

Slope (%)	0-2 2-5 5-10 10-15 10-30 > 30	
Position	(√) Position	Comments
in	( ) Summit ( ) Shoulder ( ) Backslope	
Landscape	( ) Footslope ( ) Depression ( ) Flood Plain ( ) Terrace	

PROFILE SKETCH

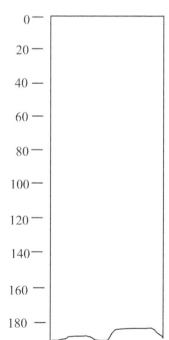

[1] Based on soil colors and redoximorphic features (e.g. gray mottles).
[2] See "Guide to Estimating Moisture Availability by Soil Texture," Appendix C.
[3] Based on surface texture and structure.
[4] Based on texture and structure of least permeable horizon.
[5] Based on slope, infiltration, and permeability.

Date _____

Name _____

Section _____

I.D. No. _____

SOIL PROFILE DESCRIPTION

Location _____   Soil Classification

Site No _____   Order _____   Great Group _____   Series _____

Depth	Horizon	Textural Class[1]	Structure			Munsell Color		Consistence[2]	pH	Boundary[3]	Comments[4]
			Strength[5]	Size[6]	Shape[7]	Dry	Moist				

[1] SL=sandy loam, LS=loamy sand, L=loam, CL=clay loam, SiL=silt loam, SCL=sandy clay loam
[2] plastic, nonplastic, sticky, non-sticky, loose, friable, firm, hard, etc.
[3] a=abrupt, c=clear, g=gradual, d=diffuse and w=wavy, s=smooth, i=irregular
[4] mottles (iron depletions or concentrations), clay skins, roots, pans, carbonates, concretions, etc.
[5] weak, moderate, strong expression of structure
[6] fine, medium, coarse
[7] granular, platy, subangular blocky, angular blocky, columnar, prismatic

45

PROFILES PROPERTIES (CIRCLE APPROPRIATE VALUES)

	very		somewhat	moderately		
Drainage[1]......................	poorly	poorly	poorly	well	well	excessively
Moisture Availability[2].........	v. low	low	medium	high		
Infiltration Rate[3]	low	medium	high			
Permeability Rate[4]	low	medium	high			
Surface Runoff[5]	low	medium	high			

Depth to hard rock (cm)   0   25   50   75   100   125   150   175   200

Parent Material	(√) Type	Specific Comments
	( ) residuum	rock: _____
	( ) alluvium	texture: _____
	( ) coastal plain sediments	age: _____
	( ) colluvium	
	( ) loess	
	( ) glacial till	
	( ) other	

SITE CHARACTERISTICS

Vegetation/Land Use:

Slope (%)	0-2 2-5 5-10 10-15 10-30 > 30	
Position	(√) Position	Comments
	( ) Summit	
in	( ) Shoulder	
	( ) Backslope	
Landscape	( ) Footslope	
	( ) Depression	
	( ) Flood Plain	
	( ) Terrace	

PROFILE SKETCH

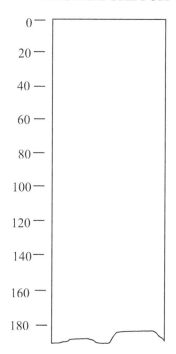

---

[1] Based on soil colors and redoximorphic features (e.g. gray mottles).
[2] See "Guide to Estimating Moisture Availability by Soil Texture," Appendix C.
[3] Based on surface texture and structure.
[4] Based on texture and structure of least permeable horizon.
[5] Based on slope, infiltration, and permeability.

Exercise 5
Use of Soil Survey Information
In Land Planning

OBJECTIVES

After completing this exercise, you should be able …

1.   Define: Soil Series, soil phase, mapping unit, soil association, soil type, soil complex.
2.   Use the satellite image map base on Web Soil Survey and Google Earth® to determine land use pattern present on the ground at the time the air-photo was made.
3.   Find and interpret mapping information such as scale, date of aerial or satellite image, etc.
4.   Use web soil survey to make an interpretive soils map of a given area.
5.   Recognize and interpret land capability symbols to the subclass level (e.g., IVe).
6.   Explain the meaning of mapping units symbols (e.g., GeB2).
7.   Explain and give appropriate consideration to the degree of purity of mapping units and the accuracy of their boundaries on web soil survey and in detailed soil survey reports.
8.   Understand the need for, access to, and uses of Web Soil Survey (WSS)
9.   Calibrate and understand the map scale on WSS
10. Search for specific locations and create an Area of Interest (AOI)
11. Understand soil map units and use them to get information about the soil
12. Use the Soil Data Explorer and understand how to interpret the data
13. Create and save a Soil Survey Data Report on an AOI on WSS
14. Download and use Google Earth®
15. Download and use the soil web kmz plugin for Google Earth®
16. Locate specific landmarks or coordinates on Google Earth®
17. Identify land uses and objects visible on vertical satellite imagery
18. Use the dating tool to see current and prior land uses
19. Create soil maps using Google Earth®
20. Access additional information about soil mapping units and soil series from Google Earth® with soils overlay kmz.
21. Use both WSS and Google Earth® to make informed decisions about the suitability of land for particular uses.

INTRODUCTION

What Is a Soil Survey?[1]

A soil survey is made to tell us what kinds of soils exist in the survey area and where they are located. The soils are mapped and described in terms of their location, their profile characteristics, their relation to each other in the landscape, their suitability for various uses, their requirements for special management practices, and their agricultural and silvicultural productivity. The detail with which soils are surveyed varies with the nature of the area and the purpose of the survey.

---

[1] See also Soil Survey Manual Chapter
3: https://www.nrcs.usda.gov/wps/portal/nrcs/detail/soils/ref/?cid=nrcs142p2_054253#terms

In many developing countries and in some non-intensively used areas of the USA, only very broad, reconnaissance surveys have been made. However, the US Department of Agriculture's Natural Resources Conservation Service has been engaged for decades in producing a detailed soil survey to cover all counties in the United States. As "detailed" soil surveys have been completed, older ones are now being updated. In the US, data from these Soil Surveys is collected in a data set call SSURGO and made available in the form of an interactive web site called Web Soil Survey (see link in sidebar). On Web Soil Survey, soil maps can be overlain on satellite imagery of any selected land area. Tables of soil information can also be displayed.

In making the soil maps of an area, a team of

Useful Soil Survey Websites

Web based soil survey maps and information for many areas of US can be found at: http://websoilsurvey.nrcs.usda.gov/app/

A KMZ file that overlays soil survey information onto Google earth images of the United States can be downloaded from: https://casoilresource.lawr.ucdavis.edu/soilweb-apps/

Site to download SSURGO soil map files for use in GIS computer programs: http://www.nrcs.usda.gov/wps/portal/nrcs/detail/soils/survey/?cid=nrcs142p2_053627

Listing of scanned paper and digital soil surveys available by US state. Note that many are not yet available in user-friendly formats. http://soils.usda.gov/survey/printed_surveys/

---

soil scientists spends months or years studying the soils. They walk over the land, using GPS to record the locations of their observations, making auger borings to determine what the subsurface soil properties are like and where the boundaries between different soils should be located. In addition, changes in topography, soil color and vegetation visible on aerial photographs and satellite images are also used to locate soil boundaries. Many soil samples from various depths and locations are analyzed in laboratories as well as in the field. Occasionally pits are dug to better characterize and describe each type of soil. Meanwhile the soil scientists also observe how the soils react to different management practices and land-uses. They study all the available information about the soils' suitability for various uses. Their experience and judgments can be summarized by constructing interpretive tables on the Explore tab in Web Soil Survey.

The overall purpose of this exercise is to familiarize you with certain online tools that will help you investigate and manage spatial geographic information about soils. This type of information is necessary in order to make wise land use decisions that consider soil conditions and some suitabilities. Soil scientists have been surveying and mapping soil bodies in the landscape using increasingly sophisticated techniques for over 100 years now. Until just a few years ago, this is information was stored and made available as paper soil survey reports with maps overlain on black and white aerial photographs. Since 2007 the USDA Natural Resource Conservation Service has offered an online tool called web soil survey (WSS) which essentially replaces and conveys the same type of information as the paper reports, but does it with interactive digital maps, tables, and reports.

Around the same time, the search engine company, Google Inc., made available free to the public an Internet-based program called Google Earth® that allows access to satellite imagery for virtually the entire land surface of the Earth. This tool displays satellite imagery and many geographic features such as roads and towns. However, it does not show soils information. Soil scientists at the University of California recently released a program that works with Google Earth® to overlay soil maps and interface with soil information from the databases of the USDA/NRCS. This "soil interface" for Google Earth® is the second Internet-based tool that we will learn to use in this exercise.

The fact that the soil maps are overlain on satellite images or aerial photos makes an incredible amount of detailed site information available to those who understand how to interpret such images. Use of recent air-photos, especially if overlapping pairs are available, can greatly enhance the site information. Viewing overlapping pairs of air photos through a stereoscope "tricks the eye" into seeing

48

the landscape in three dimensions, so the terrain relief becomes much more evident than on single "flat" photo such as the map base. A similar effect can be created for online satellite images using the "shadows" function in Google, Inc's free downloadable program, Google Earth®.

We will learn about these tools by applying them to the land encompassed by Gettysburg National Park in Pennsylvania, one of the most famous historic sites in the United States. Both of these tools involve aerial or 1 satellite imagery as well as soil maps, so this exercise will also help you learn how to get the most information from these elements.

A Word of Caution on Using Soil Maps

Before we begin, it would be wise to note some limitations associated with even these modern computer tools. First of all, the imagery used by both Web Soil Survey and Google Earth® is likely to be out of date by several months or even several years. That is, the "ground truth" may have changed since the image was made, especially in areas with rapid urban development taking place. Thus, new roads and buildings may appear, while forests may be cut down and rivers may even change their courses because of floods. Therefore, actual on the ground verification is necessary as part of a real land planning operation.

Secondly, even the most carefully constructed soil maps will have a quite a bit of uncertainty associated with the boundaries between mapping units and the actual composition of soils within any mapping unit. The soil boundaries drawn are only approximate and the mapping units they delineate are not "pure" but may contain small areas of different, even contrasting, types of soils. The mapping unit descriptions detail which soils are expected in the mapping unit, but not where these different components are located within a map unit. Making soil maps involves a certain tension between the tendencies of the "splitters" (soil scientists inclined to show split large heterogeneous map units into smaller more pure units) and "lumpers" (soil scientist who prefer to lump or combine spatially complex or uncertain information into larger, more heterogeneous mapping units).

Thus, if one goes to the actual site and investigates the soil at any particular spot within a mapping unit, there is a chance that the soil one actually finds in that spot may not be the soil for which the mapping unit was named. This uncertainty regarding the actual makeup of the areas of land delineated on the soil maps is formally recognized by mapping units called soil consocations and soil complexes. Again, before making decisions in real life, an on the ground investigation should be conducted.

MATERIALS

- Stereo pairs of panchromatic black and white air photos, preferably of locations with hills, mountains, cliffs, deeply incised streams, and other dramatic relief features)
- Pocket stereoscope (available from forestry and survey suppliers)
- An internet connected computer or mobile device with Google Earth® software installed (see 1-3 below).
  1. Do the online tutorial for web soil survey at: http://websoilsurvey.nrcs.usda.gov, click on "How to Use Web Soil Survey" under "I Want Help With..." heading on the bottom right-hand side of the screen.
  2. Download and install Google Earth® (this is different from Google Maps®) from: http://www.google.com/ earth/index.html
  3. Download the KMZ file to view soil survey data in Google Earth®: http://casoilresource.lawr.ucdavis.edu/drupal/ node/429 "SoilWeb" will be added to the "Temporary Places" folder on Google Earth®, move the folder to the "My Places" folder in the sidebar, to keep the file permanently.

After completing these steps, will you be ready to use these tools on your computer and gain some familiarity with them by doing this lab exercise.

VIEWING AIR PHOTOS IN 3-D WITH A POCKET STEREOSCOPE

1. View at least two stereo pairs of air photos using a pocket stereoscope. To do so, place obtain from your instructor a stereo pair of photos what show include the same scene viewed from two different angles. Find an obvious feature (such as a pond or rock outcrop or distinctive building) that is the shown on each photo. Place the photos, one partially overlapping the other, so that the same feature on each photo is about 10 cm apart, or the same distance apart as between the center of the two pocket stereoscope lenses. Be sure the photos are both aligned in the same manner (that is north is facing the same way on each).

2. Open the fold-out legs of the stereoscope and stand the scope so that it straddles the two overlapping photos with the same feature under each lens. Adjust the distance between lenses to match the distance between your eyes. Adjust the focus if a focus adjustment is available. Using both eyes, look through the stereoscope at the chosen feature on the air photos. Rotate the two photos slightly until the feature on one photo seems to just lie on top of or blend into the same feature on the other photo. When they coincide, the feature should "rise up" off the flat photo and appear 3-dimensionally.

3. Carefully slide the stereoscope across the overlapped pair of air photos, moving slowly along the zone showing the same land area. This strip of land should appear in relief. Identify with a pointing stylus, the ridge tops and the valley bottoms.

4. Repeat steps 1-3 for a second stereo pair of air photos.

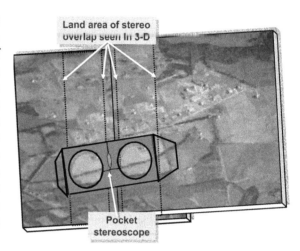

Figure 5. 1 Top-down view of a stereoscope set up on a stereo pair of air photos.

PLEASE DO NOT MAKE ANY MARKS ON THE AIR PHOTOS!

EXPLORING WEB SOIL SURVEY

Procedure

Comments

1. **Starting Web Soil Survey and Finding a location.** Navigate to http://websoilsurvey.nrcs.usda.gov/app/ and click

Be patient…the website may seem a bit slow as it is dealing with large amounts of data.

on the green "Start WSS" button. Under the quick navigation menu, click on the method by which you wish to "navigate" to your area of interest. For this exercise, choose "Address" and type in "Aberdeen, Md" for the city and state. Click the "View" button.

2. On the tool bar above the "Area of Interest Interactive Map", select the + or - magnifying glass tool, then click on the map to zoom in or out until an area of about 10,000 x 5,000 feet is displayed. Note the scale bar (in feet) near the bottom of the map.

3. **Changing the legend to make the map more readable.** Click on the legend tab located on the left side of the map window. The legend window will pop up and allow features of the map to be turned on and off.

4. **Defining an Area of Interest (AOI).** At the top of the map window, click on the "AOI button" with the red rectangle. Then take the crosshairs onto the map and draw a rectangle around the portion of the map for which you would like to obtain soil data. Make this AOI about 10,000 feet wide x 7,000 ft in size, estimating from the scale bar at the bottom of the map

5. **Viewing the Soils Map.** Once the AOI has been created and is indicated by the blue hash lines, click on the tab at the top of the page that says "Soil Map." Zoom in until you can identify individual soil map units and see their labels. To return to the full extent of the AOI, click on the button that says AOI with a green globe above it.

6. **Identifying features on the map.** Click on the blue and white "i" icon at the top of the map page. Open the legend window and click on the "Soil Map Units" category to highlight it. Then click on a specific map unit. The name and symbol of the unit will be displayed in the window at the bottom. To learn when the aerial photograph was taken, you can highlight the Aerial Photography category in the legend window, then click on the map.

You should now have a view of the area around the town of Aberdeen, Md. For example, if you scroll to the bottom of the legend window and uncheck the box next to "Transportation", the roads will no longer be highlighted and named. This is useful to make the map less cluttered, but may sacrifice some geographic awareness.

Before you can view the soil map, you will need to outline an "area of interest." There are two AOI buttons, one is for making a rectangle as described. You can also create an irregularly shaped area of interest using the polygon AOI button. Making an AOI too large will results in a map highly cluttered with unreadable map units and symbols. Making the AOI too small will result in only one or two soil map units and a warning that the scale may overly exaggerate the actual accuracy.

The soil survey map units for the defined AOI should be displayed. The summary table on the left lists the map units present in the AOI and the land area of each (in traditional English units of acres). The map unit abbreviations are the same as in the paper soil survey. You can zoom in on portions of the AOI to get a more detailed view using the "magnifying class" tool and pan around the map using the "hand" tool.

To identify and get information about certain features shown on the map, click on the blue and white "i" icon at the top of the map page. Instructions for using the identify tool ("i") pop up in a window at the bottom of the screen.

7. **Obtaining Soil Information.** Click on the tab at the top of the page labeled "Soil Data Explorer." In this tab, click on the + next to All Uses to expand the "table of contents." Click the + next to "Soils 101" near the top of the screen. Under the list of topics on the left, click to check the boxes next to the following:

✓ What is a soil survey?
✓ What is a map unit?
✓ What is a consociation, complex, association, undifferentiated group, or miscellaneous area?
✓ What is an Official Series Description?
✓ Land capability classification
✓ Then click the button for View Description.

This menu give access to a variety of information about soils and the Soil Survey. Read the selected explanations and use the information to answer questions on hand-in form at the end of this unit.

8. **Obtaining Soil Data.** At the menu of topics on the left side, click on Information for Land Users, then click to check the box for Waste Disposal Entities. Expand that menu and click on Septic tank absorption fields

This description gives background on septic tank absorption fields and how the suitability and limitations ratings were developed. As indicated by the extensive menu, soils information is available for many land uses.

9. **Making a soil interpretation map.** After investigating a soil suitability (as in 8, above), close the description box and then click on the "View Rating" button. A colored map of the suitability levels is now displayed. Click on the "Legend" tab to see what each color stands for.

The suitability soils map is color coded with red being the worst (very limited) and green being the best (not limited) soils for the selected land use. Your map of septic tank drainfield suitabilities should indicate that most soils in the area are very to moderately limited, meaning you should expect problems in siting and designing septic systems in this area. At the bottom of the page, a table of each map unit is displayed, showing its suitability rating and the reason for the rating.

10. **Making a map of soil properties.** Click on the "Soil Properties and Qualities" tab and explore the menus on the left to see the type of soil information available. Click on Water Features, then on Flooding Frequency Class. The click View Rating button.

This will easily create a map of Flooding Frequency Class…. Information that emergency agencies can use to plan ahead for flood damages and rescue operations. You can save your map as a PDF file…see making a soils report, next step.

11. **Making a Soils Report.** Now click on the "Soil Reports" tab. Browse the menus of the many different types of information available through this feature. Under "Vegetative Productivity" category, click on "Non-irrigated yields by map unit component." Select up to 5 crops of interest, then click on "View Soil Report." A table on the right-hand side of the page will display yield potentials for each map unit in the AOI.

It may take some trial and error to find the information you are looking for as the meaning of the labels is not always obvious. For example, to find crop yield potentials for different soil types, click on the "Vegetative Productivity" category, then on "Non-irrigated yields by map unit component."

12. **Ending the Web Soil Survey session.** When you are finished using the Web Soil Survey, please click on the "Logout" button at the top of the page in order to terminate your session with the data server.

Logging out will make the website run faster for other users. Congratulations, you now know how to use Web Soil Survey to explore soils related information about almost any land area in the US!

Figure 5.2. This image from *WebSoilSurvey* with soil boundaries and identification codes (thick dark sans serif lettering and lines) of West Bangor, PA area near the border with Maryland has added large white italic letters and pointers that designate features to be identified in questions 6A – 6L.

Exercise 5 Assignment:
CREATIVE LAND PLANNING USING SOIL SURVEY INFORMATION ABOUT GETTYSBURG NATIONAL MILITARY PARK

See previous three pages for information on how to locate the Park. Using Web Soil Survey and Google Earth®, determine where you would have put the Park Visitor's Center based on land capability and impacts to such things as cultural, agricultural, and natural resources. Create and print 3 or 4 maps showing the criteria that you feel are most important for making this decision, and draw on the maps where you would locate the Visitor's Center. Explain in detail the rationale you used for choosing your location of the Visitor's Center and why you chose the criteria you did to make the decision. It is important to acknowledge any factors that you intentionally did not incorporate into the decision-making process as well as impacts of your placement of the building to resources or uses that could occur, but that you feel are justified.

In summary, your assignment is to produce a report explaining where you think the best location for the Visitor's Center would have been based on land capability and such considerations as cultural, agricultural, and natural resources as they existed just before construction. Your report should include 3 to 4 maps (using both Web Soil Survey *and* Google Earth®, as per above) and an approximately 1,000 word narrative explanation. You may include tables or equations as you see fit to justify your accounting for the roles that specific soil suitabilities and resource values played in your design decisions in locating the visitor center within the Park "area of interest".

Tips for Printing Maps from Web Soil Survey

- Make sure pop-ups from Web Soil Survey are not blocked on your computer.
- When want to print a map on your screen, you may either hit the "Printable Version" button on the top of the screen to make a pdf of just that map and its legend, or you may hit the "Add to Shopping Cart" button to add it to the report you will print later. Don't worry, you won't have to actually "buy" anything in your "shopping cart."
- You may add multiple maps to the Shopping Cart and then print one report at the end. Click on the "Shopping Cart" tab and deselect items on the Table of Contents, listed on the left-hand side of your screen, to generate a report that includes only the information that you want.
- Even after narrowing the contents of the report, it will automatically include a lot of "boiler plate" information. To conserve paper and reduce hassles, print ONLY those pages that are necessary to turn in for your homework assignment. DO NOT HAND IN THE ENTIRE DEFAULT-GENERATED REPORT.

Tips for Printing Maps from Google Earth®

- In Google Earth®, go to View menu, uncheck "sidebar." This gives you a full screen image.
- Go to File menu, click "save"…then "save image" and save the images on your computer as a jpg image file.
- Print the jpg image file directly in an image software program, or insert the image into WORD® or POWERPOINT® for annotation and printing.

Exercise 5
USING SOIL SURVEY INFORMATION

The following exercises are designed to familiarize you with Web Soil Survey and other online sources to find soil survey and land feature information. To answer some of these questions you will have to make your own judgments based on information in this exercise and in the soil survey.

ACTIVIY A: Definitions and interpretations.

1. **Using Section 17.14 and the glossary in *The Nature and Properties of Soils* or the online glossary tool from the Soil Science Society of America (available at:** https://www.soils.org/publications/soils-glossary) or Soil Survey Manual at: https://www.nrcs.usda.gov/wps/portal/nrcs/detail/soils/ref/?cid=nrcs142p2_054253#terms define these terms used to describe soil differentiations on soil maps:

Pedon:

Soil Series:

Soil Phase:

Mapping Unit:

Soil Consociation:

Soil Complex/Association:

Undifferentiated Group:

Inclusion:

2. Many maps have a scale ratio. What does the map scale ratio 1:190,080

    mean?_____

a. Translate this figure into in./mile: _____ and cm/km: _____

b. How many miles are represented by 2 inches? _____

3. The Land Capability Classification system was originally developed to rate limitations for cropping but it is widely used to judge the suitability of the land for many other uses.

a. How many capability classes are there in the NRCS Land Capability Classification?

b. What are the subclasses in this system? _____

c. What is the most detailed or lowest category in the system?_____

d. How do the following differ from each other?

    i.   IIe land and IVe land: _____

    ii.   IVw and IVe land:_____

    iii.   VIs and VIIs: _____

    iv.   IIe-5 and IIe-10: _____

4. Both satellite imagery and black and white aerial photos used as background with soil maps printed over them can provide a great deal of information in addition to the location of the various soils. Use the reproduction of a Google Earth image and soil map overlay (Figure 2) to practice air photo and map interpretation by answering the following.

5. For WSS maps, how could find out what time of year and in what year was the image made?

_____

6. Identify the features marked on the reproductions by large capital letter for this exercise.

- A _____
- B _____
- C (printed characters) _____
- D (erosion control farming practice) _____
- E (erosion control farming practice) _____
- F (line) _____
- G (linear feature on land) _____
- H (group of objects) _____
- I (vegetation type – hint relate this to time of year) _____
- J (farming practice) _____
- K (lines) _____

- L (thick broken line on map) _____

7.   Using the printed scale and a ruler, determine the scale ratio of the map as printed on the page. Show calculations here:

8. One cm on the image represents _____ kilometers

9. One acre = 43,560 sq. ft. or a square area 210 ft. on each side. Find the odd shaped pond. About how

    many acres of surface are there in the pond? _____. This is equivalent to how many hectares? _____

    Show calculations here:

10. In the mapping unit symbol GcC2

                (a) "Gc" stands for: _____

                (b) "C" stands for: _____

                (c) "2" stands for: _____

ACTIVITY B: USING WEB SOIL SURVEY
Go to http://websoilsurvey.nrcs.usda.gov

Click on "Start WSS" button

Click on the "scale" button on the bar above the map and follow the instructions to calibrate the scale for your computer screen.

11. What is the scale on your screen? _____

12. Assuming the map was made at a 1:12,000 scale, the map on your computer is at a larger / smaller scale?

13. There are several ways on could use to find Gettysburg National Military Park. Try all three:

    a) Enter the address of the Visitor's Center: 1195 Baltimore Pike, Gettysburg, PA 17325
       Note: finding the park this way will not give you the park boundary
    b) Using coordinates: 39 48'40'' N, 77 13'34''W (enter without spaces or symbols: 394840N)
       Note: finding the park this way will not give you the park boundary
    c) Click on "National Park Service" on the "Search" list, and choose Pennsylvania's Gettysburg National Military Park. Click "View" on the Map that comes up using the National Park Services search option. Define your "Area of Interest" by clicking on the triangular AOI button and tracing the outline of the park that is contiguous and south of the town of Gettysburg (south of State Highway 116). Your AOI should be approximate 4500-5000 acres in size.

14. Use the *Zoom-In* tool to make a box around the southwest section of the town of Gettysburg, specifically south of the triangle formed by the intersecting US Hwy 15 BUS and State Highway 97. Once zoomed in,

use the measurement tool on the bar above the map to determine the distance between the intersection of Wheatfield Road and US Hwy 15 BUS and the intersection of US Hwy 15 Bus and State Highway 97. Record the distance here: _____.

15. Zoom to AOI Extent and click on the Soil Map tab at the top of the screen. A soil map overlay should appear. What is the dominant map unit symbol in your AOI? _____

16. What is the dominant map unit name in your AOI? _____
Click on this map unit name and answer the following questions:
      a. In what County is Gettysburg National Military Park
      located?_____
      b. Lehigh and similar soils comprise what percentage of this map
      unit?_____
      c. What is the name of the soil that makes up the minor component of this map unit?
      _____
      d. If this does not add up to 100% of the map unit, how do you account for the difference?
      _____
      e. What is the drainage class of this
      soil?_____

17. Look at the soil map again. There are two symbols that are dominant in the Park. What do these two symbols indicate (click on the map's legend, and then look at the "Special Point Features" under the "Soils" heading)?
_____

18. Zoom to the southeast corner of the park between State Highways 134 and 116, where one of these symbols predominates. What do you see just outside of the park boundary?
_____
_____

19. Click on the "Soil Properties and Qualities" tab and expand Soil Qualities and Features to click on Parent Material Name. Click "View Rating." What trend is easily observable with respect to the parent materials on this map?
_____
_____

20. Based on the type of parent material nearby, what is being removed at the site discovered in Question
18? _____

21. What is common in the parent materials of the soils found to the north of US HWY 15?

_____

22. Click on the "Soil Data Explorer" tab, and then choose "Land Classifications/Farmland Classifications" and "View Rating." What does the Farmland Classification tell us? (Click on View Description)
_____

23. As you can see from the map, a lot of farmland surrounds Gettysburg. Explore how suitable the land is for farming. Do you see any similarities to other information we have looked up today?

_____

_____

_____

24. The Gettysburg Visitor Center is located south of town in the triangle between State Hwy 97 and State Hwy 134. Zoom to this area. You should now be able to see the structure to the south of Hunt Avenue. Click on the "Suitabilities and Limitations for Use" tab and click on "Sanitary Facilities".

Is this location suitable for septic tank absorption fields (remember to use the legend to understand how symbols and colors are displayed on the map)? _____

25. Can you find a type of sanitary facility that is suitable at this site?

_____

26. How do you think the Visitor's Center treats their sewage?

_____

_____

USING GOOGLE EARTH®

27. Open Google Earth®. If you have not done so already, download the KMZ file to view soil survey data in Google Earth® from: https://casoilresource.lawr.ucdavis.edu/soilweb-apps/ "SoilWeb" will be added to the "Temporary Places" folder on Google Earth®, move the folder to the "My Places" folder in the sidebar, to keep the file permanently

28. Under the *Places* sidebar, make sure "SoilWeb" is checked. This will display soil map units as an overlay when you are zoomed in (scale of 1:35,000 or larger).

29. Under the Layers sidebar, click the arrow to display the layers under "More", and then click the arrow to display "Parks/Recreation Areas". Make sure the boxes next to "Parks/Recreation Areas" and "US National Parks" is checked. This will display the park boundaries.

30. Use the search function to find Gettysburg National Military Park.

31. Find the map unit labeled NaB and click on it. A window will open showing the components of the map unit and diagrams of the soil profiles for these soil series.

32. What soil series make up this map unit? _____

33. Clicking on the soil series names will open up links with information about the soil series.

    a. Using the map unit WaB:

    b. What is the name of the map unit? _____

    c. What type of map unit is this? _____

    d. What does the Wa stand for? _____

    e. What does the B stand for? _____

f. What is (are) the major component(s) of this map unit? _____

34. Use the search function to find the following coordinates. Identify the features from the aerial photographs. (Hint: when entering the coordinates into the search toolbar leave a space instead of the ° symbol, for example: 39°50'18.42"N 77 14'21.83"W)

   a. 39°50'18.42"N 77o14'21.83"W _____

   b. 39°48'1.37"N 77o11'33.81"W _____

   c. 39°48'23.51"N 77o14'53.52"W _____

   d. 39°49'0.79"N 77o15'16.25"W _____

   e. 39°46'51.67"N 77o11'54.50"W _____

   f. 39°54'30.35"N 77o19'16.38"W _____

   g. 39°49'58.47"N 77o9'58.73"W _____

   h. 39°49'28.30"N 77o19'42.20"W _____

35. Find the visitor center using the coordinates 39°48'41.35"N 77°13'33.84"W. Along the top tool bar there is a clock icon that opens the historical imagery toolbar. Move the slider bar to look at older aerial photographs. Use the slider bar to scroll through the older aerial photographs and determine when the visitor center was built. _____

36. Prior to construction of the visitor's center, what was the land use at this site? _____

37. Go to the most recent image and look at the soil map. There are two polygons labeled "W". What is this map unit? _____

38. Is this consistent with the current land cover/use? _____

39. Use the historical imagery to explain why the W mapping unit was used at this location

   _____

   _____

   _____

Exercise 6

Getting to Know a Catena in the Field

OBJECTIVES

After completing this exercise, you should be able to …

1. recognize a catena of soils in the field.
2. define and distinguish the terms catena and toposequence.
3. make an auger hole and collect soil using a bucket auger.
4. examine soil during augering to recognize horizon changes.
5. use soil color, texture, landscape position and horizon changes to associate an auger hole with a soil description in a soil survey report.
6. associate soil suborder names with drainage status of several soils in a catena.
7. determine the drainage class by the depth of redoximorphic features observed while augering.
8. explain how soil morphological features might be used to rate a soil as well, moderately-, or poorly- suited for use as a septic filter field or as a fruit orchard.

INTRODUCTION

Hands-on experience is an important part of learning about soils. That is why most introductory soil science courses include a weekly laboratory. While many analyses can be performed on soil material brought into the lab, to understand soils as natural bodies in the landscape one must go out into their natural habitat. Therefore, the lab portion of introductory soil science courses commonly includes one or more field trips. Examining a catena of soils in the field is an excellent way to broaden your knowledge of soil profiles and soil-landscape relationships. *Catena* is a term first coined in East Africa to describe a grouping of different soils that occur together in the landscape, each soil in a catena differing from the others principally because of the effect of topography. These soils may be in the same soil order, or the topography may have so affected their development as to set them off in different soil orders.

Your instructor will have chosen a site that contains a set of soils whose drainage characteristics vary with the topography so that soils belonging to at least three drainage classes occur side by side. Drainage classes are given names such as 'well drained' or 'excessively drained' if water moves readily through the entire profile and no evidence of water logging is seen in the upper 100 cm (see Table 6.1). A 'moderately well drained' or 'somewhat poorly drained' member of a catena will have restricted water movement through the profile, and as a result, will show evidence of *water logging* within 50 or 25 cm of the surface. A 'poorly drained' or 'very poorly drained" member of the catena would be waterlogged to within less than 25 cm of the soil surface for a significant portion of the average year. These soils are likely to be *hydric* soils associated with *wetlands*.

"Water logging' is a colloquial term that suggests a water saturated condition.[1] To cause the formation of redoximorphic features in the soil profile, the water saturated conditions must occur during parts of the year when soil temperatures are high enough for microbial activity to use up all the oxygen dissolved in the soil water, thus creating anoxic conditions. Under anoxic conditions, certain redoximorphic features can form in the soil. Examples of these features include gray colors (iron reduction and depletion), mottles of contrasting rust-red (iron concentrations) and gray colors, black

---

[1] To learn more about changes that occur when a soil becomes waterlogged, see Chapter 21.

humus accumulations, grayish humus depletion spots, and reddish zones around root channels made by hydromorphic plants.

In one type of catena, known as a *toposequence*, all the soils have formed from the same or related parent materials. However, if you are investigating a catena in which the parent material changes along with the slope, you should be able to observe the main effects of topography, as well as the interaction of two factors of soil formation (topography and parent material). The total topographic variation need not be very dramatic; often just a meter or two difference in elevation will provide major changes in soil profile characteristics. Prior to this field experience, you may not have attached much importance to small topographic variations in the landscape. After this field trip, you should be more aware of how important small changes in relief can be. If conditions at the site are right, some of the auger holes may allow you to observe ground water *in situ.*

This exercise will be of greatest educational value if it follows a field trip in which you examined one or more soil profiles using soil pits. Ideally, you will have seen a pit profile of at least one of the soil series included in the study catena. The previous experience in the soil pit should help you relate the pieces of soil material that the auger brings up to the appearance of the soil in place. This field exercise will go more smoothly and be more meaningful if you have already completed exercise in which you learned to determine texture by feel, use the Munsell color book, and determine pH.

MATERIALS

- Appropriate field site: The site should contain a set of soils whose characteristics clearly vary with the topography. In most regions, these characteristics will be largely related to soil drainage. In dry regions, other characteristics such as depth to carbonate layers or soil texture changes may be more important. If possible, use a site where soils belonging to at least three drainage classes occur side-by-side: a well drained or excessively drained member, a moderately well or somewhat poorly drained member, and a poorly or very poorly drained member. Choosing a site and time of year that will allow students to observe ground water in some of the auger holes will further enhance the experience. The instructor should make sure that the profile and drainage features desired are actually in the positions where they are expected to occur. If possible, choose a site for which a soil survey map is available. The pedons to be augered along the drainage catena should be marked with labeled flags (1,2, 3, 4 and series name if known).
- A bucket type soil auger with a T-handle (generally a 1.5 m long handle is sufficient). The auger head should bore a hole between 7 to 10 cm in diameter. For coarse or medium textured soils, a closed bucket auger can be used. For clay soils, an opened sided bucket auger will allow easier removal of the soil material. Good alloy augers are lightweight, strong, and capable of staying sharp.
- Munsell Color books (one book for every three or four students).
- pH dye kit or portable pH meter with plastic beakers (one for every three or four students).
- A large knife or spatula (a butter knife will do in a pinch) to help remove soil from auger
- A measuring tape as long as the auger handle (at least 1.5 m).
- A set of three or four troughs made by slicing 10 cm (4") diameter PVC piping in half lengthwise. Troughs should be as long as the deepest profile augered (1.5 m) and marked with centimeters (or inches) to facilitate placing the soil to scale. An optional enhancement is to glue a square piece of Plexiglas on either end of the trough to prevent it from rolling over and to hold in the soil.
- Squeeze-type water bottle (500 mL) filled with distilled water (one for every three or four students). The distilled water can be used both in pH determination and to moisten soil for texture by feel.
- A dropper bottle filled with 10% HCl (one for every three or four students). Necessary only if it is possible that free carbonates will be encountered in the profiles.
- A plastic dishpan for catching soil from the auger (optional).
- Surveying level and rod to enable students to measure the elevation difference between auger holes.
- A soils map of the area and soil series descriptions, if available.

PROCEDURE	COMMENTS

1. Standing at the highest position on the landscape to be investigated, look around you and briefly discuss how the five soil forming factors have affected this landscape.

   In particular, discuss changes in elevation and parent material, and the geological causes for these changes. At each site, briefly describe the landscape position (e.g. summit).

2. Begin augering the hole about 30 cm away from the marker flag. First, remove the surface vegetation, and then use your body weight to push the auger bit into the soil as you turn the T-handle clockwise. Usually, it only requires three or four rotations of the auger to fill the auger bucket. Listen carefully to the sound the auger makes as it cuts through the soil and note and change in the difficulty of turning the auger.

   Although the auger bucket may be 20-25 centimeters long, it will fill with soil after penetrating only 10 to 12 cm into soil. Do not overfill. The auger makes a grinding/scraping sound when it hits a sandy or gravelly layer. Such auger noises, and changes in the difficulty of augering (as when encountering a clay accumulation), provide important clues about the profile to the soil scientist even before the auger is removed from the hole.

3. Before removing the soil from the auger, point the bit end of the auger towards the group to allow your classmates to closely inspect the relatively undisturbed soil.

   The patterns of color, roots, pores and, to some degree, the soil structure, are more clearly visible here where the material has broken cleanly away from the soil mass than in the soil material after being removed from the bucket.

4. Invert the auger so that the T-handle meets the ground at about a 45-degree angle and tap it against the ground causing the soil to fall out of the back of the bucket. Catch as much of this soil as possible (in a dishpan or in your hand). Use a steel tape to measure the depth of the hole, and determine the length of the soil increment just collected. Then lay the soil from this increment in the trough so that it takes up the same length as the increment of profile from which it came.

   It is best if two or three people work together. Look for horizon boundaries by observing differences in soil properties. Discuss the probable horizon designations. Features to look for in the well-drained soil include the thickness of the A horizon (and O horizon if one is present) and the colors of the subsurface horizons. In a well-drained soil, these colors should be fairly bright browns, reds or yellows (having a high Munsell chroma number), indicating good aeration.

5. Repeat steps 2-4, rotating duties with your classmates so that everyone has a chance at each task.

   As each soil increment is laid in place, a full-scale profile of the soil will be assembled in the trough

6. Once the trough is filled with the entire profile, work in teams of three or four to describe each soil horizon with regard to its colors, texture, structure (as far as possible), presence of carbonates and pH. The main properties should be noted on Figure 6.1 to the right of the appropriate profile diagram.

   The horizon designations and boundaries should be added to the appropriate profile diagram in the form (Figure 6.1). Since the augered material has been broken up, the original structure may no longer be evident.

7. Pick up the trough of soil and carry it down the slope to the second flagged position, where steps 2-6 are to be repeated. The newly filled trough, along with the previous one, is carried to next site, where steps 2-6 are again repeated.

8. When the last site is augered, lay your collection of three or four soil profiles side by side. In most landscapes, a number of soil features can be observed to change systematically from the well drained to the poorly drained positions. See if you can observe the types of changes listed at right as the soils go from the upper to the lower catena members.

At each flagged site, the soil in the trough is described, paying particular attention to the color chromas in the subsoil, the depths of the A horizon, and the color hue of the A horizon. The last soil should have chroma 1 or 2 colors < 25 cm deep.

a) Increasing A horizon thickness (due to both sedimentation and to greater organic matter);
b) Darkening color of the surface horizon due to the slower and less complete decomposition of organic matter in wetter soils;
c) Decreasing chroma values in the subsurface horizons and increasing frequency of mottles or other redoximorphic features in these horizons;
d) Evidence of redoximorphic features closer to the soil surface (see Table 6.1);
e) Change in soil odor: aromatic earthy smell in the well-drained soil and a putrid, sulfide odor in the most poorly drained member.

9. If possible, use the auger to reach the groundwater level at the lowest elevation site. Observe that the soil increments are nearly saturated when the auger begins to sample the capillary fringe above the water table. Look down the hole, see the reflection of the sky in the free water, and then use the steel tape to determine the depth of the water table immediately after augering. Measure the depth to the water table again after about ten minutes have passed.   Depth to GW: _____ cm.
Depth to GW after ___minutes: _____ cm.

Note the semi fluid state of the saturated soils, the free water that appears when this material is jarred, and the cool temperature of the water, which if the water table is several meters deep, approximates the mean annual temperature for the region.

The rate of rise in the ground water level gives some indication of the recharge rate and the soil permeability. The groundwater you are observing is either "perched" on an impermeable layer or it is in a surficial, unconfined aquifer.

10. Before leaving the field site, be sure to go back to the holes with the troughs of soil and pour the soil, bottom horizon first, back into the hole. Also, use push in any soil remaining around the hole.

Filling the holes prevents a hazard to people or animals. Horses are especially susceptible to breaking a leg in an auger hole. Filling the holes also protects ground water from surface contaminants that might wash in.

Table 6. 1 Soil drainage classes defined by most shallow depth with redox characteristics.

Class	Characteristics
Very Poorly	Thick (>20-25 cm) black surface and iron-depleted matrix (chroma ≤2) below the A horizon
Poorly	Dark gray or thin black surface horizon, all subsurface horizons are chroma ≤2, value ≥4
Somewhat Poorly	Redox depletions or a depleted matrix (chroma ≤2) beginning between 25 and 50 cm.
Moderately Well	Redox depletions (chroma ≤2) beginning between 50 and 100 cm
Well	Redox depletions (chroma ≤2) do not occur above 100 cm
Excessively	High hydraulic conductivity and low water retention, usually sandy or gravelly; no evidence of a seasonally-high water table

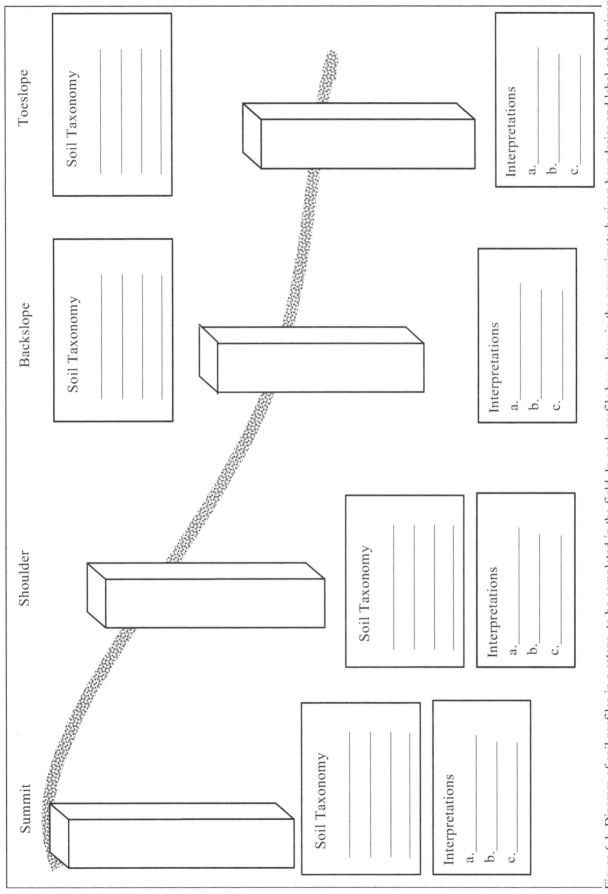

Figure 6.1 Diagram of soil profiles in a catena, to be completed in the field. In each profile box, draw in the approximate horizon boundaries and label each horizon identified using standard symbols for genetic horizons (Ap, Bt, etc.). To the right of each profile box, note the textural class (e.g., scl for sandy clay loam) and Munsell color (e.g., 7.5YR3/4). Under Soil Taxonomy, write in the soil series and the Soil Order, Suborder, Great Group and Subgroup. Under interpretations, give (a) drainage class, (b) suitability (good, moderate, poor) for septic filter field, and (c) suitability (good, moderate, poor) for fruit orchard.. See Tables 6.1-3.

Table 6.2 Suitability for Septic Tanks

Factor Affecting Use	Degree of Limitation		
	Slight	Moderate	Severe
Flooding Frequency	None	Rare	Common
Slope	<8%	8-15%	>15%
Depth to seasonally-high water table	>180 cm	120-180 cm	<120 cm
Depth to bedrock	>180 cm	100-180 cm	<100 cm
Depth to cemented pan	>180 cm	100-180 cm	<100 cm
Hydraulic conductivity (60-150 cm)*	Moderate	Low	Very low or high

*Hydraulic conductivity estimated from soil properties:
> Very low – clays, sandy clays, and silty clays with weak or moderate structure
> Low – clays, sandy clays, and silty clays with strong structure;
>> Or clay loams, silty clay loams, and sandy clay loams with weak structure
> Moderate – sandy loams, silt loams, loams;
>> Or silty clay loams, clay loams, and sandy clay loams with moderate or strong structure
> High – sands and loamy sands

Table 6.3 Suitability for Dwellings with Basements – sands and loamy sands

	Degree of Limitation		
Factor Affecting Use	Slight	Moderate	Severe
Flooding frequency	None	-----	Rare or common
Slope	<8%	8-15%	>15%
Depth to seasonally high water table	>180 cm	75-180 cm	<75 cm
Depth to bedrock	>150 cm	100-150 cm	<100 cm
Depth to cemented pan	>150 cm	100-150 cm	<100 cm

EXERCISE 6

Getting to Know a Catena in the Field

Results and Conclusions: See Figure 6.1.

Questions:

1. Briefly explain specific ways that the five soil forming factors have influenced the soils *in your study catena.*

   a.   parent material:

   b.   organisms:

   c.   climate:

   d.   time:

   e.   topography:

2. Compare the well-drained to the most poorly drained member of *your study catena* with regard to:

   a.   Thickness of A horizon.

   b.   Depth to redoximorphic features.

   c.   Matrix (main) color of the B horizon.

3. Which soil in *your study* catena appeared to be least weathered (that is with the least well developed profile, the fewest horizons, or the thinnest, least distinct B horizon)? Explain why you think the soil in that particular landscape position has undergone the least development.

4. If you were able to observe and measure the depth of the groundwater at your field site, comment on the correlation between the presence of groundwater and the presence of redoximorphic feature in the soil profile. Also, calculate the rate of recharge in cm/minute based on your two depth measurements and comment on the relationship of this recharge rate to the soil textures of the lower horizons.

Exercise 7
Soil Texture:
Mechanical Analysis of Particle Size

OBJECTIVES

After completing this exercise, you should be able to....

1. Explain the application of Stoke's Law to the analysis of particle sizes in soils.
2. Disperse a soil sample physically and chemically and explain how this occurs.
3. Use a hydrometer to measure the amount of silt and clay in a suspension of soil.
4. Calculate the percentages of sand, silt, and clay particles in a soil when given the appropriate hydrometer readings and temperatures.
5. Use the soil "textural triangle" to find the textural class of a soil.
6. Describe and recognize the sorting of different **size** fractions during **sedimentation.**
7. Define the terms: *soil separate, sand, silt, clay.*

INTRODUCTION

The relative amounts of different sizes of mineral particles present profoundly influences the behavior of a soil. The particle size distribution of a soil is referred to as its *texture.* The *textural class* of a soil (i.e., loam, sandy clay, etc.) is determined by the percentages by weight of sand, silt, and clay sized particles. These three percentages sum to 100% because organic matter and water are *not* included in the determination. Particles larger than 2.0 mm in diameter (such as gravel or stones) are also *not* included in the determination of texture, but their presence can modify textural class names (e.g., *gravelly* loam or *stony* silt loam, etc.). Sand is defined in the USDA system as being mineral particles of 0.05 to 2.0 mm diameter. *Silt* is defined as having diameters 0.002 to 0.05 mm and *clay* as being smaller than 0.002 mm in diameter. See Figure 4.2 for abbreviations such as sil (silty loam).

Fine sand can be separated from coarse sand, or sand can be separated from the rest of the soil by means of mechanical sieving. However, 0.05 mm holes are very small indeed and the sieving of fine sand is quite an arduous task. How then can the still smaller silt and clay fractions of the soil be separated and measured? Certainly a sieve so fine would not work even if it could be made! The answer lies in *Stoke's Law* which describes the rates with which spherical particles of different sizes settle through a fluid in response to gravity.

$$V = \frac{2(D_p - D_l)gr^2}{9\eta}$$

Where V = velocity of fall (cm/sec)
D_p = density of soil particles (g/cm^3)
D_l = density of liquid (g/cm^3)
g = gravitational acceleration (cm/sec^2)
r = particle radius (cm)
η = absolute viscosity of liquid

If standard conditions are imposed so that it can be assumed that the η, D_l and D_p components do not vary, then all the above terms except radius (*r*) can be combined into a single constant (*K*) in a simplified equation:

$$V = K * r^2$$

Stokes Law tells us that "the bigger they are, the faster they fall" i.e. the settling velocity will increase as the square of the radius of the particle. Armed with this relationship we are now ready to measure the amounts of even very small size particles in a soil. We will simply shake up a sample of soil in a tall cylinder of liquid (water) and let the particles settle out. Using Stoke's Law to predict the settling velocity of a given size of particle we can calculate how long it will take for particles of that size to fall a given distance. For example, after enough time has elapsed for sand size particles to settle below the 10 cm mark, we can sample the suspension at 10 cm and determine the amount of soil still present. This soil will be silt and clay only, the sand having settled farther down already.

Two methods are commonly used to determine the amount of soil particles still in suspension at a given depth and time. These are the pipette method and the hydrometer method. In the former method a pipette is used to sample a portion of the suspension at a known time and depth. The water in the sample is then evaporated, and the amount of soil material determined by weighing. In the hydrometer method a hydrometer is used to measure the density of the suspension which varies with the amount of soil material suspended. The latter, though not quite as accurate, is simpler and is the method used in this exercise. Special Bouyoucos hydrometers are used which are calibrated to read in "g solids in suspension." The procedure is given below, slightly modified to fit into a convenient time period.

MATERIALS

Note to Instructor: If soil organic matter is high (>3% organic matter), you may want to do the hydrogen peroxide procedure (step 3) a week ahead. Otherwise this step can be skipped with only minor effects on accuracy of particle size determination.

At each bench:

- 1 Bouyoucos cylinder (or 1 L hydrometer cylinder)
- 1 agitator paddle similar to shown below, must be 5 mm smaller inside of above cylinder.
- 1 Bouyoucos hydrometer
- 1 thermometer
- 1 wash bottle
- 1 dropper bottle of amyl alcohol
- 1 - 25 mL graduated cylinder
- 1 - 250 mL beaker
- 1 stirring rod
- hand lense

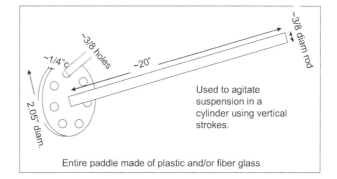

Shared by class:

- Electric blenders (restaurant milk shake maker will work, but special blending blades for soil are available from Soil Test, Inc.)
- Metal blender cups (cups with special baffles soldered inside are available from Soil Test, Inc.)
- Air-dry soils (crushed and passed through a 2 mm sieve)
- Balances (capable of weighing 100 to nearest to 0.1 g)
- Sodium hexametaphosphate (formerly Calgon®) solution (NaPO₃)₆. Place 95 g of sodium hexametaphosphate and 5 g of $NaCO_3$ in a 1 L container with ~900 mL water. Dilute to 1 L with distilled water. Commercial Calgon®, should *not* be used as it no longer contains $(NaPO_3)_6$.
- 6% hydrogen peroxide (optional)

PROCEDURE

1. Choose a soil from those provided. Note: the soil identification and % moisture: _____ . Use a separate portion of soil to estimate the texture by the feel method as described in Exercise 4 and record the textural class in Table 7.4.

2. If your soil is coarser than a sandy loam, weigh 100g of it into a 250 beaker. If your soil is a sandy loam or finer use only 50g. Weigh soil accurately to the nearest 0.1g.

3. **OPTIONAL:** (Before doing this step, **check with your instructor** and read the adjacent "comments"). To the 250mL beaker containing your soil (50 or 100g—see step 2). Add 100mL of 6% hydrogen peroxide. Mix well and allow to stand overnight. Then warm gently in a water bath until the reaction subsides. Frothing can be controlled by adding 2 drops of amyl alcohol. Cool for a few minutes. Then, after reaction has subsided, boil (but not to dryness for 5 minutes. Cool. Proceed with step 4.

4. Add 100 ml distilled water and 25 ml of (NaPO₃)₆ solution (NaPO₃)₆ to the beaker with soil and stir well for 5 minutes.

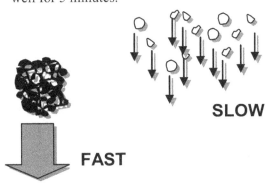

SLOW

FAST

5. Using distilled water from a wash bottle, *completely* transfer the contents of the beaker to a metal blender cup. Fill the cup about ½ to 1/3 full using distilled water

6. Place metal cup on blender, being certain to orient it correctly so that the stirring paddle will not touch the baffles in the cup. Blend for 5 minutes if coarse textured soil is used, 10 minutes if fine textured. Turn off blender.

7. Using your wash bottle, transfer the contents of the blender cup *completely* to a Bouyoucos cylinder. Fill cylinder about 2/3 full with distilled water.

COMMENTS

The air-dry soils appear dry but may contain a small amount of water absorbed from the atmosphere. If your instructor does not provide the moisture content, determine the % moisture on a separate sample as described in Appendix D.

Remember to tare the beaker first, then add soil until the balance reads 50.0 or 100.0 g.

This step destroys (i.e. oxidizes) organic matter in the soil. Texture is based on the size distribution of mineral particles; if an appreciable amount of organic matter is present, it will either interfere with the hydrometer readings and/or the calculations which assume that a known weight of (sand + silt + clay) was used to begin with.

If step three is carried out, the "weight of oven dry soil" used in calculating the percentage of each particle size must be corrected by subtracting the organic matter from the 50 or 100 g weighed out. Therefore the % soil organic matter must be known.

The Na^+ in the (NaPO₃)₆ replaces Ca^{2+} from the soil clays causing them to disperse. This is a *chemical dispersion*. The PO_3^- anion causes cations such as Ca^{2+} to precipitate and thus avoids flocculation. For clayey soils this mixture should stand overnight to allow complete wetting and slaking of aggregates. The electric blender is used to achieve mechanical dispersion of the soil aggregates. These clumps of clay and silt particles must be completely broken up or dispersed, for the clay aggregates would settle rapidly like sand particles. The individual clay and silt particles will settle very slowly, if at all. You will use their relative settling rates to measure the amounts of sand, silt and clay in your soil.

8. *Very gently* place the hydrometer into the suspension in the cylinder. *While it is floating,* add enough distilled water to bring the volume up to the 1130 ml mark (if 50g of soil were used) or the 1205 mark (if 100g were used). If a 1 L cylinder is used, bring the liquid up to the 1 L mark without floating the hydrometer.

CAUTION: The hydrometer is fragile and may break if it hits the bottom of the cylinder. Do not let go of it until you are sure it is floating—this may be deeper than you expect. The purpose of floating the hydrometer at this time is simply to allow you to add the proper volume of water with the volume displacement of the hydrometer bulb accounted for.

9. Carefully remove the hydrometer (do not rinse) and place it on a paper towel, making sure it will not roll off the bench. Agitate the suspension in the cylinder with 10 vertical strokes of an agitator paddle, being sure to completely suspend all particles. Gently remove the paddle, making sure all soil and water drips back into the cylinder and immediately start a stopwatch or record the start time here in Table 7.1.

The cylinder now contains 50g or 100g of soil material. The agitator is designed to ensure that all the various sized particles become evenly dispersed throughout the liquid before their settling tomes are measured.

10. Quickly, but carefully, insert the hydrometer into the suspension, holding on to the stem until it begins to float. If froth is present on the liquid surface, add a few drops of amyl alcohol. With the hydrometer floating, read the water level on the stem at 40, 50, 60, 70 and 80 seconds after sedimentation began and record in Table 7.1.

11. Plot the readings from Table 7.1 on the graph in Figure 7.2, and draw a line through the five readings, so that the line intersects the heavy diagonal line printed on the graph. Draw a horizontal line from the intersection of these two lines to the Y axis. The value of the Y axis where it is intersected by your horizontal line is your "raw" *silt + clay hydrometer reading* (example shown by a dashed line on the graph). Record this reading in Table 7.1 and 7.3.

Stoke law tells us how long it will take for the smallest sand particle to travel a given distance.[1] The distance we are interested in is that from the liquid surface to the middle of the hydrometer bulb. However, as the particles settle out, the suspension becomes thinner and less buoyant, so the hydrometer sinks deeper, so the distance is increasing. If almost no sand were present, the hydrometer would be floating very high (reading near 50) and the smallest sand could settle past that distance in 40 seconds. However, if the soil were all sand, the hydrometer would sink rapidly until it read near 0. It would take the smallest sand particle approximately 80 seconds to settle this longer distance to the middle of the bulb. Figure 7.2 provides a way to estimate what the reading would be when the smallest sand particle in your soil sample passes the hydrometer bulb.

12. Carefully remove the hydrometer (do not rinse) and measure the temperature of the suspension by inserting the thermometer tip a few cm into the suspension taking care not to disturb the suspension. Record the temperature (°C) in Table 7.1 Wipe the thermometer clean and place it where it will not roll off the bench.

Since the hydrometer sinks more deeply if the liquid is warmer (therefore "thinner"), the temperature is used to "correct" the hydrometer reading from Figure 7.2. The hydrometer is calibrated to read "g soil remaining in suspension at 19.5 °C".

---

[1] The standard hydrometer method (G. Bouyoucos. 1964. Hydrometer method improved for making the particle size analysis of soils. Agronomy Journal 54:464-465) calls for readings at 40 seconds and two hours, but these times are at odds with Stoke's Law, and result in considerable error. (See comment next to step 17). Except for the modification explained here in step 10, pitfalls and improvements for the hydrometer method are discussed in: W.P. Miller, D.E. Radcliffe, and D.M. Miller, 1988. An historical perspective on the theory and practice of soil mechanical analysis J. Agron. Educ. 17:24-28.

13. Correct the raw silt and clay hydrometer reading for temperature using the equation at right. Write out this calculation in the space provided for Calculation 1 in your hand-in sheet.

"**temperature-corrected reading**" =
   raw reading + 0.36(°C – 19.5),
where °C is the measured temperature of the suspension from Table 7.1.

14. If your instructor has not already done so, set up another large cylinder to contain 25 mL of $(NaPO_3)_6$ solution (10% by weight) plus either 881 mL or 862 mL of distilled water depending on whether you used 50 or 100g of soil, respectively. Add no soil to this cylinder, but gently float the hydrometer and take the reading. Also determine the temperature of the solution. Record both the hydrometer reading and temperature for the correction cylinder in Table 7.2.

15. Using the data from Table 7.2 and the equation at right, calculate the **sodium hexametaphosphate correction factor**. Write out this calculation under Calculation # 2 in the space provided in your hand-in sheet and record this correction factor in the fourth column of Table 7.3.
Subtract the **$(NaPO_3)_6$ correction factor** from the temperature-corrected hydrometer reading for silt and clay. Write out this calculation in the space provided for Calculation # 2 and enter the value into Table 7.3.

$(NaPO_3)_6$ correction factor =
   correction hydrometer reading + 0.36(°C – 19.5)

where °C is the measured temperature of the *correction cylinder* from Table 7.2.

Note that this $(NaPO_3)_6$ correction factor is also corrected for temperature.

16. Examine the layering of the sediment in the bottom of the cylinder. Use a hand lens to get a closer look. Draw the layers in the diagram provided on the back of the hand-in sheet.

You should observe a sharp boundary between the bottom layers of sand in which the grains are visible and the next layer of silt which seems smooth (without individual visible grains).

17. To take the final reading, record the time elapsed since the beginning of sedimentation here: _____ (See Table 7.1 for start time). Two hours is commonly used, but see comments at right.

Carefully reinsert the hydrometer into the suspension and read when the bobbing has ceased. Record this "Raw" reading under the clay reading column of Table 7.3. Remove the hydrometer and wipe it clean.

At the time of the final reading, the silt-sized particles should have all settled past the middle of the hydrometer bulb, and the reading will therefore indicate only the g of *clay* left in suspension. If the time used is much shorter than the approximately 6 hours and 52 minutes calculated by Stoke's Law, some of the silt will still be suspended and will be mistaken for clay. Thus, taking the final reading after only two hours, as is often done, will considerably overestimate the clay and underestimate the silt fractions. Because the smallest particles settle very slowly, a much smaller error is incurred by lengthening the time as long as 24 hours if needed for convenience.

18. Correct the raw clay reading for temperature using the equation in step 13 using the initial temperature reading in Table 7.1. Record this value in Table 7.3 and write out your calculation in the space provided for Calculation 3.

Subtract the sodium hexametaphosphate correction factor calculated in step 15 from the temperature corrected reading. Record this value in Table 7.3 and write out your calculation in the space provided for Calculation 4.

Since it will take a long time before the silt has completely settled out, check with your instructor about doing another exercise in the interval, or possible leaving the lab and coming back for the final reading at a specified time.

Table 7.1 Data for Initial Hydrometer Reading

Soil I.D.			
Start time:			
Silt+Clay Hydrometer Readings			
40 sec			
50 sec			
60 sec			
70 sec			
80 sec			
Y Intercept from Figure7.2			
Temperature, °C			

19. Subtract this correction factor from each of your temperature corrected soil suspension hydrometer readings. Calculate the percentages of sand, silt and clay using the following equations. Write out these calculations in the space provided in your hand-in sheet and record their values in Table 7.3.

$$\%silt + clay = 100 * \frac{corrected \ initial \ reading}{oven \ dry \ weight \ of \ soil \ sample \ (g)}$$

$$\%sand = 100 - (\%silt + clay)$$

$$\%clay = 100 * \frac{corrected \ final \ reading}{oven \ dry \ weight \ of \ soil \ sample(g)}$$

$$\%silt = (\%silt + clay) - \%clay$$

We have to subtract the reading for "Sodium hexametaphosphate alone" because the it adds to the buoyancy of the solution, making the hydrometer float a bit higher and indicate suspended soil when there is none.

Table 7.2 **Data for (NaPO₃)₆ Correction Cylinder**

	if 100g soil	if 50 g soil
Hydrometer Reading		
Temperature, °C		

20. Clean all your equipment and return it to its original location.

21. Fill in the Data Sheet to be handed in at the next lab.

If you are using your own soil, record the sand, silt and clay percentages in Appendix G, Table G2.

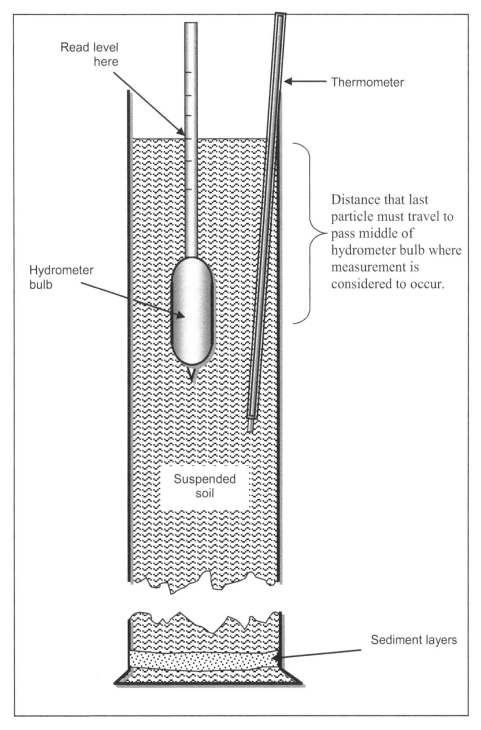

Figure 7.1 Set up for determining particle size distribution using a hydrometer.

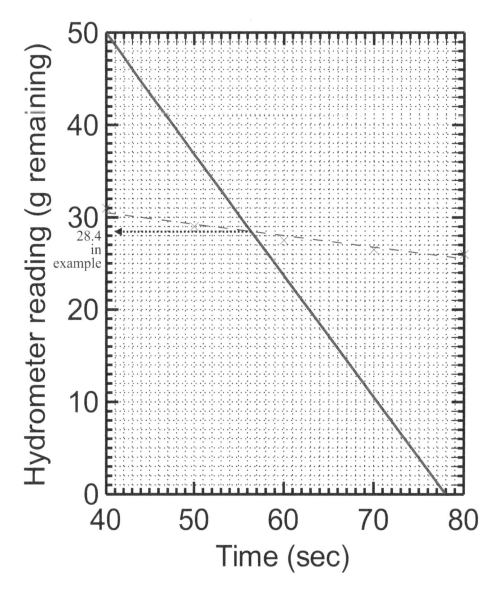

Figure 7.2 Graph to determine silt + clay reading for step 11. Plot at least 5 hydrometer readings (40, 50, 60, 70 and 80 sec.) on the graph and draw a "best fit" line through your points. Draw a horizontal line connecting the Y axis to the intersection of your plotted line (thin dashed line in the example) with heavy diagonal line, as shown by the arrow for the example data. In the example shown, the "raw" initial hydrometer reading for "silt + clay" would be 28.4. In this example it would take a 0.05 mm particle (smallest sand) about 57 seconds to pass the middle of the hydrometer bulb.

Date _____

Name _____

Section _____

I.D. No. _____

EXERCISE 7

Soil Texture:

Mechanical Analysis of Particle Size

Table 7.3 Results of Mechanical Particle Size Analysis. Fill in one row in the table for each soil sample analyzed. Show your calculations on hand-in sheet #2 in spaces provided.

Soil I.D.*	Air-dry soil (g)	Oven-dry soil (g)[†]	(NaPO$_3$)$_6$ Correct factor	Silt & Clay Reading			Clay Reading			Silt + Clay (%)	Sand (%)	Clay (%)	Silt (%)	Textural Class (USDA)[‡]
				Raw (from Table 7.1)	Correct for temp.	Correct for temp. and (NaPO$_3$)$_6$	Raw	Correct for temp.	Correct for temp. and (NaPO$_3$)$_6$					

* Underline your own data. Data for other soils may be obtained from your classmates if the instructor so directs.

† See comment for procedure step #1f soil used was only air dry, not oven dry: **g oven dry soil = (100) · (g air-dry soil used) / (100 + % H$_2$O)**

‡ See textural triangle—Figure 7.3.

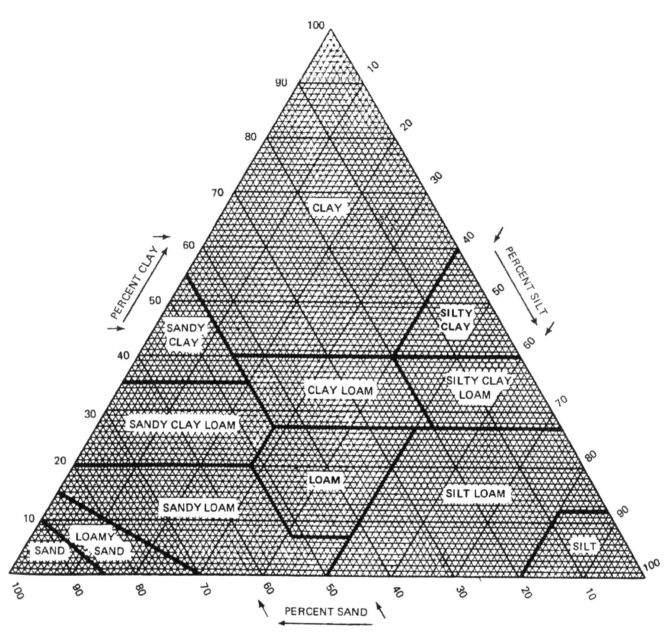

Figure 7.3 USDA Textural Classes. Read the percent sand, silt and clay in the direction indicated by the respective small arrows.

Date_____   Name_____

Section_____   I.D. No. _____

EXERCISE 7 (Sheet #2)
Soil Texture:
Mechanical Analysis of Particle Size

Table 7.4 Texture by Feel Results. Fill in one row for each soil sample analyzed. Record your best estimate of % sand, clay, and silt as well as the USDA texture class based on the texture by feel method.

Soil Designation	%Sand	% Clay	% Silt	Textural class (USDA)*

*See textural triangle – Figure 7.3.

Calculation 1: Silt and Clay reading temperature correction

Calculation 2: Silt and Clay reading Sodium hexametaphosphate correction

Calculation 3: Clay reading temperature correction

Calculation 4: Clay reading Sodium hexametaphosphate correction:

Calculation 5: % SILT + CLAY

% SAND calculation:

% CLAY calculation:

% SILT calculation:

QUESTIONS

1. What assumptions have been made in this determination of particle size distribution?

2. What were the likely sources of error in this procedure?

3. On the texture triangle graph (Figure 7.3) draw in one or more small colored circles to represent the location of your sample(s).

4. Draw and label a diagram illustrating the size-sorting action of sedimentation as seen in the sediment in the bottom of the large cylinders during this procedure. Describe and explain your diagram in a couple of sentences.

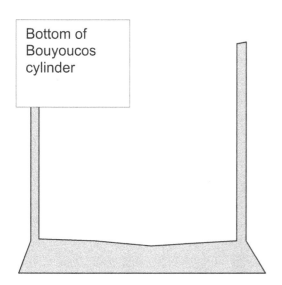

Bottom of
Bouyoucos
cylinder

Exercise 8
Soil Density, Porosity and Structural Stability

OBJECTIVES

After completing this exercise, you should be able to...

1. Define and differentiate bulk and particle densities.
2. Explain in principle how the measurement of bulk density (D_b) and particle density (D_p) can be made.
3. Calculate D_b and D_p if given the appropriate volume and weight measurements.
4. Calculate % Pore Space given the necessary data.
5. Explain why the bulk density method used in this exercise works well for sand but not for most soils.
6. Recognize that even a solid-appearing clod of soil has considerable pore-space within it.
7. Explain the environmental significance of aggregate stability in surface soils.
8. Relate structure type and organic matter content to water stability of structural peds.
9. Visually estimate percent of aggregate remaining intact after slaking in water.

INTRODUCTION

Soil is a mixture of solid, liquid and gaseous materials. The liquid (soil solution) and the gases (soil air) are very important for plant growth and are located in the space between solid particles. Also, spaces or pores between the solid particles are necessary if the soil is to allow the movement of roots and water. The more tightly the solid particles are packed together, the less pore space will remain. The bulk density (D_b) of a soil is the weight (g) per unit volume of *dry* soil (cm3). This volume includes both the spaces between solid particles and the particles themselves. The bulk density is an often-measured soil property because it gives an indication of the amount of pore space in a soil. High bulk densities greater than 1.6 /cm^3 generally exhibits restricted root penetration, impeded water infiltration and poor aeration. Very light, porous organic matter rich soils may have bulk of densities 1.0 g/cm^3 or less.

The density of the solid particles themselves may also be measured and this latter is called the particle density (D_p). The D_p of a soil is the weight (g) per unit volume where the volume is that of the solid particles only and does not include the volume of the pore spaces. Hence the D_p of quartz sand is the same as that of a large boulder of solid quartz. The D_b of the sand is a much lower value because it is the density of the sand particles and the pore spaces combined. Equations 6.1 through 6.4 define D_b and D_p and show how the percent pore space in a soil may be calculated once D_b and D_p are known.

$$\textbf{Bulk density } (\textbf{\textit{D}}_b) = \frac{\text{mass of dry soil}}{\text{volume of solids \& pore spaces}} \qquad \text{Eq. 8.1}$$

$$\textbf{Particle density } (\textbf{\textit{D}}_p) = \frac{\text{mass of dry soil}}{\text{volume of solids only}} \qquad \text{Eq. 8.2}$$

$$\% \text{ solid space} = \frac{D_b}{D_p} \times (100)$$ Eq. 8.3

$$\% \text{ pore space} = 100 - \left(\frac{D_b}{D_p} \times (100) \right)$$ Eq. 8.4

To determine the D_b of a soil one must find the dry weight of a known volume of soil. Special core sampling tools are available that remove a known volume from a natural soil with a minimum of physical disturbance to the sample. Alternatively, a small hole can be dug in a soil and all the soil removed, carefully dried, and weighed. The volume of the hole can then be measured by lining it with plastic film and determining the volume of water needed to fill it.

It would be instructive, in addition to the lab procedure outlined here, to determine the bulk densities of soils from a field site using one of the above techniques. If convenient, it would be interesting to analyze undisturbed soil cores taken from a foot path and from an area just a few meters off the path. Increased bulk density, hence decreased porosity is a major effect of trampling by people, animals, or machinery.

In this exercise you will use loose sand instead of undisturbed soil to demonstrate, in the lab, the concepts of bulk density, particle density, and porosity. Sand is used because it does not present problems of trapped air when determining the volume of solids by displacement of water. Particle density is usually determined by weighing the water plus a known weight of soil required to fill a precise volume in a special flask called a "pycnometer." Air is removed from the water and pore spaces by vacuum suction or boiling. The simplified method used in this exercise would not work very well for most soils because of the likelihood of some air remaining trapped in the pores. However, it is reasonably accurate when using sand instead of soil.

This exercise will also introduce the concept of structural stability and as resistant to slaking. Slaking is the process by which a dry clod or aggregate of soil falls apart (appears to "melt") when it is placed in water. The observations of soil slaking made in this exercise help us understand how stable and resistant to erosion a soil will be when impacted by falling rain.

MATERIALS

- Balance accurate to 0.1 g
- 50 ml graduated cylinder (preferably plastic)
- Sheet of smooth paper (8½ × 11")
- Blocky peds from a Bt horizon (air-dry)
- Small clods or granular peds from a A horizon rich in humus (air-dry)
- Three 50 mL glass beakers or similar, transparent containers
- Alcohol (isopropyl or denatured ethanol) or acetone
- Quartz sand (attention: some commercial "play sand" is make from coral or limestone and has a slightly higher particle density than the quartz used in this exercise)
- Air-dry soil aggregates about ¼ inch in diameter (preferably from the soil sample represented in Appendix G).
- Three or six mini-sieves made from PVC pipe and aluminum window screening (Figure 8.1).
- Small plastic parts or tackle box with at least 6 compartments large enough to accommodate a mini-sieve (Figure 8.1).
- Stopwatch (or watch or cell phone with stopwatch function)

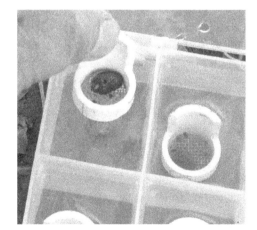

Figure 8.1 Mini-sieves in plastic parts box.

PROCEDURE	COMMENTS

Bulk Density

1. Weigh out 40.0 g of dry sand and carefully transfer to a *dry* 50 mL graduated cylinder, using a sheet of paper as a "funnel."

This is the "weight" of dry soil referred to in the Equations defining bulk density and particle density.

2. Place a book or notebook flat on the lab countertop and gently tap the cylinder on the book, 5 times to settle the sand. With the sand leveled-off, read the volume.

FOR SAFETY HOLD GLASS CYLINDER NEAR THE BASE WHILE TAPPING.

3. Repeat step 2 until the volume is no longer decreased by further tapping. Record this volume as "bulk volume of dry sand" in Table 8.2.

This volume is the *bulk* volume of the sand and includes both the volume of the particles and the volume of the pore spaces.

4. Transfer the dry sand to a sheet of paper and save.

5. Calculate the bulk density of the sand using equation 8.1, recording both your calculation and the result in Table 8.2, line c.

$$Bulk\,density(D_b) = \frac{mass\,of\,dry\,sand}{volume\,of\,solids\,\&\,pore\,spaces}$$

Approximate Particle Density

6. Add exactly 30 mL of water to the 50 mL graduated cylinder. Record this volume in Table 8.2 line d.

7. Transfer the 40.0 g of sand from step 4 to the cylinder.

8. Stir the sand-water mixture to remove trapped air. Tapping gently will help.

9. Read the volume (i.e., the level of the water surface).

10. Repeat steps 8 and 9 until the volume remains unchanged between two successive readings. Record this volume in Table 8.2 line e as "volume of water and sand solids."
The difference between this volume reading and the 30 mL of water originally added is due to the volume of the sand *particles*. The pores are now filled with water.

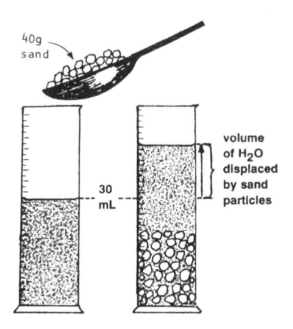

Figure 8.2 Determination of particle volume by water displacement.

Porosity and Stability of Natural Soil Peds

11. Fill 3 50-mL beakers ½ full with tap water. Fill a fourth beaker ½ full with alcohol or acetone.

Water is a high surface tension polar solvent that is strongly attracted to the mineral surfaces of soil particles. Alcohol (or acetone) is not.

12. Choose two blocky peds from the B_t horizon of a soil. Also collect a few granular peds (or aggregates) from the A horizons of two similar soils, one having a long history of permanent vegetation (grassland or forest) and the other from a continuously cultivated (tilled) agricultural field.

The blocky B horizon peds consist of soil particles held together principally by clays and oxide coatings. The A horizon peds are largely held together with organic matter. Hastened decomposition and crop harvest have reduced the amount of organic matter in the soil from the cultivated field.

13. Closely examine each ped using a hand lens. Draw an actual size sketch of each type of ped in the spaces provided on Table 8.3 and label the type of soil structure represented

Note especially the tiny pores or openings in the peds. Look for shiny clay coatings on the surface of the blocky B_t horizon ped. These are called clay skins. Figure 4.1 may help in labeling your sketch.

14. Place one of the blocky B_t peds in the beaker of alcohol (or acetone). Observe carefully and note the results in Table 8.3.

Unlike the sand used earlier, to the casual observer
The blocky ped may appear to be quite solid. The
Escaping air bubbles, displaced by the alcohol,
Prove that the ped actually contained much air
space and in fact, is probably more porous than the sand.

15. Line up the three beakers of water. Place the remaining blocky ped, the cultivated A-horizon peds and the uncultivated A-horizon peds into respective beakers of water. Observe closely and compare their behavior in the water. After a minute or so, gently swirl the beakers to test the stability of the various peds.

As water, with its high surface tension and affinity for the soil soaks into the ped from all sides, air is compressed into pockets within the ped. The pressure eventually is sufficient to burst apart the blocky ped resulting in the miniature "explosions."
The low surface tension of the alcohol used in Step 13 allowed the air to escape freely without bursting the ped. In comparing the two types of A-horizon peds, does organic matter content seem to affect aggregate stability?

16. Record your observations in Table 8.3.

Aggregate Stability by Slaking Test[1]

17. Fill in sample ID in Table 1 and select three or six *dry* aggregates each about 6-7 mm across. Place each aggregate in a separate sieve. We will refer to these aggregates as "sub-samples" of the soil you are testing.

18. Fill the empty (no sieves) box with deionized or distilled or rain water so each compartment has 2 cm depth of water.

Make sure the samples are dry before testing. Depending on the amount equipment and time available, your instructor will indicate whether to use 3 or 6 sub-samples (aggregates) per sample tested. Using more sub-samples gives more accurate results.

The water should be approximately the same temperature as the soil.

19. Start a stopwatch and lower the first sieve with the sub-sample into the respective water-filled compartment— upper left corner of sample box to upper left corner of water. From the time the sieve screen touches the water surface to the time it rests on the bottom of the box, 1 second should elapse. Start the stopwatch when the first sample touches the water. Use Table 8.1 to assign samples to stability classes and enter the results in Table 8.4.

20. After five minutes, follow the sequence of immersions on Table 8.4, adding one sample every 30 seconds. Observe the fragments from the time the sample hits the water to 5 min (300 sec) and record a stability class based on Table 8.1 Raise the sieve completely out of the water and then lower it to the bottom, but without touching the box bottom. Repeat this immersion a total of five times.

21. Calculate the average rating for your soil and enter in Table 8.4. The rating to use is the higher of the two ratings for each sub-sample.

It should take 1 second for each sieve to clear the water's surface and 1 second to return to near the bottom of the box. Do step 20 even if you have already rated the sample a 1, 2 or 3 *(you may change your rating if after sieving, >10% of the original soil remains on sieve)*. Hydrophobic samples (float on water after pushed under) are rated 6.

Table 8.1 Stability class descriptions.	
Stability class	Criteria for assignment to stability class
1	50% of structural integrity lost (melts) within 5 seconds of immersion in water, **or** soil too unstable to sample (falls through sieve).
2	50% of structural integrity lost (melts) 5-30 seconds after immersion.
3	50% of structural integrity lost (melts) 30-300 seconds after immersion **or** < 10% of original soil remains on the sieve after five dipping cycles.
4	10–25% of original soil remains on the sieve after five dipping cycles.
5	25–75% of original soil remains on the sieve after five dipping cycles.
6	75–100 % of original soil remains on the sieve after five dipping cycles.

[1] Modified from slaking stability test for rangeland soils described in Herrick, J.E., J.W.V. Zee, K.M. Havstad, L.M. Burkett, and W.G. Whitford. 2005. Monitoring manual for grassland, shrubland and savanna ecosystems. Volume 1:Quick start. USDA/ARS Jornada Experimental Range, Las Cruces, New Mexico. pp 23-29.

Sequence for stability class = 1.

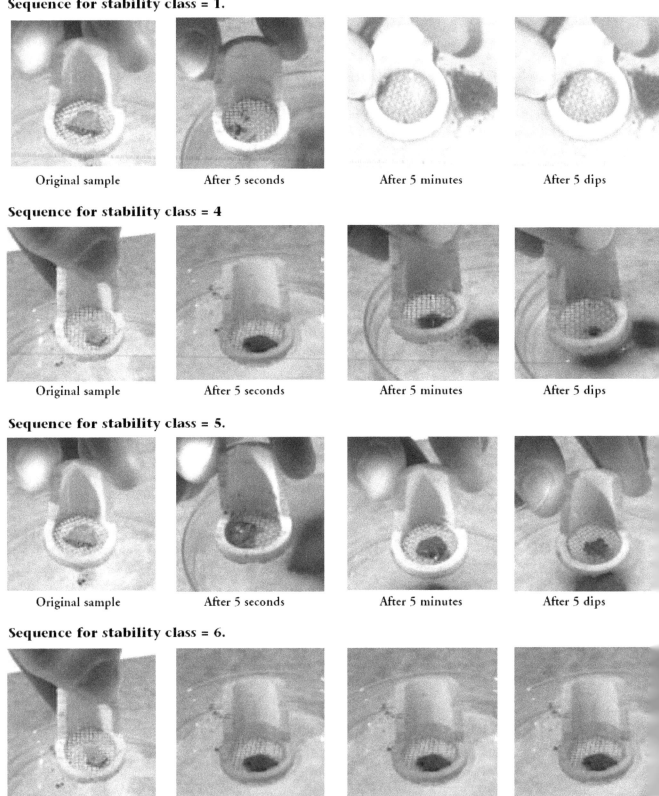

Original sample   After 5 seconds   After 5 minutes   After 5 dips

Sequence for stability class = 4

Original sample   After 5 seconds   After 5 minutes   After 5 dips

Sequence for stability class = 5.

Original sample   After 5 seconds   After 5 minutes   After 5 dips

Sequence for stability class = 6.

Original sample   After 5 seconds   After 5 minutes   After 5 dips

Figure 2 Illustration of soil stability classes. Note that actual soil clod or aggregates should be about 6-7 mm in diameter. From US Department of Interior/Bureau of Land Management. https://www.blm.gov/nstc/library/techref.htm

Date_____   Name_____

Section_____   I.D. No._____

Exercise 8
SOIL DENSITY, POROSITY AND STRUCTURAL STABILITY

Table 8.2 Density calculations.

What is the bulk density of the sand?		
a. Weight dry sand		g
b. Bulk volume of dry sand		cm^3
c. *Bulk Density* of sand		g/cm^3
What is the particle density of the sand?		
d. Volume of water		cm^3
e. Volume "water & sand solids		cm^3
f. Volume of sand solids		cm^3
g. *Particle Density* of sand		g/cm^3
How much of the volume is solid or porespace?		
h. Percent solid space in dry sand*		%
i. Percent pore space in dry sand*		%
How heavy is sand when dry or wet?		
j. Weight of 1 cu. Ft. of dry sand[†]		kg	lbs
k. Weight of 1 cu. Ft. water saturated sand[‡]		kg	lbs

*See definition formulas in the introduction to this exercise. [†]28,316 cm^3 = 1 cu ft.; 454 g = 1 lb [‡]1 cm^3 = 1 g; 1 cu ft. of water = 62.4 lbs.

1. Is the bulk density of the sand higher or lower than that of most topsoils? Why?

2. What are the main sources of error in the simplified procedure used in this exercise to determine D_b and D_p? Do these errors tend to over or underestimate these parameters?

3. Compare the particle density calculated for the sand in this procedure to the density of quartz listed in exercise #1.

4. In reference to Table 8.3, what caused the air bubbles to emerge from the soil ped?

5. Which ped was most stable in water? Why?

6. Why did the clayey B-horizon ped seem to almost "explode" as it fell apart?

7. Why was the stability of the structure in the non-polar solvent different from that in water?

87

Table 8.3 Observations on Natural Soil Peds

Horizon	B_t Horizon	Cultivated A horizon	Uncultivated A horizon
Type of Structure (see Fig. 4.1)			
Shape of Ped (sketch actual size)			
Behavior in alcohol (or acetone)			
Behavior in water			
% Organic Matter (from Exercise #17, or see instructor)			

8. What was the effect of cultivation on soil structure?

Table 8.4 Data table for soil aggregate stability test (table has spaces for 6 peds from 1 soil or 3 peds from 2 soils).

Sub-sample number[b]	1	2	3	4	5	6	Avg. stability ratings[a]
Soil I.D.: _____							
Stopwatch time aggregate placed in water.	0:00	0:30	1:00	1:30	2:00	2:30	
Aggregate Stability Class (1-3)							
Stopwatch time start to dip in and out of water 5 times.	5:00	5:30	6:00	6:30	7:00	7:30	
Aggregate Stability Class (3-6)							

[a] $Average\ stability\ rating = \dfrac{\sum_{1-n} highest\ stability\ rating}{n}$, where n is the number of sub-samples tested for a soil sample.

[b] Use either 3 or 6 sub-samples per soil sample tested, according to your instructor's directions.

Exercise 9
Investigating Capillary Rise

OBJECTIVES

After completing this exercise, you should be able to…

1. Explain the meaning of $h = \dfrac{2\gamma cos\theta}{r\rho g}$.
2. Predict the effect of pore size and particle size on the *rate* and eventual *height* of rise of water by capillary action.
3. Describe the relationships in objective #2 by means of an appropriate graph, or conversely, interpret a graph of these relationships.
4. Compare the characteristics of thin glass tubes to soil pores.
5. Describe and explain the pattern of upward movement of a capillary wetting front.
6. Explain why a taller pot of soil is less likely to be water logged than a shorter port of soil.

INTRODUCTION

Unsaturated water movement in the soil is the result of capillary forces that cause water to move toward areas where the water will have a lower free energy (i.e. water moves toward areas where the soil particles will hold it with the greatest degree of tension). A capillary is any small tube or pore. We can measure the strength of capillary forces by observing the height to which they will draw water above a free water surface. Capillary movement is the result of two forces which have components acting in the same direction; namely, (1) attraction between the water molecules and the pore material (glass wall of tube or soil particle surface) and (2) the attraction of water molecules for one another. The first force is called *adhesion* and the second is *cohesion*. A special case of cohesive forces plays a major role. This is the surface tension caused by the unbalanced forces of cohesion at the liquid-air interface. As adhesion attracts the water to the capillary walls, surface tension acts like a rubber membrane to "pull up" the body of water. The upward movement continues until the capillary forces are balanced by the weight of the column of water drawn up. The capillary forces and hence the height of rise are affected by the radius of the pore and the surface tension of the liquid. This relationship is expressed mathematically as follows:

Eq.9.1 $\quad h = \dfrac{2\gamma cos\theta}{r\rho g}$

h = maximum height of rise (cm)
γ = surface tension (dynes/cm; approx. 72 for H_2O)
θ = angle between the liquid and solid surfaces
ρ = water density (1.0g/cm^3)
g = gravity acceleration (980 cm/sec^2)
r = radius (cm) of the capillary pore (not of the soil particle)
cos = cosine of the angle

89

For water under normal conditions in the soil equation 9.1 can be simplified to read:

$$h(\text{cm}) = \frac{0.15}{r(\text{cm})}$$

Eq. 9.2

Equation 9.1 may be simplified if one makes some assumptions that are valid for water in soil pores under normal conditions. That is, we can assume that $\gamma - 72$ dynes/cm, the surface tension of pure water. For a wettable surface like quartz or glass, the angle between the water and the solid surface is nearly zero, i.e., $\theta = 0$ and therefore, $\cos \theta = 1$. The density of water $(\rho) = 1.0$ g/cm^3 and the gravitational acceleration, $g = 980$ cm/sec^2. Substituting these values in equation 9.1 we get:

$$h = \frac{(2)(72)(1)}{r(1)(980)} \quad \text{or}$$

$$h \text{ (in cm)} = \frac{0.15}{r(cm)}$$

Eq. 9.2

The capillary rise equation tells us, therefore, that water will rise higher and be held more tightly in small radius pores than in larger pores. This and other principles of capillary water movement in soils will be demonstrated in this exercise.

MATERIALS

- 5 glass tubes about 8 cm long, each with a different inside radius. The inside radii should range from approximately 0.025 cm to 0.25 cm. Medical capillary tubes work well for the smaller radii.
- 1 ruler 30 cm long with 1 mm delineations
- 1 8 x 8 cm plastic weigh-boat or small glass beaker to hold 30 mL of colored water.
- 1 grease pencil or marker that will mark on glass
- 3 glass or clear plastic tubes, each 40 cm long with an inside diameter of about 0.5 to 1 cm
- 1 support for the 3 large tubes (This can easily be fashioned by drilling 3 holes of appropriate diameter in a small strip of plywood and attaching this to a lab stand with a clamp)
- cheese cloth
- 3 rubber bands
- 1 12 x 12 cm plastic weigh boat or other shallow pan to hold about 100 mL water
- Calgon or similar dishwasher low-suds detergent
- 2 large sponges (approximately 4 cm x 10 cm x 15 cm), preferably made of cellulose
- 1 pan large enough to hold the 2 sponges submersed in water
- 1 500 mL beaker, preferably plastic
- 1 graduated cylinder to measure up to 50 mL
- sand -- well graded, quartz (not micaceous). To be dry-sieved into the three size classes shown in Figure 9.3. Construction sand or pool filter sand should do.

PROCEDURE

Capillary Rise in Glass Tubes

1. Fill a small pan (such as an 8 x 8 cm weigh boat) approximately 2/3 full of water. One at a time, place one 8 cm long glass tube of each radius upright in the water. Carefully observe the movement of water into the tubes, noting both the rate of rise and the final height. Tap each tube gently until the water column height stabilizes. NOTE that the tubes must be clean on the inside. Any grease from prior handling could prevent the normal attraction of the water to the tube walls.

2. Using the ruler, measure and record (in Table 9.1) the height (to the nearest 0.1 cm = 1 mm) to which the water rose in each tube above the water level in the beaker. See Fig. 9.1. Alternately, you can gently lift the tube vertically out of the water and measure the length of the water column that remains in the tube. If you do this, do *not* place your finger over the end of the tube or touch the ruler to bottom of the tube.

3. Remove the glass tubes and dry them gently with a towel.

4. Add a pinch of detergent to the water in the beaker and stir.

5. Repeat steps 1 and 2. Record these data in Table 9.1 under "soapy water". Compare these Heights to those obtained with pure water.

6. Measure the radius (cm) of each tube as accurately as possible with a ruler or wire gauge. Record under "Measured Radius" in Table 9.1 Then return each tube to the container labeled for the correct radius.

COMMENTS

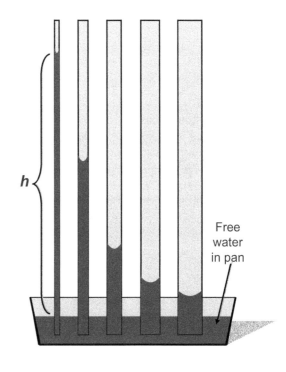

Figure 9. 1 Set of glass tubes showing the effects of inside (pore) radius on height (*h*) of capillary rise.

The soap or detergent reduces the surface tension (γ) of the water—"it makes water wetter." Be sure your tubes are dry inside before standing Them in the soapy water. You may need to blow out any water remaining in the tubes.

Facts to remember when using these units:
radius = ½ diameter
1 cm = 10 mm

91

7. Using Eq. 9.2 and your data from step 2, calculate the radius of each tube and record under "Calculated Radius" in Table 9.1. Are these values close to those measured in step 6?

8. Calculate the surface tension (γ) of the soapy water using Eq. 9.1 (assume cos θ = 1) and your data from step 5. record below Table 9.1.

Eq. 9.2 assumes the water is pure. Solve Eq. 9.2 for r (in cm):

$$r = \frac{0.15}{h}$$

Solve Eq. 9.2 for γ, again assuming a wet-table surface and therefore cos θ =1. Use the values given in the introduction for ρ and g.

$$\gamma = \frac{h\rho gr}{2}$$

Capillary Water in a Sponge

9. Obtain 2 sponges and a large pan of water. Let the sponges soak in the water. Then lift one sponge from the water horizontally until it stops dripping. Then squeeze it over the 500 mL beaker to remove as much as possible of the water remaining in the sponge. Measure the amount of water collected using a graduated cylinder and record in Table 9.2 under "Horizontal Sponge". Return the sponge to the pan of water.

10. Once again remove the sponge horizontally. Then when the dripping stops, turn the sponge to the vertical position. After the renewed dripping stops, squeeze the sponge over the beaker as in step 9, but record the amount in Table 9.2 under "vertical sponge". Return the sponge to the pan of water.

11. Remove both sponges and hold them separately in the vertical position until they stop dripping. Then, without squeezing them, place one sponge above the other so that they are in vertical end-to- end contact. After the renewed dripping ceases, squeeze the upper sponge over the beaker and record the volume collected in Table 9.2 under "upper of two vertical sponges."

Using a ruler, measure the vertical dimension of the sponge(s) in each situation to document the capillary height of rise necessary to hold moisture at the top edge of each sponge. Enter the values in Table 9.2.

The sponge serves as an analogy for soil. The water will stop dripping when the weight of the columns of water in the sponge's pores is equal to the capillary forces holding the water in those pores. The largest pores exert less capillary attraction than would be necessary to hold a column of water as high as the sponge is thick and so the water drains out from the pores leaving them filled with air.

Be careful not to squeeze the sponge while letting it drip. Note that the sponge holds less water when in the vertical than when in the horizontal position. In the vertical position the water columns are longer and so smaller pores will be drained.

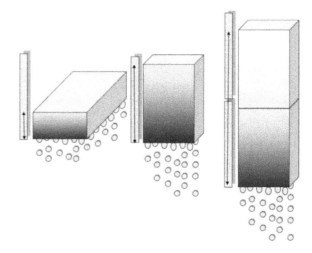

Figure 9. 2 A sponge holds different amounts of water and air depending on the vertical length of capillary columns in the sponge (as measure by the double arrow in each ruler).

The Effect of "Soil Texture" on Capillary Rise

12. Add about 500 g of dry, well graded quartz sand to the top sieve in a nest of sieves like that shown in Figure 9.3. Shake in mechanical shaker until good separation is achieved. Transfer the contents of the 40, 80, and 100 mesh sieves to separate beakers.

Note :This step may be done before class by the instructor. The 3 sizes of sand should then be available at the front of the lab.

13. Cover one end of each of 3 glass tubes with a *small* piece of cheese cloth folded in three layers and secure with a rubber band. Be sure you use enough layers of cloth to prevent the fine sand from leaking out.

14. Using a small funnel or paper cone, fill each tube with a different size of sand and label. During filling, tap the tubes gently to settle the sand.

15. Place the tubes in a dry pan, cloth-covered end down, and hold upright with the supporting rack.

16. Be ready to note the time. Add about 1 cm depth of water to the pan and immediately record the start time: _____.

17. Observe closely the rise of water in the sand-filled tubes. At the time intervals indicated in Table 9.3 below, mark the sides of the tubes to show the height of water rise at those times. After the 10-minute reading your instructor may want you to begin to carry out a second exercise concurrently with this one.

18. After you have completed Table 9.3 you should graph the results in the place provided and answer the questions.

19. Clean up materials. Put sand columns in oven to dry so other classes can use the sand over again. Take care not to mix up the different sand sizes.

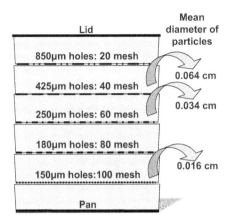

Figure 9. 3 Nest of sieved used to separate the various sizes of sand used in this exercise.

The large tubes are of a diameter far too large to allow the tubes themselves to exert a noticeable capillary influence. However, the spaces between sand grains will be of capillary size.

See Figure 9.4

To maintain a depth of about 1 cm of water in the pan, you may need to add a little more water after a few minutes.

Work in pairs. Try to mark all three tubes at nearly the same time. The wetting front may not be even, so always mark on the same side showing the average level of rise.

The curves should level off at the respective effective maximum height of capillary rise for each size sand.

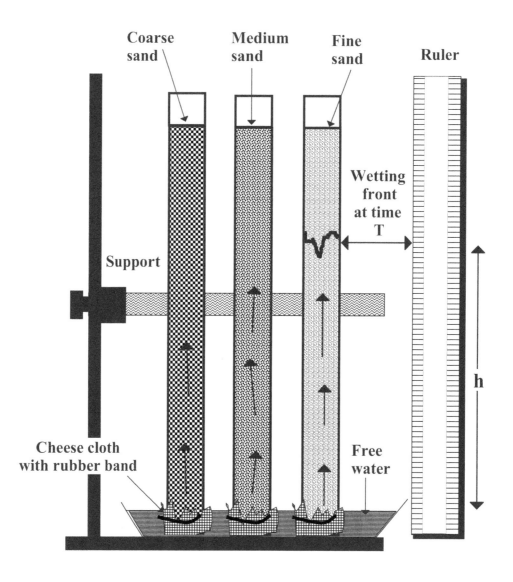

Figure 9. 4 Experimental set-up to demonstrate capillary rise in sand of various grain sizes.

Date _____   Name_____

Section_____   I.D. No._____

Exercise 9
INVESTIGATING CAPILLARY RISE

RESULTS

Table 9.1 Data for capillary rise in glass tubes.

Variable	Tube 1	Tube 2	Tube 3	Tube 4	Tube 5
			---------- cm ----------			
Measured radius, cm					
Calculated radius, cm					
Height w/ pure water, cm					
Height w/soapy[1] water, cm					

[1] calculated surface tension of soapy water:

Table 9.2 Volume of water held in a sponge after drainage as influenced by orientation of the sponge and resulting length of vertical capillary columns.

	Horizontal sponge	Vertical sponge	Upper of two vertically joined sponges
Vertical length of capillary column, cm			
Volume of water squeezed from sponge, mL			

Table 9.3 Capillary rise data for columns of coarse, medium and fine grained sand.

Sand size	Mean sand diameter[1]	Effective pore radius[2]	15 sec	30 sec	1 min	2 min	5 min	10 min	20 min	30 min	40 min
			Height of capillary rise above water level in pan (cm)								
coarse											
medium											
fine											

[1] See Figure 9.3 or the label on sand provided by instructor. [2] See calculations in question 4.

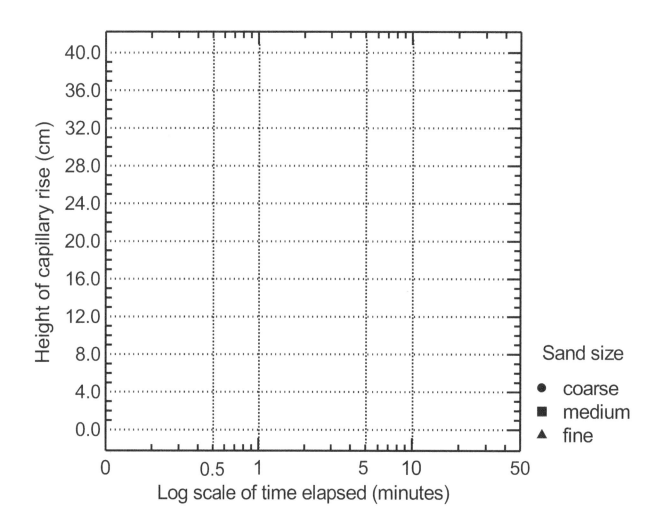

Figure 9.5 Graph for plotting data (from Table 9.3) for capillary rise in three sand sizes. Use the symbols indicated, and then connect the symbols with a smooth curve. Note the log scale of time on the X-axis. This allows you to show the early readings of less than 1 minute.

Exercise 9

INVESTIGATING CAPILLARY RISE

QUESTIONS

1. Describe how the water moved up in the sand columns. Was the rise an even or a jerky motion?

   _____

2. Explain why you think the movement was smooth or jerky, as observed?

   _____

   _____

3. Does particle size affect pore size? If so, explain how.

   _____

   _____

   Draw a diagram showing
   how you think this pore
   size is related to the
   particle size.

4. Calculate the effective pore radius for each sand column using Eq. 9.2 and record in Table 9.3. Show your calculations here.

5. Describe some practical implications of this exercise for designing the following:

    a. a concrete slab building foundation

    _____

       . _____

    b. a garden with a shallow water table

    _____

    _____

    c. a golf green

    _____

    _____

    d. a bottom watered green house bench

    _____

    _____

6. Relate the sponge experiment to the influence that the shape of a flower pot has on the aeration or water logging of the soil in it. Use the drawing of two pots to help explain by showing the zones of saturation ("capillary fringe") and the relative amount of air filled pores in the potting medium. This "drowning" phenomenon is one of the most commons reasons for poor growth of house plants!

_____

_____

_____

_____

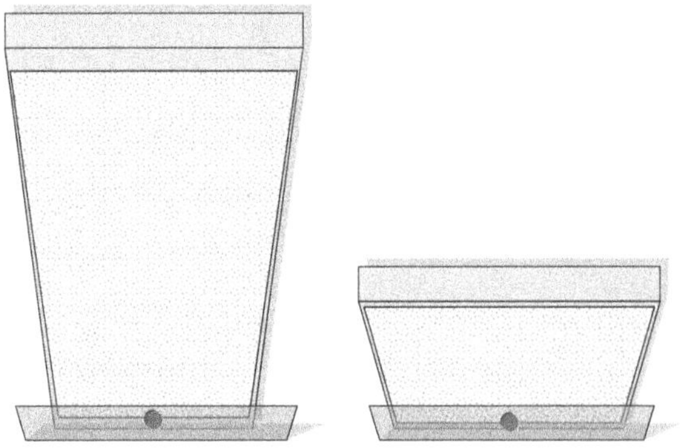

Figure 9. 6 Tall and short flowerpots have very different aeration properties. Show why.

98

Exercise 10
Effect of Soil Composition on Percolation and Retention of Water

OBJECTIVES

After completing this exercise, you should be able to...

1. Describe the relative effects of sand, organic matter (peat) and clay on the percolation rate and retention of water in soil.
2. Calculate the percolation rate and water content (by mass and by volume) given the necessary measurements.
3. Explain how to determine soil water content by the gravimetric method.
4. Explain how the length of a water column hanging from a soil is related to the soil water potential and pore sizes occupied by the water.

INTRODUCTION

The movement of water through soils (percolation) and its retention in soils (water holding capacity) are key aspects of how soils perform their environmental functions of supporting plant growth and protecting groundwater supplies. The concepts of water retention and water percolation are key to understanding how various soils will behave in a wide range of applications, including field irrigation and drainage, containerized plant production, landfill stabilization caps and waste lagoon liners.

Water retention by soils is essential to the survival of land plants and plays an important role in watershed runoff yield, soil productivity, and resistance to loss of chemicals by leaching. Among the factors that greatly influence water retention are the texture and organic matter content of the soil material. Clay and soil organic matter both possess tremendous amounts of surface area per unit mass or volume. Water is attracted to and held by these surfaces. Generally, the more clay and/or organic matter in a soil, the greater its water holding capacity will be.

Percolation is the downward movement of water through the soil pore system. In the field, downward water percolation through soils occurs because of the "pull" of both gravity and the attraction of water to small pores in deeper soil layers. In containers, the latter effect is largely absent. Very small pores hold water against the pull of gravity but contribute little to the movement of water. Medium and large pores are the ones that conduct nearly all the water that percolates.

The percolation rate (expressed as cm/hr or inches/hr) is an important factor in the functioning of natural watersheds, wetlands, natural and artificial drainage systems, and septic tank filter fields. The rate of flow through a porous material increases exponentially with the diameter of the pores (think of water flow through a fire hose versus and garden hose!). The size of the pores available for water movement is determined largely by the size of the particles composing the soil (the soil texture), as well as the manner in which they are packed together (the soil structure). Large particles like sand generally will have relatively large spaces between them; while the spaces between very small particles like clay will generally be very small (think of the spaces between basket balls in a bin versus golf balls).

In this exercise you will demonstrate water percolation and retention, as affected by gravity and the water potential generated by a hanging water column (that is very much like the hanging water columns in field soil profiles generated by the pores in deeper soil layers). In this exercise, you will alter the pore sizes through which water travels by changing the size of the particles in the material. It should become quite evident that a small increase in the clay content of a soil can *greatly* slow down percolation. In addition, the measurements and calculations you will perform also demonstrate the concepts of soil water content based on volume (θ_v) and mass (θ_m) of water and soil.

MATERIALS

- Desiccator with dry desiccant.
- Drying oven
- Leaching column (~2 cm I.D.)fit with one-hole white (soft) rubber stopper and 3 cm long glass or stiff plastic drain tube (a 65 ml plastic syringe without plunger can also be used a leaching tube)
- 50 cm length of Tygon tubing to fit over leaching column drain tube
- Lab stand with clamp
- 10 ml graduated cylinder
- 50 ml graduated cylinder
- Disposable specimen container with top (120 to 150 mL)
- Timer or watch showing seconds
- Cheesecloth or 1.5 cm diameter filter paper disk
- 50 ml glass beaker
- Teaspoon measure
- Tongs (to remove beaker after microwaving)
- Medium to fine sand (well graded grains, with less than 2% silt or clay). Concrete mixing sand. Air dry before using. If fines are present (handling the sand leaves the hand "dirty"), use a 100 mesh sieve to remove them.
- Horticultural peat (or finished compost), dried and ground to pass a 2 mm sieve.
- Clay soil from a B horizon (subsoil, low in organic matter, approx. 50% clay content), air dried and ground to pass 2 mm sieve.
- Natural mineral soil, preferably of medium or coarse texture, air dried and ground to pass 2 mm sieve. This can be student's personal soil.

Table 10.1 Soil materials used and their composition.

Soil Material	Components of test material	Description of resulting material
Sand	30 cm^3 sand	Sand (<2% clay)
Sand + peat	25 cm^3 sand + 5 cm^3 ground peat	Peat-sand potting mix (16% peat by volume, ~ 4% peat by mass)
Sand + clay	25 cm^3 sand + 5 cm^3 clay soil	Sandy loam (~ 8% clay by volume and mass)
Sand + natural soil	25 cm^3 sand + 5 cm^3 soil	Natural mineral soil (personal soil) % clay = _____ (from Ex. 7)

PROCEDURE

1. Using a *dry* 10 mL graduated cylinder to measure the volumes, prepare 30 cm³ of each of the four air-dry soil materials listed in Table 10.1 Tap 3 times to settle material in cylinder when you measure each volume. Add the materials to a screw- top jar and slowly roll end over end 15 times to mix the materials thoroughly. Thereafter, avoid vibrations that might cause the material to segregate again.

2. Set up 4 leaching columns as shown in Figure 10.1. Label them 1-4 for the soil materials in Table 10.1. Using a stirring rod or pencil, place a moistened filter paper disk (diameter just a bit smaller than that of the column inside diameter.) in the bottom of the column. Adjust the clamp height to accommodate a 25 mL graduated cylinder beneath the column. Add a soil material to each leaching column. A funnel made from a sheet of paper may facilitate the transfer of the dry soil material. Tap the column on the bench three times to uniformly settle the material. Place another small, moistened filter paper disk on top of the soil material.

3. Using a 25 mL graduated cylinder, *slowly* add 20.0 ml of water to each leaching column. Place the empty cylinders under the columns to collect and measure the leachate.

Watch the movement of the wetting front in the columns. Does the water flow smoothly or unevenly?

Does it tend to flow down the edges between the soil and the column wall?

COMMENTS

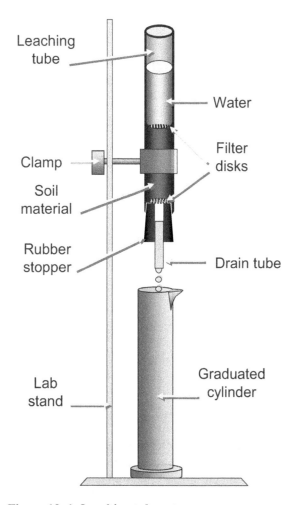

Figure 10. 1 Leaching tube setup.

4. When rate of dripping slows down to 1 minute between drops, replace the cylinder beneath each column with an empty beaker. In Table 10.2 column A record the volume of this "1st leachate" in each cylinder. Then pour all the leachate collected in each graduated cylinder back onto the soil in the same column and catch the new (2nd) leachate in the beakers.

5. Record (in Table 10.2, column B) the time of the first drop of drainage following the re-application of the leachate. This will be almost immediately after re-adding the leachate. When rate of dripping slows down again, note the time that each drop falls (use form at right). When the interval between drops is greater than one minute, consider the time recorded for the previous drop to be the time that drainage ceased. Circle that time at right and enter this time in column C of Table 10.2 as the time when 2nd leaching ceased.

6. Use a 10 ml graduated cylinder to carefully measure the volume of the 2nd leachate in each beaker. Record this volume in column E of Table 10.2: volume of leachate at saturation.

7. The amount of water retained, under essentially saturated conditions is 20 mL minus the mL collected in the 2nd leaching. Recorded this value in column G of Table 10.2.

8. After the dripping has ceased and the beakers have been emptied, attach a straight 50 cm length of soft plastic tubing to the outlet at the bottom of each leaching column. A small weight such as a steel nut may help it hang without curling. Set the stand on a shelf or the edge of the bench so that the tube hangs straight and ends in a small empty beaker.

During the first leaching much of the water may have flowed between the clay aggregates without soaking into them completely. By the time of the second leaching the soil mix should have become well moistened, and any clay present will have expanded.

Sand	Sand + peat	Sand + clay	Sand + Natural soil

The rate of water movement that you are now measuring is essentially the "percolation rate" of your soil material. Compare the rates of percolation of the various soil materials that you and/or your classmates are using. Note the effect on the percolation rate of adding a small amount of clay.

For these steps to work properly, the tube connection must be air-tight. The 50 cm long tube should slowly fill with water without the presence of any air bubbles or air gaps in the water column. If done properly, the 50 cm long column of water in the tubing will "hang" from the water in the soil, causing a negative pressure or "pull" on the water remaining in the soil equal to the weight of 50 cm

9. Carefully add exactly 25 ml of water to the soil in each column. Observe the water movement and appearance of soil mix. Take care that all the leachate is collected in the beaker.

10. After all water movement has ceased, carefully detach the Tygon tubing from the drain tube, allowing the leachate to drain from the tubing into the beaker. Then transfer the leachate to a graduated cylinder and record the volume in Table 10.2., Column H.

11. Label a dry, clean 50 ml glass beaker with your name, section, and soil material no. Weigh the beaker accurately and record in Table 10.3 column A.

12. Transfer the soil mix from the leaching column to the beaker (blowing hard through your hand cupped around one end of the column may help remove the soil). Immediately weigh the beaker of moist soil. Record weight in Table 10.3 column B. Then dry the soil and beaker. **Using a microwave oven**, place the beakers of moist soil on a turntable. Set the output power to "high" and microwave for 5 minutes. Then weigh the beaker and stir the soil. Be sure not to lose any soil on the stirring rod. Repeat this procedure for several more 5-minute exposures until the weight is nearly constant. Then repeat once more and proceed to step 13.

13. Remove the dried beaker of soil from oven and place in a desiccator a few minutes to cool. Obtain accurate final dry weight when cooled to near room temperature and record in column C of Table 10.3.

14. The amount of water retained by 30 cm^3 of soil mix at -5kPa (close to "field capacity") is calculated as (ml water added in steps 3 and 9) – (ml water in leachate from steps 6 and 10). Record this in column I of Table 10.2.

of H_2O. Since 1000 cm H_2O = 1 bar pressure, the water remaining in the soil will be under -0.05 bars ≈ -5kPa pressure. As this force is applied, you should be able to see air filling the larger soil pores.

A conventional oven should be set at 105 °C (above the boiling point of water) to drive off all water from the sample.

Up to 25 samples may be dried at once in a medium size 750-watt microwave oven, but the amount of microwave energy applied must be increased as the total amount of water and soil in the oven increases.

See appendix D for details on soil drying for water content determination.

USE GLOVES AND TONGS TO HANDLE THE BEAKER WHICH MAY BE HOT!

This estimate of θ_v is made by subtracting all the water drained from all the water added. An independent estimate of θ_v can be made by multiplying bulk density x θ_m calculated by the weight loss on drying.

15. Complete Table 10.3. The weight of water that had been in the soil is the difference between the weights before and after drying in the oven. Compare this to the volume of water that was estimated to have been retained (see step 14).

16. If one of the soils used was your own soil, calculate the approximate water holding capacity for the soil as the volumetric percent water held when the water potential is -5 kPa (-0.05 bar). Use the data you have entered in Table 10.3 as follows. Remember that you mixed 5 cm^3 of soil with 25 cm^3 of sand to give 30 cm^3 of a mix:

cm^3 water in 5 cm^3 soil at -5kPa equals:
    (Mix water content * volume of mix) – (Sand water content * volume of sand)

which (using the values from Table 10.3) equals:
    (line 4, col. G) * (30 cm^3 mix)) – (line 1, col. G) * (25 cm^3 sand))

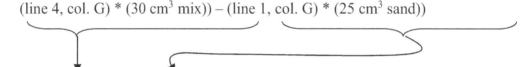

= (_____) – (_____) = _____ g water/5 cm^3 soil.

Divide the result from above by 5 to give cm^3 water /cm^3 soil at -5 kPa = _____

Enter this last value in Appendix G, Table G2 as your soil's water holding capacity at -5 kPa.

Exercise 10
Effect of Soil Composition on Percolation and Retention of Water

RESULTS

Table 10.2   Percolation and Water Retention as Affected by Soil Composition

	A	B	C	D = C-B	E	F = E/D	G = 20-E	H	I = 45- (E+H)	J = (I/30)
Soil Mat'l	Vol. of 1st leachate	Time 1st drop	Time last drop	Duration of 2nd leaching	Leachate volume at sat'n	Perc. Rate	Vol. Retained at sat'n	Leachate -5 kPa[†]	Retained -5 kPa	Volumetric water content, θ_v
	mL	--- hh:mm ---		min	mL	mL/min	--------------- mL ----------------			cm^3/cm^3
Sand										
Sand + peat										
Sand + clay										
Sand + natural soil										

[†] Note that -5kPa $\approx$ -50 cm H_2O (the length of the water column hanging in the tube). This condition is wetter than 'field capacity', which is usually considered at -10kPa or 100cm H_2O.

Table 10.3   Gravimetric and Volumetric Moisture of Final Soil at $\approx$ -50 cm H_2O Water Potential

	A (step 11)	B (step 12)	C (step 13)	D = B-C	E $= \dfrac{D}{C-A}$	F $= \dfrac{C-A}{30}$	G = E*F
Soil Material	Wt. Beaker alone	Wt. Beaker + moist soil mix	Wt. Beaker + Dry soil-mix	Wt. H_2O lost	Wt. Water Content (θ_m)	Bulk density	Vol. Water Content (θ_v)
	-------------------- g --------------------				g/g	g/cm^3	cm^3/cm^3
Sand							
Sand + peat							
Sand + clay							
Sand+Natural soil							

Write out calculations for your soil here:

cm^3 water in 5 cm^3 soil at -5kPa equals:
(Mix water content * volume of mix) – (Sand water content * volume of sand)

which (using the values from Table 10.2) equals:
(line 4, col. J) * (30 cm^3 mix))   (line 1, col. J) * (25 cm^3 sand))

= (_____ * 30) – (_____ *25) = _____ cm^3 water/5 cm^3 soil.

cm^3 water /cm^3 soil at -5 kPa = _____ / _____ = _____ .

QUESTIONS

1. What relationships would you expect to find between the clay content of a soil and its percolation rate and water retention capacity?

2. Were the expected relationships apparent in your class' data? If so give an example. If not, explain why not.

3. For <u>your personal soil</u>, calculate θ_v at -0.05 bars (or -5kPa) as cm H_2O/cm soil and inches H_2O/ft. soil retained using your calculations from top of this page.

4. For each soil material, calculate θ_v, the volumetric water content (cm^3 H_2O/cm^3 soil) using data from Table 10.3.

5. Are values in Table 10.2, column J comparable to those in Table 10.3 column G? Explain.

6. Why were the dried samples cooled in a desiccator?

Exercise 11

Using Tensiometers to Monitor
Soil Moisture Status

OBJECTIVES

After completing this exercise, you should be able to ...

1. Describe the uses, advantages, and disadvantages of tensiometers as compared to other soil moisture monitoring methods.
2. Identify the parts of a tensiometer.
3. Explain how a tensiometer works and what specific soil property it measures.
4. Relate the vacuum gauge readings on a commercial tensiometer to the plant-availability of soil moisture and the need for irrigation.
5. Prepare and install a tensiometer.
6. Explain the effect of soil texture on the availability of moisture at a given water content.
7. Describe how tensiometers should be installed and used to control irrigation of a) turf, b) trees or c) row crops.

INTRODUCTION

Just as a thermometer or thermostat helps a manager cool or heat a greenhouse to the proper temperature, instruments that measure soil moisture can help an irrigator provide the right amount and timing of water for optimum plant growth. Many different methods are available for monitoring soil moisture status. They range from the old-fashioned "art" of feeling soil moisture to high-tech instruments such as neutron probes and capacitance sensors.

Some methods measure the *amount* of water in the soil. Others measure how tightly the water is absorbed to the soil particles. The ease with which plant roots can obtain water is inversely related to how strongly the water is absorbed to the soil surfaces. *Soil moisture tension* (SMT) or *moisture potential* (ψ) are terms used to describe the force of adsorption that roots must overcome in order to pull water away from the soil. Soil moisture tension indicates how easily available the water in the soil is, but it does not indicate how *much* water is available. Knowing the *amount* of water available in a soil would enable a manager to estimate the number of days a soil can keep plants supplied.

A tensiometer is a simple mechanical instrument which responds directly to the "pull" of soil particles on soil water, the SMT. Basically, it consists of a sealed water-filled tube with a porous ceramic tip on one end and a vacuum gauge at the other end. When the ceramic tip is in contact with soil, water moves from inside the tube through the ceramic tip and into the soil. As water leaves the tube, the water level in the tube is lowered slightly, creating a partial vacuum in the air-tight upper end. This vacuum is registered on the face of the vacuum gauge. The drier the soil, the more strongly it attracts water from the tube, and the greater the vacuum registered on the gauge. If the soil is moistened (as by irrigation or rainfall) the added water is not held as tightly by the soil and the vacuum in the tube will pull some of it in through the porous tip. This extra water will partially refill the tube and cause the vacuum to decrease. Thus the negative pressure (vacuum) in the tube is equal to the negative pressure (tension) of the water in the soil. Changes in this soil moisture tension can read directly on the gauge.

On most tensiometers, the gauge reads in centibars (cbar) or kiloPascals (kPa) from 0 (saturated soil, no tension) to 100 (fairly dry soil, enough tension to cause moisture stress for most plants). Actually, the highest reading possible in practice is about 85 kPa. At greater tensions (drier soils) air is drawn in through the ceramic tip and breaks the vacuum in the tube. Therefore, should the soil become drier than 85 kPa, the gauge needle would drop back to zero. For most irrigation-control purposes this characteristic is not a serious problem since irrigation for most plants should begin while the soil moisture tension reading is well below 80 kPa. For measurement of moisture in drier soils, electric resistance blocks, time-domain reflectrometry probes, a neutron probe, or a psychrometer can be used, though these instruments are generally much more expensive and/or laborious to calibrate.

In this exercise you will learn to prepare, install, read and care for a tensiometer. We will use tensiometers to demonstrate the effect of soil texture on soil moisture tension. Optionally, we will also use this instrument to observe the depletion of soil water by evaporation and growing plants and the recharge of soil water at two depths by rain or irrigation.

MATERIALS

- 3 tensiometers with vacuum gauges, 15 to 30 cm length (additional tensiometers may be used for an outdoor demonstration). These instruments are available from Irrometer Co., P.O. Box 2424, Riverside CA 92516, and from Soil Moisture Equipment, Inc., P.O. Box 30025, Santa Barbara, CA 93105, as well as many farm and forestry suppliers. Soak the tip in clean water for 48 hours before class.
- Hand vacuum pump for servicing tensiometers. Must have a suction cup or other fitting to fit top of tensiometer tube. Supplied by most sources that supply tensiometers.
- Lab stand with clamp to hold tensiometer upright while testing with tip in water.
- Plastic squeeze-type wash bottle, 500 to 1000 ml.
- Fine emery cloth, sandpaper or stiff brush.
- Water-based, NOT oil-based, food coloring dye (supplied by some tensiometer manufacturers).
- 2 large funnels
- 2 plastic buckets (5 L or 1 gallon size)
- PVC pipe 1/2" I.D. and 12 inches (30cm) long with 10-20 slots cut around the pipe along the lower 10cm. Cut slots with a hack-saw blade on all sides of the pipe, but no more than 1/3 of the way through the pipe.
- 1 plastic container, I L (I qt) size
- 1 screw-top specimen cup
- 8 L of air-dry loamy sand soil or fine construction sand (< 5% clay). Sieve through 5 mm mesh.
- 8 L of air-dry sandy loam, texture soil (<10% clay, 2 to 3 % organic matter). Sieve through 5 mm mesh. Use a soil with substantial organic matter, but little clay. Test to be sure water will soak in and spread to throughout bucket within 30 minutes.
- Standard galvanized steel pipe, 1/2" I.D., 7/8" O.D., 18" long.
- Heavy hammer and block of wood for driving steel pipe into soil outdoors.
- Small plastic bags and rubber bands.
- Absorbent paper towels.
- (Optional if outdoor installation not possible) Two potted "house" plants (Dieffenbachia is a suitable species) in large (at least 1 gallon) pots of soil or potting mix.

PROCEDURE

1. Select a tensiometer that has been soaking at least over night clean water. Identify the parts of the tensiometer shown in Figure 11. 1. Pay particular attention to the nature of the three parts most likely to give problems during operation of the instrument: the rubber seal at the top of the tube, the vacuum gauge, and the ceramic tip.

2. Unscrew the filler cap and check the *rubber seal* for cracks or brittleness. Replace it if necessary. In some models the rubber seal is a number 0 laboratory rubber stopper. Record your observations in Table 11.2.

3. Check the *vacuum gauge* for visible damage to its weatherproof casing or glass front. Droplets of moisture inside the gauge usually indicate a damaged gauge. Second, check the operation of the gauge with a hand vacuum pump. Be sure the tensiometer is filled with water or colored solution. Moisten the pump suction cup or fitting to make it easier to form an air-tight seal. With the tensiometer filler cap removed, apply the pump suction fitting to the top of the tensiometer and pump several quick strokes. A properly working gauge should give a reading of 80 to 90 kPa.

COMMENTS

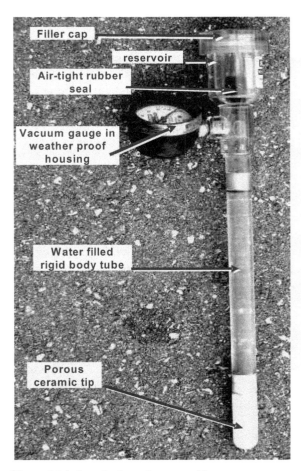

Figure 11.1 A typical tensiometer with vacuum gauge. Different brands have slightly different construction and features. For example, some vacuum gauges have a zero-calibration screw, and some do not. Some have a large reservoir, and some do not.

4. *Slowly* release the suction fitting and check that the gauge needle drops back to 0. Record your observations in Table 11.2.

Never allow the vacuum gauge needle to drop back too rapidly as this may damage the gauge. The gauge is a delicate mechanical instrument. Do not jar or drop it.

5. To check the *ceramic tip,* stand the tensiometer in clean water and screw on the cap with rubber seal. Seal, but do not over tighten. The gauge should read 0. Now lift the tensiometer from the water and wrap the tip tightly in a dry paper towel and watch the gauge. Within about 5 minutes the needle should have moved to 15 - 30 kPa. Remove the towel and re-submerge the tensiometer tip in the water. Within a minute the needle should swing back to the 0 position. Record your observations in Table 10.2.

For the instrument to respond to changes in soil moisture tension, water must be able to flow freely in and out through the ceramic tip. Never let the dip dry out after field use as this may result in the precipitation of salts from the soil solution which can clog the ceramic's pores. Oils from your hands can also clog the pores and make the tip hydrophobic. A well maintained tensiometer tip should have a useful life of many years unless used in very salty soils. Avoid storing the tensiometers in a metal bucket as rust can also clog the ceramic.

6. If the tip fails the above test and appears dirty, clean it by scrubbing with a stiff brush, a handful of wet, sandy soil, or a piece of fine emery cloth or sandpaper. Wash it in clean water. Then fill the tensiometer tube just to the level of the gauge, (do not seal), stand up-right in a plastic container with about 5 cm of water and allow the water in the tube to drain out through the tip.

If the water level in the tube falls by 1 or 2 cm in 30 minutes, the tip is clean. Otherwise, it may need replacing or further reconditioning.

Measurement of Soil Moisture Tension as Affected by Soil Texture

1. Prepare a pre-soaked tensiometer (15 or 30 cm tube length) for installation. Fill the tube and half the reservoir with colored water. Apply the pump and pump several quick strokes to pull an 80 to 90 cbar vacuum while standing the ceramic tip in a container of clean water. Allow the pump to remain in place under 30 vacuum for seconds. Tap the side of the tensiometer to facilitate the removal of the bubbles.

The coloring agent in the water is designed to make the water level in the tensiometer more visible. In the field as the soil dries out, it draws water from the instrument. When the water level has dropped 5 to 10 mm below the rubber seal the top of the tube contains air, the seal should be loosened, allowing the air to bubble out and water from the reservoir to refill the tube.

2. After 30 seconds of applying the vacuum, slowly release the suction. Then screw on the cap, tightening only enough to form a good seal (about 1/4 turn after the seal engages). Keep the ceramic tip wet at all times by covering the tip with a wet paper towel and plastic bag held in place by a rubber band until it is installed.

Notice the air bubbles that emanate from the water under vacuum. The more of this dissolved air that can be removed, the more sensitively the instrument will operate. Notice that, when the vacuum is released, the bubbles disappear. Can you explain what causes the bubbles to appear and disappear?

Do not over-tighten the rubber seal as this reduces its life.

3. Obtain a 5-L plastic bucket, two 30 cm sections of slotted PVC pipe, and 4 L of air-dry medium textured soil. While holding the pipes upright, slotted end down, near the center of the bucket, pour in the 0.4 L of dry soil around the pipes. Tap the bucket several times to settle the soil evenly.

When the wetting front reaches the ceramic tip, the vacuum reading should drop as water is drawn from the soil.

4. Mark the tensiometer tube at a point 15 cm from the middle of the ceramic tip. Remove the plastic bag and towel from the tip. *Gently* insert the tensiometer vertically to the 15 cm mark at a place mid-way between the two pipes (see Figure 11.2). DO NOT HANDLE BY THE GAUGE. If the soil is soft push the tensiometer in by pressing down on the filler cap. If the soil is hard, first make a hole to 15 cm with a 22.2mm (7/8 inch) O.D. pipe and then push the tensiometer into this hole for a snug fit. Pack the soil around the tensiometer as shown in Figure 11.2.

5. Place a funnel in the top end of the PVC pipe and *slowly*, a little at a time, pour in 0.4 L of water. Part of this water may also be gently poured around the walls of the bucket.

6. Begin timing when the 0.4 L of water has all been applied and soaked into the soil. Read the tensiometer gauge every 10 minutes for 60 minutes or until there is no change. Tap the tensiometer filler cap gently before reading the gauge. Plot the results in Figure 11.3.

The initial reading should be very high since the soil is almost completely dry. Note how long it takes for the water to soak into the "medium textured" soil and move out from the slotted pipes to the tensiometer tip (the arrival of the wetting front at the tip will be indicated by a decrease in the vacuum reading).

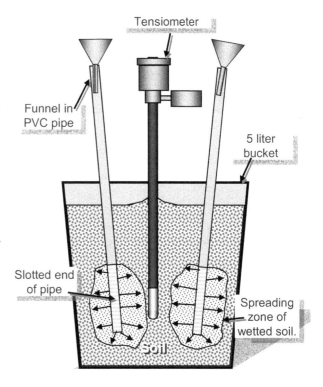

Figure 11.2 Experimental set up using tensiometers to measure the soil moisture tension in two soils (only one shown) of the same water content but different textures. The slotted pipe will help spread water throughout the soil. Note the soil is slightly mounded and firmed around the tensiometer tube to prevent false readings from surface water flowing down along the tube.

By adding 0.4 liter of water to 4 liters of dry soil a soil 1/10 water by volume is created, i.e.,10% moisture (v/v) *on average*. In the medium texture soil, the water will eventually spread out thinly over the large surface area of the clay and silt particles, resulting in a relative high vacuum gauge reading. **Note:** *it may a long time for the water to evenly distribute throughout the soil, therefore the soil may still be wetter or drier than the 'average' near the tensiometer when you read it.*

7. Between readings in step #6 obtain a second tensiometer, bucket and pair of pipes. Set up as in steps 1-5 but use a very "coarse textured" soil such as a loamy sand or sand. Take timed readings of this second tensiometer as in step 6. Plot the readings in Figure 11.3.

Be sure to keep track of the time intervals for each soil. Compare the time required for the water to reach the ceramic tip in the coarse-textured to that required in the medium textured soil. Also compare the value at which the reading stabilized each soil.

8. Once the tensiometer readings have stabilized, slowly add an additional 0.4 L of water to each bucket of soil. Once this 0.4 L of water has soaked, take a tensiometer reading for each soil at 5 minute intervals until the readings stabilize. Record your results in Figure 11.3.
    Answer questions #1-6. Clean up your bench and materials.

    The additional 0.4 L of water will bring each soil to 0.8/4 or 20% moisture (v/v) *on average*. For the medium textured soil, this should be about "field capacity" or 10 to 20 kPa. For the coarse soil 20% moisture may be near saturation (0 kPa). Again, remember *it may a long time for the water to evenly distribute throughout the soil, therefore the soil may still be wetter or drier than the 'average' near the tensiometer when you read it.*

9. *If possible* (check with your instructor) leave the tensiometers in the buckets of soil and check the tensiometer readings daily for several days. You can plot these results on Figure 11.4, using the symbol "X" to distinguish these data from the outdoor readings.

    It may a day or two for the water to evenly distribute throughout the soil and for the tensiometers readings to stabilize completely. The readings should then begin to increase as the soil slowly dries by evaporation of water from the surface.

Installation of Tensiometers in the Field

1. Check and prepare two tensiometers as described in steps 1 and 2 above. One tensiometer should be 15 cm long and the other 30 to 60 cm long. After pumping to remove the dissolved air, cap the tensiometer snugly and protect the ceramic tip with a towel and plastic bag.

    In controlling irrigation, it is usually advisable to use tensiometers in pairs, one set to measure the moisture in the upper part of the rooting zone and other in the lower. Irrigation is generally begun when the upper tensiometer registers stressful levels of moisture tension (e.g., 50 kPa). Enough irrigation water should be applied to affect the reading on the deeper tensiometer. That way the irrigator knows that the entire root zone has been moistened.

2. With your instructor, choose a site outdoors to set up a tensiometer station. Mark a 7/8" O.D. pipe at the appropriate depths for the two tensiometers. Also mark the tensiometer tubes. Using a heavy hammer and wood block, drive the 7/8" O.D. galvanized pipe into the ground and pull out to make two holes about 30 cm apart, one hole for the short tensiometer and a deeper one for the long tensiometer.

    The site may be in an irrigated field or on a lawn. It may even be in a landscaping container or near a tree. Wherever they are installed, the tensiometers should be protected from damage by covering them with a wooden box or a section of concrete pipe. The location should be clearly marked with a notice to passersby to not disturb.

3. Using soil from the depth at which the tensiometer tip will be set, make a 2:1 soil: water slurry in a specimen cup. Shake well, then pour about 25 mL of the slurry down the hole.

    Contact between the tensiometer tip and the soil will be improved by nestling the tensiometer tip into a slurry in the bottom of the hole.

4. Insert the tensiometers into their respective holes, being careful not to press on the gauge. Be sure the tensiometers are pushed all the way to the bottom of the hole.

    Within a few minutes the gauges should begin to register a vacuum. Tap on the filler cap if the needle appears "stuck".

112

5. Record the gauge readings after they have about 30 minutes to stabilize. Discuss the interpretation of the gauge readings in terms of moisture availability to plants in the root zone and the need for irrigation (Refer to Table 11.1).

6. If possible, leave the tensiometers installed for several weeks. Record all rainfall or irrigation water inputs using a rain gauge or instructor-provided information. Observe and record the gauge readings every few days, especially after a rain event or irrigation. Graph the tensiometer readings on Figure 11.4. Write a brief report discussing the *infiltration and percolation* of water in this soil and the *evapotranspiration* of water from the root zone. Relate the tensiometer reading to rainfall and irrigation events and plant growth and vigor.

Probably the most useful way of recording tensiometer readings is to plot them on a chart every 3 to 5 days (see Figure 11.4). In this way the trends can be perceived and the need for irrigation predicted ahead of time by extrapolation.

Never expose a tensiometer to freezing temperatures as ice forming inside the gauge will damage the gauge. If tensiometers must be stored where they may freeze, be sure to empty all water from the gauge as well as from the tube. Always thoroughly clean the instrument, especially the tip, before storing.

> **Do not leave the tensiometers out during periods of possible freezing temperatures!**

Using Tensiometers to Monitor Water Status of Potted Plants[1]

1. Obtain a two potted leafy "house" plants growing in large (at least 1 gallon) plastic containers. Water both slowly until water drains out the bottom drain holes. Then label one pot "dry" and the other "wet". Use a 7/8 inch O.D. pipe to make a pilot hole 15 cm deep in the soil (or potting medium) in each pot.

2. Mark two tensiometers tubes at a point 15 cm from the middle of the ceramic tip. Remove the plastic bag and towel from the tip. *Gently* insert one tensiometer vertically into each of the 15 cm pilot holes in the two pots. DO NOT HANDLE BY OR PRESS ON THE GAUGE. Press down gently on the filler cap for a snug fit. Pack the soil around the tensiometer. After about 15 minutes, record the two tensiometer readings.

Make sure to both holes are exactly the same depth. The soil (medium) will tend to be wetter near the bottom of the pot, so be sure the tensiometer tip is not installed too deeply.

Note: This exercise may allow one of the plants to die.

3. Place both potted plants with their tensiometers near a bright window or under a grow-light. Water the "wet" plant by adding 500 mL of water once each week. Do not water the "dry" plant at all. Record the tensiometer readings weekly before adding water (record in Table 11.3 and Figure 11.4)

Record the amount and times of all water additions to the "wet" plant.
Observe both plants to assess their condition at least once per week. Look for signs of wilting or waterlogging stress in the plants. Record your observations in Table 11.3

---

[1] This section may be especially useful if conditions do not permit outdoor installation of tensiometers.

Table 11.1 Interpretation of Tensiometer Gauge Readings in Terms of Availability of Soil Moisture to Plants (Adapted, with permission, from literature of Irrometer Company, Riverside, CA).

Gauge Reading (kPa or cbar)	Interpretation
0-10	Saturated soil. Often occurs for a day or two following irrigations. Continued readings in this range indicate over irrigations-danger of water-logged soils, inadequate root aeration, root rot or high water table.
10-20	Field capacity. Sprinkler and furrow irrigations are discontinued in this range to prevent wasting water and nutrients. In drip irrigation water is applied frequently in low volume to maintain moisture readily available to the plant. This range (10-20 kPa) should be maintained 30" – 45 cm from the emitter.
30-60	Usual range for starting irrigations, except in drip irrigation. Root aeration is assured anywhere in this range. In general, irrigations start in the lower part of this range in hot dry climates, and in coarse-textured sandy soils. Irrigation starts in the upper part of this range in cool, humid climates or In soils with water high water holding capacity. Starting irrigations in this range insures maintaining readily available soil moisture at all times, which is essential for maximum growth. It also provides a safety factor ... a reserve of soil moisture to compensate for such practical problems as delayed irrigations and inability to obtain uniform distribution of water to all portions of the section controlled by the station
70 and higher	Stress range. A reading of 70 does not necessarily indicate that all avail moisture is used up, but that readily available moisture is getting dangerously low for maximum growth. Top range of accuracy of the tensiometer is 80-85 kPa

EXERCISE 11

Using Tensiometers to Monitor Soil Moisture Status

Table 11.2 Observations during Check of Tensiometer Condition

Component	Observations	Status
Rubber seal	Visible damage?	O.K. _____ replaced_____
Vacuum Gauge	Visible damage: yes/no describe: _____ Reading after a pumping: _____ Gauge reading after release of vacuum:____ Correction factor*: add/subtract ___ to reading	O.K. _____ replaced_____ repaired_____
Ceramic Tip	Visible damage: yes/no Tip clean? yes/no If no, what type of coating? _____ Max. gauge reading within 5 min. of drying tip: _____ Time (min.) to return to zero after re-submerged: _____	O.K. _____ replaced ____ cleaned _____

*Optional. Can be determined by comparison to test gauge if available on pump.

Table 11.3 Soil Moisture Tension as Affected by Plant Use and Replenishment of Water.

Time after start	Gauge Reading		Plant and soil conditions
	"wet" pot	"dry" pot	
days	kPa		Observations

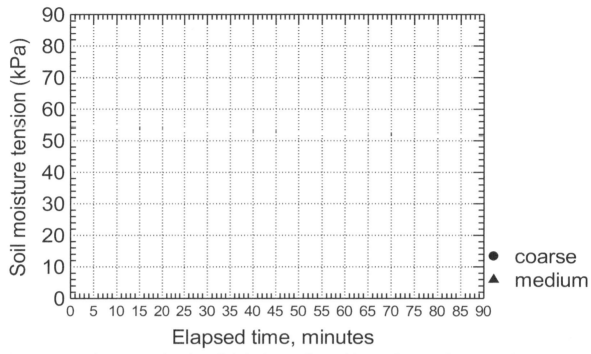

Figure 11. 3 Tensiometers readings for soils in buckets. Indicate with a small arrow when 0.4 L of water was added for the second time.

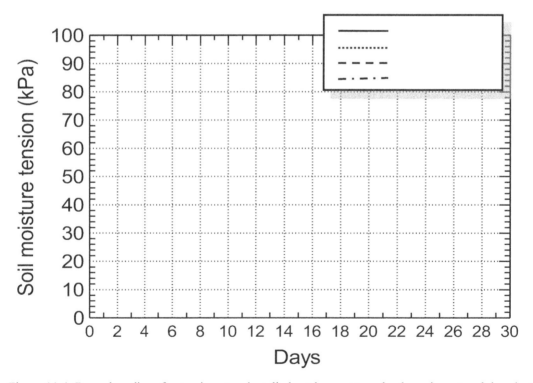

Figure 11.4 Record readings for tensiometers installed outdoors at two depths or in wet and dry plant containers. Indicate tensiometer tip depths and/or watering treatments in legend. Use arrows to indicate days on which rain occurred or water was applied.

EXERCISE 11
Using Tensiometers to Monitor Soil Moisture Status

Questions

1. What soil property does a tensiometer measure?

_____

2. Explain how you could perform auxiliary measurements that would use a tensiometer to determine not only *how available* the water in a soil is, but also *how much* water is in the soil.

_____

_____

_____

3. What three parts of a tensiometer are most likely to need repair/maintenance?

a. _____

b. _____

c. _____

4. What is the highest reading that a tensiometer can register accurately? Why?

_____

5. Why did bubbles of air appear when the pump was used to apply a vacuum to the water-filled tensiometer?

_____

_____

6.   Based on your data recorded in Figure 11.3, compare the amount, rate of distribution and plant availability of water in the two soils.

_____

_____

_____

7.   Explain why your tensiometer readings differed between two soils with the same average moisture percentage?

_____

_____

_____

8.   Discuss how the plants changed in appearance as the tensiometer readings changed (if your class used potted plants).

_____

_____

_____

9.   If you were able to set up a field tensiometer station, use the space below to discuss what you learned from the behavior of the tensiometers in the field.

_____

_____

_____

_____

Exercise 12
Effect of Cations on Flocculation

OBJECTIVES

After completing this exercise, you should be able to . . .

1. Predict the effect of sodium and calcium on the flocculation of soils.
2. Explain why the sodium-treated soil passed through the filter paper while the calcium-treated soil did not.
3. Graphically represent the effect of sodium on soil permeability.

INTRODUCTION

Flocculation of clay particles is often the first step in the formation of soil structure. During the flocculation process, individual clay particles (colloidal in size) coagulate together into tiny clumps or floccules. The floccules can then be bound together by cementing agent such as microbial glues or iron oxides forming the stable granular structure that is so prized in highly productive surface soils.

Since like charges repel, negatively charged clay particles tend to disperse if their negative charges are not completely balanced by positive charges from adsorbed cations. If clay particles can approach each other very closely, short-range forces of inter-atom attraction, called van der Waals forces, cause the particles to cohere. In soils, however, the colloids are surrounded by a swarm of adsorbed (exchangeable) cations with positive charges that negate some or all of the negative charge on the clay. Furthermore, these cations are hydrated. That is, each ion carries a shell of water molecules which affects how close to the clay surface the charged ionic nuclei can approach. Depending on how closely these cations are held to the colloid, the swarm of hydrated cations surrounding each colloid particle may prevent the particles from getting close enough together for van der Waals forces to come into play.

Divalent and trivalent cations tend to be most tightly attracted and therefore form a compact ion swarm that allows the particle to approach quite closely. In contrast, monovalent ions, especially sodium, are weakly attracted and tend to form a very widely spread-out swarm around the colloid. In addition, every Ca^{2+} ion would be replaced by two Na^+ ions, each carrying a shell of hydration water. All these "fat" hydrated Na^+ ions intervene between adjacent colloid particles, preventing their flocculation (see diagram). In addition, di- and trivalent ions can form cation "bridges" between colloid particles, but monovalent ions cannot. Because of its large hydrated-radius and small charge, Na is held much more loosely than any other cation commonly found in the soil. Soils with high amounts of sodium therefore tend to become dispersed.

In the dispersed state, the clay particles are spaced far apart, giving rise to a gel-like condition that is almost impermeable to water. When a sodium-affected soil dries out, it tends to form a hard, impermeable surface crust. Few plants can survive in such a soil, and it is almost impossible to leach out any excess salts (including the sodium) that may be present.

An additional factor that influences flocculation and dispersion is the concentration of ions or salts. A high concentration of total ions tends to cause the swarm of exchangeable ions to become compressed close to the particle surface, thus encouraging flocculation. This effect of high salt concentration occurs even if the cations are largely sodium. The opposite occurs when salts become too diluted. The exchangeable cation swarm spread out away from the particle surface and dispersion is encouraged. Thus, in this exercise inured to demonstrate the dispersion of soil we will use a very dilute solution and further dilute the salts by leaching the soil with distilled water which simulates the effect of rainwater.

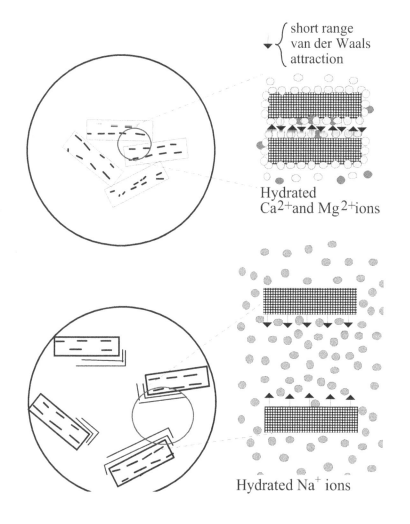

short range van der Waals attraction

Hydrated Ca^{2+} and Mg^{2+} ions

Hydrated Na^+ ions

If soil colloids come very close together, short range van der Waals forces cause them to cohere. Because hydrated Ca^{2+} ions have two positive charges and only a moderately large shell of water, they are strongly attracted to the colloids and stay very close to the colloid surface. This allows the colloids to come close enough together to be held together by van der Waals attraction. The soil is in a flocculated state as the colloids are clumped together.

Because they have only a single charge and a relatively large shell of water molecules, hydrated monovalent Na^+ ions are only weakly attracted to soil colloids. The swarm of exchangeable Na^+ ions therefore is quite spread out with most of the ions vibrating at some distance from the colloid surface. Such a swarm of weakly held ions therefore prevents the colloids from coming close enough together for van der Waals forces to act. The colloids are not held together, and their negative charges repel each other, giving rise to a dispersed soil condition.

Figure 12.1 Diagram of cation roles in colloid flocculation. Di- or tri-valent cations (top) tend to promote flocculation while monovalent cations (bottom) tend to reduce flocculation and increase dispersion.

MATERIALS

- soil (air dry, sieved to < 2mm, non-saline, clay loam, 20-30% clay)
- distilled water
- 0.002 M NaCl
- 0.001 M CaCl$_2$
- 4 filter funnels
- 8 folded filter papers (medium speed, e.g., Whatman #31 or Fisher P5)
- 4 50-mL graduated cylinders

- 1 filter stand (to hold 4 funnels)
- scoop (approximately 1 teaspoon)
- timer with second hand (or wristwatch)
- 4 large (50 mL) glass culture tubes or clear plastic centrifuge tubes (with tops)
- test tube rack to hold 4 tubes
- china marker

PROCEDURE	COMMENTS

1. Set up 3 funnels with folder filter paper. Moisten each paper with a few drops of water. Arrange so that each funnel will drain into a graduated cylinder. Label the funnels "DW", "Ca" and "Na", respectively.

The filter paper is moistened so that it will adhere to the sides of the funnel.

2. Add a level teaspoon of soil into each of 3 test tubes. Label them DW, Ca, and Na, respectively.

3. To the 3 labeled test tubes add 20 mL of distilled water, 0.001 M $CaCl_2$, or 0.002 M NaCl, respectively. Stopper and shake each tube vigorously ten times so that all the soil is completely wetted and brought into suspension.

Note that equal volumes of 0.002 M NaCl and 0.001 M $CaCl_2$ provided equal numbers of Na^+ and Ca^{2+} ions, respectively. Can you explain why this is so?

4. After shaking the tubes, sit them upright in a test tube rack and allow the soil to settle for 1 minute. Watch closely. Observe the upper part of the suspensions. Record your observations and answer question 4 on the results and conclusions sheet.

Dispersed clay produces a turbid or cloudy suspension of brown, gray or reddish color depending on the color of the clay. A clear, brown-colored solution (like tea) may be formed from organic compounds dissolved from the soil, especially by NaCl.

5. SLOWLY pour the supernatant suspension from each tube into the appropriate filter funnel.

Use care to avoid allowing any of the suspension to overflow the filter paper.

6. Observe the filtrates as they collect in the cylinders, noting their relative turbidity. Carefully set aside the three filter papers with soil. Note the appearance of the soil on the papers now and after they have had 20 minutes to dry out. Record your observations in Table 12.1 and *clean your funnels and glassware.*

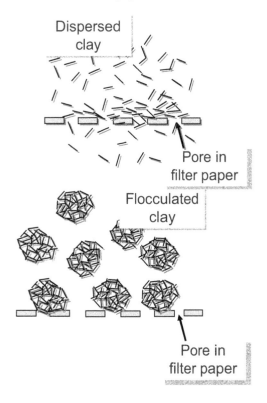

7. Set up 4 funnels with fresh (moistened) filter papers and graduated cylinders to catch the filtrates. Fold filter paper in fluted fashion. To each funnel add 1 level teaspoon of dry soil. Using the spoon, make a slight indentation in the middle of the soil. "DW-DW", "Ca-DW", Na-DW and "Na-Ca", respectively.

8. To the respective funnels, *SLOWLY* add 25 mL of *either* distilled water (DW), 0.005 M $CaCl_2$ (Ca-DW) or 0.01 M NaCl (both Na-DW and Na-Ca). Allow the soils to soak for 5 minutes. Carefully pour off and discard any liquid remaining above the soil in the funnel. Also discard any filtrate that collects in the cylinders. The cylinders should be empty before the next step is begun.

While the soil is soaking, cations from the added salt solution are replacing cations held by the clays. The $CaCl_2$ treated soil becomes **saline** (salty) and the NaCl treated soils becomes **saline-sodic** (high in exchangeable Na and total salts).

9. Little by little, add 50 ml distilled water to each funnel of soil and allow it to leach, catching the leachate in cylinders. After drainage has ceased, discard the leachate.

This step washes out the soluble salts, leaving relatively salt-free Na-saturated, Ca-saturated, and control soil, respectively. Without the excess salts, the Na-saturated clay becomes dispersed. The Ca-saturated soil remains flocculated. Lowering the ionic strength with DW may also cause dispersion.

10. Being certain to not allow the solution to creep up over the filter paper, carefully add 40 mL distilled water to the "DW-DW" soil and record in Table 12.2 the time this was added.

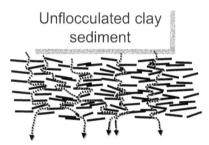

Unflocculated clay sediment

11. Repeat this step for the other 3 funnels, adding 40 mL **distilled water to Ca-DW and Na-DW**, but adding 40mL of **$CaCl_2$ to Na-Ca**. Record the times the solution was added to each funnel.

Dispersed clay particles lay flat as soil settles, creating an impermeable condition with only very small, tortuous pores for water movement (see diagram above).

12. Carefully observe and record the time at which each 5 mL increment of leachate collects in each cylinder. Record these times as hour:minute:second (hh:mm:ss) in Table 12.2.

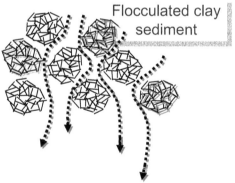

Flocculated clay sediment

13. For each 5 mL increment, calculate seconds elapsed since that solution was added and plot your results in Figure 12.2.

    Please clean your workspace and materials (rub off the china marker labels with a dry paper towel).

Flocculated clay has a porous, open structure with large pores between floccules that allow rapid water movement (see diagram above).

Exercise 12
Effects of Cations on Flocculation

Results and Conclusions

Table 12.1 Observation of Relative Flocculating Abilities of Na and Ca

First solution shaken with soil	Relative Turbidity of 2nd Filtrate	Appearance of Soil on Filter Paper
Distilled Water		
$CaCl_2$		
NaCl		

Table 12.2 Time of Collection for Increments of Filtrate. Record hour, minute and second.

Trt	First solution	Second solution	Time 2nd solution Added	Time at Which Increments (mL) of Filtrate Were Collected						
				5 mL	10 mL	15 mL	20 mL	25 mL	30 mL	35 mL
				------------------------------ hh:mm:ss ------------------------------						
A	Distilled Water	Distilled Water								
B	$CaCl_2$	Distilled Water								
C	NaCl	Distilled Water								
D	NaCl	$CaCl_2$								
				------------------------ calculated seconds elapsed ------------------------						
A	Distilled Water	Distilled Water								
B	$CaCl_2$	Distilled Water								
C	NaCl	Distilled Water								
D	NaCl	$CaCl_2$								

123

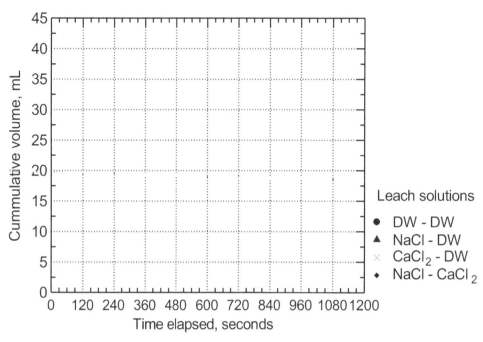

Figure 12.2 Filtrate volumes to estimate permeability of soils treated with Na and Ca salts.

Questions:

1. Why would flooding with seawater have a detrimental effect on the structure of coastal soils?
    _____
    _____

2. What might be added to such soils to improve their structure after the seawater has receded? Explain with reference to the results for "treatment D" in this exercise.
    _____
    _____
    _____

3. Can you think of any application in which compounds containing Ca^{2+} or other multivalent ions could be helpful in causing the flocculation and settling of soil materials from muddy water? Explain.
    _____

4. In step 4, which soil settled most rapidly? Why? _____
    _____. In which did the clay stay in suspension for the longest time?
    _____

5. Summarize your conclusions from this exercise with respect to the effect of the kind of salt in irrigation water on the permeability of the soil. _____
    _____

6. What physical explanation can you give for the fact that the curves in the above graph are not straight lines? (Hint: Is the water pressure head constant during leaching?)
    _____
    _____

124

Exercise 13

Cation Exchange Properties of Soil

OBJECTIVES

After completing this exercise, you should be able to...

1. Define the terms "cation" and "anion" and relate these terms to the + and - terminals of a battery.
2. List the cations and anions measured in this exercise and name the source of each in the filtrates.
3. Explain how and why the sand behaved differently from the soils in this exercise.
4. Interpret the meaning of white precipitates formed by the addition of barium chloride, ammonium oxalate and sodium cobaltinitrite to soil leachate solutions.
5. Estimate the cation exchange capacity of a soil by the adsorption of a colored dye.
6. Explain why gentian violet is adsorbed by soil, but other organic compounds may not be.
7. Discuss several ways in which cation exchange in soils is important for plant nutrition and environmental quality.

INTRODUCTION

The purpose of this exercise is to demonstrate the occurrence of cation exchange reactions in soils and to show that they are associated with the clay and humus fractions of the soil in particular.

In most soils, the colloidal fraction has negatively charged surfaces as a result of isomorphous substitution in crystal lattices (in certain clays) and the dissociation of H^+ ions from exposed oxygen ions (in both humus and clays). These negative charges are normally balanced by positively charged ions (cations such as Ca^{2+}, Cu^{2+} or K^+) from the soil solution (Figure 13.1). The charge balancing is not a static condition but rather is a dynamic equilibrium process. Cations from the soil solution oscillate about the negatively charged sites on the colloidal surfaces. Cations held in this oscillating state are said to be "exchangeable cations." Since all ions in solution are in continual movement, it is likely that another cation from the soil solution will move into the oscillation volume around a negative charge and become attracted to that charge, replacing the previously held cation which is then free to diffuse out into the soil solution (Figure 13.2). Thus, exchangeable cations are in a dynamic equilibrium with the cations in the solution. Anions (negatively charged ions such as Cl^- or SO_4^{2-}) do not participate in exchange reactions to nearly as great an extent as do cations because in most soils (the subsoils layers in some Ultisols, Oxisols and Andisols being major exceptions) colloids have many more negative sites than positive ones.

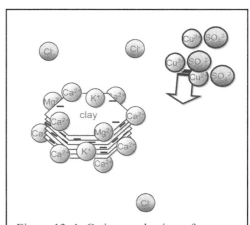

Figure 13. 1 Cations and anions, for example as $CuSO_4$, are washed into a soil.

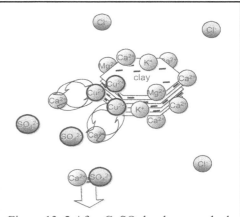

Figure 13. 2 After $CuSO_4$ has been washed through a soil, Cu is adsorbed, replacing the Ca, which then leaches down

125

The importance of cation exchange in soils can be readily appreciated if one imagines a soil without this property. It would be much like pure quartz sand. Water percolating through sand dissolves any soluble ions and washes them down and away. Soon the water in the sand is devoid of nutrients. Under these conditions most terrestrial ecosystems as we know them would never have come into being because soils could not hold the nutrients needed by trees, grasses and agricultural crops. Fortunately, in most real soils, nutrient cations held by attraction to negatively charged colloids are not washed out by pure water. The ions held by the negative charges on soil particle surfaces are called "exchangeable ions" and act as a reservoir of ions that can replace those removed from the soil solution by leaching or plant uptake.

The negatively charged colloids in soils also attract cations added as fertilizer or powdered limestone. Organic cations such as certain herbicides are attracted to the colloids as well, sometimes so strongly that they fail to be available for uptake by weeds. Therefore, to kill weeds effectively, people may have to apply more herbicide to soils that have a higher amount of negative charges. By the same token, by adsorbing positively charged organic compounds, soils may help protect groundwater from contamination by toxic organic materials such as pesticides or industrial products that might be applied or spilled on soils.

In the first part of this exercise you will demonstrate that the soil components clay and organic matter carry a net negative charge, and that the dye molecule, gentian violet, carries a net positive charge. In the second part you will demonstrate that cations are adsorbed (held) by soil while anions are much less so. In the third part you will use these principles to analyze a soil sample to quantify its negative charge or capacity to hold cations in exchangeable form.

Gentian violet (also known as "crystal violet") is a positively-charged organic compound that is strongly adsorbed by the negatively charged colloids in soils. The chemical structure of gentian violet is shown in Figure 13.3. Note the positive charge on the nitrogen atom that is double-bonded to a six-carbon ring structure. In this lab exercise, you will use the adsorption of this violet-colored dye from solution to estimate the amount of negative charge in a soil.

Figure 13. 3 The chemical structure of gentian violet dye. Note the positive charge (+). Gentian violet (a.k.a. crystal violet) has a formula weight of 408 g/mol, which includes a Cl- anion, not shown.

Cation exchange is a dynamic process. As the name implies, cations of different types exchange places during the process. Those adsorbed to the colloid surfaces are freed to go into solution as cations from the solution take their places on the colloid surfaces. Therefore when a dilute solution is equilibrated with a soil, as in the last part of this exercise, only a portion of the cations from the solution are adsorbed at any time, but the amount adsorbed is proportional to the total amount of negative charge available. This amount is termed the cation exchange capacity (CEC) of the soil or other material. Although the adsorption of the dye is not a precise way to determine the capacity of a soil to adsorb cations, it should enable you to easily distinguish between soils with high CEC from those with comparatively low CEC. This method may not be appropriate for some very acid soils because under very low pH conditions, the gentian violet can become irreversibly bound to soil, giving a falsely high reading for CEC.

In summary, the cation adsorption capacity, or CEC, is a very important soil property, as it helps us predict how well a particular soil can store nutrient cations or protect water supplies from contamination.

MATERIALS

- 2 lengths of medium gauge copper electrical wire stripped of insulation on both ends.
- 2 9-volt batteries
- finely ground clay soil (surface horizon of a clay or clay loam texture, pH 6 or greater)
- 4 funnels to fit folded 12.5 cm filter paper
- Rack to hold 4 filter funnels
- 4 Graduated cylinders (50 mL)
- 14 test tubes (10-20 mL)
- 8 graduated cylinders (25 mL). Label 1 with soil ID and three with gentian violet standard concentrations.
- Plastic specimen cups (100 to 150 mL) with leak-proof lid, 1 per soil sample.
- Beaker, glass or plastic, about 50 mL, 1 per soil sample + two used in steps A1-3 and four used in step B1.
- Filter paper (Whatman #1, Fisher #Q2, or VWR # 494). Use the same type and batch of filter paper for standards and samples in a batch of gentian violet CEC analyses.
- Clean quartz sand ($\leq$ 2% clay), sieved, and dried. Be sure to avoid certain "play sand" made from limestone or coral.
- Medium textured soil mineral soil (dried and sieved), with 2-4% organic matter and 10 to 20% clay
- Additional air-dried soil of interest, sieved to < 2mm. Can be student's personal soil.
- Distilled water in wash bottle
- Ethanol (96% in water, denatured) in wash bottle
- Potassium sulfate solution (0.02 M K$_2$SO$_4$; 3.48 g K$_2$SO$_4$. in 1 L distilled water)
- Barium chloride solution (3.0 g BaCl$_2$ · 2H$_2$O in 100 mL distilled water)
- Wax pencil or glass marker for labelling
- Ammonium oxalate solution (0.025 M (NH$_4$)$_2$C$_2$O$_4$, 0.31 g in 100 mL distilled water)
- Sodium cobaltinitrite powder Na$_3$Co(NO$_2$)$_6$
- Flat-type wooden toothpicks
- Balance to weigh 30 g $\pm$ 0.1 g
- Gentian violet solutions.
    - Stock solution: Mix 10.0 g gentian violet with 20 mL ethanol. Bring to volume with distilled water in a 500 mL volumetric flask. Mix well. Store in a bottle labeled "gentian violet stock solution, 49 mmol/L".
    - Working solution: Pipette 5.0 mL of stock solution into a 1000 mL volumetric flask and bring to volume with distilled water. Mix well. This *working* solution now contains 100 mg GV/L or 0.245 mmol/L. Store in glass bottle labeled as "gentian violet working solution., 0.245 mmol/L"
    - Standard solutions: Pipette 0, 25, 50 and 75 mL of the *working* solution into a 100 mL volumetric flask and bring to volume with distilled water. Mix well. Pour into bottles labeled as 0 (blank), 0.061, 0.123, or 0.184 mmol/L gentian violet, respectively.
- Spectrophotometer set at 580 nm wavelength
- Cuvettes or test tubes for spectrophotometer
- Cuvette rack that prevents cuvettes from touching each other or any hard surface.
- Sealable waste container labeled "barium sulfate"
- Sealable waste container labeled "gentian violet, < 0.1 mmol/L"
- Waste container labeled "waste soil"

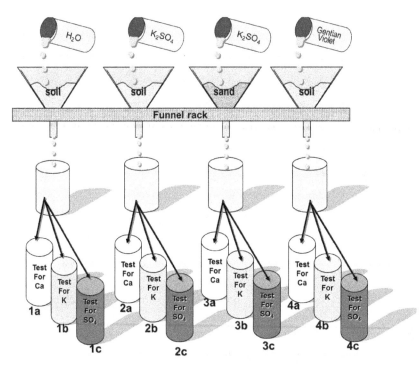

Figure 13. 4 Scheme for demonstrating relative sorption of cations and anions on soil cation exchange capacity (controls without soil or sand not shown).

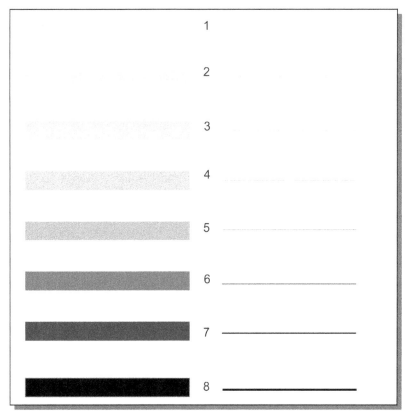

Figure 13. 5 Chart for rating turbidity of suspensions. Hold page vertically with test tube in front of figure. Record the lightest line or bar that is visible through suspension.

| PROCEDURE | COMMENTS |

PART A: Demonstration of Charges on Soil Colloids and gentian violet Dye

1. Attach one 15 cm length of medium (16 gauge) copper wire each the positive terminal of a 9-volt battery (look for the + symbol printed on the battery). The wire may be attached directly using a pair of needle noose pliers or with alligator clips. Attach a second copper wire to the negative terminal. **Adjust the wires to assure that they do not touch each other**. Repeat for a second 9-volt battery.

2. While stirring, slowly add a teaspoonful of finely ground clay soil to a 50 mL beaker ½ filled with water. Stir well. Set up the battery so that the two wires are dipped into the clay suspension on opposite sides of the beaker.

3. Pour 30 mL of gentian violet working solution into a second 50 mL beaker. Set up the second battery so that the two wires are dipped into the gentian violet solution on opposite sides of the beaker.

4. Allow the battery wires to stay in the clay and gentian violet beakers for 10 minutes. You may begin the next part of this exercise (steps 5-6 below) while you wait. After 10 minutes, pull the wires out of the beakers and observe the ends closely. Neatly tear out the hand-in sheet at the end of this chapter. Carefully fold the sheet so that one wire is folded in its appropriate area in Table 13.2. Wipe the wire to leave evidence of clay or dye in the appropriately labeled box in Table 13.2. Repeat with the other set of wires. Observe and compare the marks left by wiping the wires.

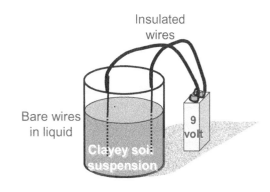

Figure 13. 6 Set-up using a 9-volt battery and wires to demonstrate the charge on clay. The positive battery terminal is called the "**an**ode" and attracts negatively charged "**an**ions." The negative terminal is the "**cat**hode" which attracts positively charged "**cat**ions."

What does the greater accumulation of clay or gentian violet dye on one of the wires than on the other tell you about the charge on these materials?

Part B: Demonstration of Relative Adsorption of Anions and Cations to Soil

1. Fit 4 funnels with filter paper and label them 1 through 4. To funnels 1, 2, and 4 add a scoop (25-35 g) of loam soil. To funnel 3 add a scoop of quartz sand. Form an indentation in the center of each material using the bottom of a clean, dry test tube. Place a clean 25 mL graduated cylinder beneath each funnel.

   The soil consists of sand, silt, clay and humus, the latter two being the soil colloids responsible for cation exchange. The sand by itself should have little or no cation exchange capacity. The indentation is made to ensure that the solutions will percolate through the soil mass and not along the funnel.

2. To each funnel, *very slowly* add 15 mL of the appropriate solution to the depression in the soil as listed below, *letting about 2 mL soak in before adding more*. The idea is for the liquid to soak into the soil or sand without causing ponding that might allow the liquid to creep up the sides of the funnel. Clean the graduated cylinder thoroughly between different solutions.
   Funnel 1: add distilled water
   Funnel 2: add K_2SO_4 solution
   Funnel 3: add K_2SO_4 solution
   Funnel 4: add gentian violet working solution

   Distilled water should only leach out soluble, but not exchangeable, cations from the soil. The gentian violet solution contains positively charged organic molecules while K_2SO_4 in solution provides both cations ($2K^+$) and anions (SO_4^{-2}). The K^+ and positive gentian violet should exchange with (replace) some of the cations initially held on the exchange complex of the soil. See Figure 13.2.

3. Once the solution has soaked in, *very slowly* add distilled water, a little at a time, to the indentation in the soil in each funnel until approximately 15 mL of filtrate has been collected from each. Take care not to add the water so fast that it climbs up the filter paper and funnel. Record your observations on Table 13.1 on the data sheet, comparing the colors of the filtrates to those of the originally added solutions.

   The excess distilled water will wash out any soluble ions not held in the soil by the cation exchange complex, including those cations initially held by colloids but subsequently displaced by the cations added in step C2.

4. Label 12 test tubes as 1a, 1b, 1c, 2a, 2b, 2c, 3a, 3b, 3c, 4a, 4b and 4c (as in Figure 13.4). To each test tube add about 3 mL of the filtrate from the correspondingly numbered funnel. To a 13th and 14th test tube add 3 mL of K_2SO_4 solution.

   Note that the exact volume added is not critical, so long as all test tubes receive the *same* volume (i.e., are filled to the same depth with their respective solutions).

5. To test tubes 1a, 2a, 3a and 4a test for Ca^{2+} by adding 3 drops of the ammonium oxalate solution. Swirl. Then hold the tube vertically against Figure 13.5 to estimate the amount of Ca^{2+} by recording the lightest line or bar on the chart that is visible through the suspension. Record your observations in Table 13.1.

   If Ca^{2+} is present a white precipitate of CaC_2O_4 will form. The Ca present is proportional to the amount of precipitate formed. Since no Ca^{2+} was added, where did it come from?

130

6. To tubes 1b, 2b, 3b and 4b one of the tubes of K_2SO_4 test for K^+ as follows. Add 1 mL alcohol (96%) and shake well. Using a flat toothpick, add a small lump (size of pin-head) of sodium cobaltinitrite, $Na_3Co(NO_2)_6$, to each tube with the end of a toothpick. Swirl. Then hold the tube vertically against Figure 13.5 to estimate the amount of K^+ by recording the lightest line or bar on the chart that is visible through the suspension. Record your data in Table 13.1.

The presence and amount of K^+ in the filtrate is indicated by the formation of suspended crystals of $Na_3Co(NO_2)_6$ giving a cloudy appearance to the filtrate. The alcohol promotes precipitation by lowering the dielectric constant of the solution.

> Dispose of $Na_3Co(NO_2)_6$ in labeled hazardous waste container.

7. To tubes 1c, 2c, 3c and 4c and remaining tube of K_2SO_4, add 4 drops of barium chloride solution ($BaCl_2$). Swirl. Then hold the tube vertically against Figure 13.5 to estimate the amount of SO_4^{2-} by recording the lightest line or bar on the chart that is visible through the suspension. Record your observations in Table 13.1.

Any SO_4^{2-} ion present will precipitate as white barium sulfate particles.

> Dispose of $BaCl_2$ in labeled waste container.

PART C: Estimating Cation Exchange Capacity (CEC) of a Soil[1]

1. *To make a standard curve*, set up 4 separate funnels fitted with filter paper moistened with distilled water. Filter about 25 mL of the four gentian violet (GV) standard solutions (0.0, 0.061, 0.123, and 0.184 mmol/L). Collect the first 10.0 mL in a 25 mL graduated cylinder, then quickly set that cylinder aside and use a *clean, labeled* 25 mL graduated cylinder to catch another 9.0 mL of filtrate. Once the 9.0 mL is collected, switch back to the first cylinder to catch (and later discard in labeled waste container) any remaining filtrate. Using a squirt bottle carefully add 16.0 mL of distilled water to the cylinder containing the 9.0 mL of filtrate. This will bring the volume up to the 25 mL mark.

> **This step may be done for the class by the instructor.**

The standard solutions are filtered before reading their absorbance because the soil suspensions will also be filtered This way the standard curve will take into account the GV absorption by the filter paper.

If your cuvettes are square, do NOT touch the smooth clear sides. For any cuvette, be sure nothing scratches the sides of the cuvette. Use a plastic (not metal) rack that prevents cuvettes from touching each other.

2. Then, fill a cuvette to about ½ full with the 0.0 mmol/L solution (distilled water without any GV). Wipe the outside of the cuvette clean. Insert the cuvette into the cuvette holder of the spectrophotometer and close the cover. Be sure the orientation of the cuvette is correct according to the instructions for the specific machine. Adjust the absorbance to read zero, then remove and rinse the cuvette several times with water. Now use the cuvette to obtain the absorbance reading for the three GV standard solutions in

Observe the even progression of color intensity with increasing concentration in this series of known GV concentrations.

---

[1] This is a modification of the procedure proposed by Guertal,W.R. and P.A. McDaniel. J. Agron. Educ. 19:189-190 (1990).

order of increasing concentration. Be sure to clean the cuvette and wipe the outside between each reading. Record the readings here *and plot them* in Figure 13.8. Abs readings for mmol/L GV:

0: _*0.0*_, 0.061:___, 0.123:___, 0.184:___.

This step makes a standard curve (which should be a straight line) by reading the absorbance of a series of gentian violet concentrations. The linear relationship between GV conc and absorbance will be used to estimate the concentration of GV from future absorbance readings.

3. For most soils, weigh 0.5 g of air-dried soil into a screw-top container. If your soil is very high in organic matter and/or clay, then use 0.25 g instead. If your soil is very sandy and low in OM use 1.00 g of soil. Record the g of soil used here:

   _____.

If you used 1.0 or 0.25 g, do not forget to adjust the CEC for the amount of soil when using the standard curve. See caption to Figure 13.7.

4. Using a 50 mL graduated cylinder, add 50 mL of gentian violet *working* solution to the soil in the container.

Gentian violet is an eye irritant and a very strong dye, so **wear goggles** and be careful not to get any in your eyes or on your hands or clothes.

5. Cover the container tightly and shake for exactly 10 minutes. Then set aside for a few minutes to allow the soil to settle.

Watch for any change in the intensity of the violet color. As the gentian violet dye is adsorbed to the soil's colloids, less of the dye remains in the solution to give a purple color to the liquid.

6. Set up a clean filter funnel in a filtering rack and fit a folded piece of dry filter paper. Place an unlabeled 25 mL graduated cylinder under the funnel. Slowly, a little at a time, pour the supernatant (with as little sediment as possible) from the soil-gentian violet mixture into the filter funnel, using care not to allow any of the liquid to flow over the edge of the paper. Collect the first 10.0 ml of filtrate, then immediately switch to a clean, labeled 25 mL graduated cylinder to collect another 9.0 mL of filtrate for analysis. When the 9.0 mL is collected, immediately replace this cylinder with the one previously set aside in order to collect (and later discard) any additional filtrate produced. Compare the color of your filtrate with that of the original gentian violet solution and with the filtrates from your classmates' soils.

The first 10 mL is discarded as that portion is greatly affected by the absorption of color by the filter paper. Be certain that your labeled collection cylinder and funnel start out clean...a small amount of ethanol may be required to clean residues of gentian violet from previous uses.

As you compare your solution color with that of your classmates', try to determine what soil properties in the various soils were associated with the removal of high and low amounts of gentian violet from solution.

7. To the labeled cylinder containing the second 9.0 mL of filtrate, add 16.0 mL of distilled water to bring the volume to the 25.0 mL mark.

This dilution will bring the color into a range that the spectrophotometer light beam can penetrate. **Note that this diluted *filtrate must be a clear, colored solution* –not cloudy or with visible particles. If it is cloudy, steps 3-7 must be repeated.**

8. Fill a cuvette or spectrophotometer test tube about 2/3 full with the diluted filtrate. Insert the tube or cuvette into a spectrophotometer well, close the cover and read the absorbance at 580 nm wavelength. Record the abs: _____. *If your abs reading is < 0.15 or well below the lowest standard, then repeat from step #C3 onward using 0.25 g soil. If the abs reading is > 1.65 or near the maximum standard, then repeat from step #C3 onward using 1.0 g soil.*

Be sure that the glassware is clean to start with, and that any fingerprints are wiped off with tissue paper. Higher the absorbance number (from 0 to about 2.0) means that more gentian violet remains in solution and less was adsorbed by the soil.

Absorbance readings near the ends of the scale will not be accurate. If your abs reading is too low, you need to use less soil to get an accurate reading. If your abs reading is too high, you need to use more soil. In these cases, you will need to repeat the procedure starting with step #C3, using 0.25 or 1.0 g soil, respectively, instead of the 0.5 g generally used.

9. Plot your absorbance reading on the "standard curve" in Figure 13.8 and estimate the concentration of the GV by extrapolation.

Record conc. here and under #5 on hand-in sheet: _____ mmol/L

10. Use the GV concentration value from step #C8 to determine the CEC of your soil, by interpolating on the "standard curve" given in Figure 13.7.

Record the "raw" CEC (in soil) here for 0.5 g sample. (_____ cmol (+)/kg)

11. For soils high in clay and/or organic matter, which might have a CEC above the range of the curve, using 1/2 as much soil (0.25 g) should bring the result to within the range on the graph (see step #C3). However, you will have to multiply by 2 to compensate for the smaller sample size.

Record the adjusted CEC for your sample size on hand-in sheet and in Table G2 of Appendix G.

The standard curve was developed using mixed mineralogy soils with CEC values between 3 and 18 cmol (+)/kg.

Your instructor may wish to develop a "standard curve" using local soils whose CEC is known. The relationship between CEC and adsorption of the gentian violet is only approximate and may be affected by soil pH and soil organic matter levels.

12. Clean all your materials. Rinse any purple stain from glassware using a small amount of ethanol. Answer the questions on the hand-in sheet.

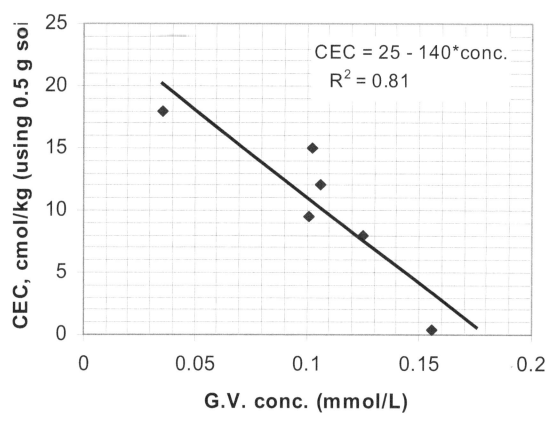

Standard curve with 6 soils of known CEC

CEC = 25 - 140*conc.
R^2 = 0.81

Figure 13. 7 Standard curve construction with 6 soils of known CEC. This curve allows prediction of CEC from gentian violet concentration. You can extrapolate graphically or use the equation of the straight line as shown in the graph (CEC = 25-140*GV concentration). The "R^2 =0.81" is a statistical expression that tells us that the equation explains 81% of the variation in CEC among the 5 soils. This graph assumes an adsorption reaction using 50 mL of 0.245 mM gentian violet solution with 0.5 g soil. Therefore, if 0.25 g soil was used (see step # C3), multiply the CEC from graph x 2. If 1.0 g soil was used (step #C3) then divide the CEC from graph by 2. Note that the CEC is expressed here as the number of centimoles of + charges that can be held per unit mass (kg) of soil.

Exercise 13

CATION EXCHANGE PROPERTIES OF SOIL

Results and Conclusions

Table 13.1 Observations on cation exchange reactions with sand and soil.

Funnel No.	Material in Funnel	Solution Added	Appearance of solution added	Appearance of filtrate	Relative Amount of Ion *		
					Ca^{2+}	K^+	SO_4^{2-}
1	Loam soil	Distilled H_2O					
2	Loam soil	K_2SO_4					
3	Quartz Sand	K_2SO_4					
4	Loam soil	Gentian violet					
None	Control	K_2SO_4					

* Rate this on relative scale of 0 (none) to 8 (high) for each ion based on the amount of white precipitate formed in the respective tests. See Figure 13.5.

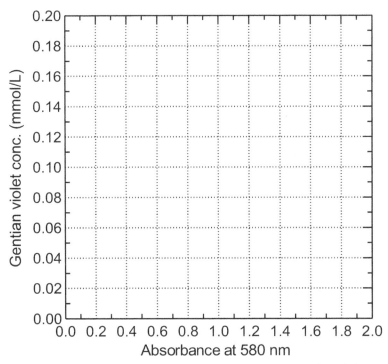

Figure 13. 8 Graph for making standard curve to predict gentian violet concentration from absorbance readings. Plot your class data and draw a straight line that best fits the points (or calculate the linear regression equation).

Write your sample absorbance here: _____

Table 13.2 Observations and evidence on amount of clay and gentian violet attracted to + and - charged wires. See step #A4.

	Fold wire in appropriate area below and wipe to leave evidence of clay or dye
Clay soil ___ Charge _____ ion	+ wire ___ode ───────────── ‑ wire ___ode
Gentian violet	+ wire ___ode ───────────── ‑ wire ___ode

Questions

1. What do your observations recorded in Table 13.2 lead you to conclude about the sign of the predominant charge on clay and gentian violet?

2. Define "cation" and "anion" and list the ions of each type used in this exercise. What are the + and – terminals on a battery called?

3. Describe and explain the behavior of anions and cations added to sand and soil, respectively, using K^+ and SO_4^{2-} as examples.

4. What was the source of the Ca^{2+} found in tubes 1-4, respectively?

    a. Tube 1:

    b. Tube 2:

    c. Tube 3:

    d. Tube 4:

5. Why did the sulfate behave different from the potassium or gentian violet?

6. Did the colored compound, gentian violet, behave as a cation or anion? Explain, giving evidence from the behavior of gentian violet in the soil.

7. CEC estimated from adsorption of gentian violet.
a. Record the concentration of GV in your filtrate after reacting with your soil. Extrapolate using your standard curve in Figure 13.8:
    _____mmol/L.

b. Record the cation exchange capacity for your soil, as estimated by gentian violet adsorption, by extrapolating the CEC from Figure 13.7 (or using the regression equation) and adjusting for sample size, if necessary:
    _____cmol(+)/kg.

c. Discuss how your CEC value compares with the CEC expected for soils of similar organic matter and clay content in your region. For example, typical ranges (in cmol (+)/kg soil) are 2 to 18 for Ultisols, 4 to 24 for Alfisols, 5 to 18 for Spodosols, 5 to 24 for Aridisols, 10 to 35 for Mollisols, 30 to 45 for Vertisols, and 80 to 200 for Histosols. Very sandy soils low in organic matter will generally have a CEC at the low end of each range.

Exercise 14
Soil Acidity and Alkalinity (pH)

OBJECTIVES

After completing this exercise, you should be able to . . .

1. Properly calibrate and operate a pH meter.
2. Determine the pH of a soil using a pH meter.
3. Determine the pH of a soil using an indicator-dye kit.
4. Explain the effects of measuring soil pH in water vs. a salt solution.
5. Describe the effect of dissolved CO_2 on the pH of a solution.
6. Explain the difference between heavy and light textured soils with regard to their pH buffering.
7. Graph and explain the results of the titration of soil acidity with NaOH.

INTRODUCTION

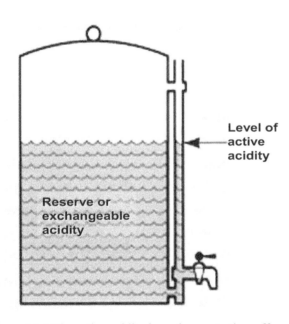

Figure 14.1 The active acidity is analogous to the coffee in the indicator vial on the outside of a coffee urn. The pH measures the active acidity. The reserve acidity is a function of the C.E.C., the % base saturation, free Aluminum, etc. (Adapted from Weil and Brady, The Nature and Properties of Soils. 15th Ed. Prentice Hall, 2016).

The pH of the soil is a measure of the active acidity of the soil, which results from free H^+ (or more correctly, H_3O^+) in the soil solution. Soils also have a great deal of reserve or potential acidity which includes exchangeable H^+, and hydrolysable –OH groups on clays and organic matter. In addition, aluminum ions will react with water to release H^+:

$$Al^{3+} + 3HOH \rightarrow Al(OH)_3 + 3H^+$$

Thus, if H^+ in solution is neutralized (as by liming) other acidity will be released from the reserve to replace the active acidity. The reserve acidity is usually many times greater than the active acidity as illustrated diagrammatically in Figure 14.1.

The pH of the soil is a very important property with respect to plant growth. Some plant species such as Jack Pine and Blueberries are adapted to very acid soils with a pH 4.5 to 5.0 being optimum. Others, such as Asparagus and Sweet Clover, do well in slightly alkaline soils. Most crops, however, grow best in soils between pH 6.0 and pH 7.0. Soil pH affects the availability of nutrients. For example, the nutrients Mo, S, Ca, and Mg are most available above pH 6.0. Others like Fe, Mn, Zn, and Cu are most available below pH 6.0. Aluminum is often toxic below pH 5.0.

The pH is a soil property over which we may exert considerable control. Lime ($CaCO_3$) can be added to soils to raise the pH by forming water from the H^+ ions, replacing them with Ca:

$$\boxed{\begin{array}{l}\text{Clay or} \\ \text{humus}\end{array}}\begin{array}{l}H^+ \\ H^+\end{array} + CaCO_3 + H_2O \longrightarrow \boxed{\begin{array}{l}\text{Clay or} \\ \text{humus}\end{array}}Ca^{2+} + \underline{H_2O} + CO_2\uparrow$$

$$\qquad\qquad\qquad\qquad \underset{\text{Limestone}}{} $$

Limestone
(calcite)   water

Sulphur (S°) can be added to lower soil pH. Elemental S° is oxidized microbially to sulphate (SO_4^{2-}) which reacts with water to form sulfuric acid (H_2SO_4). The difference between the optimum soil pH and the present soil pH helps us estimate the amount of these materials needed, but information on the CEC of the soil must be used in conjunction so as to take the reserve acidity into account.

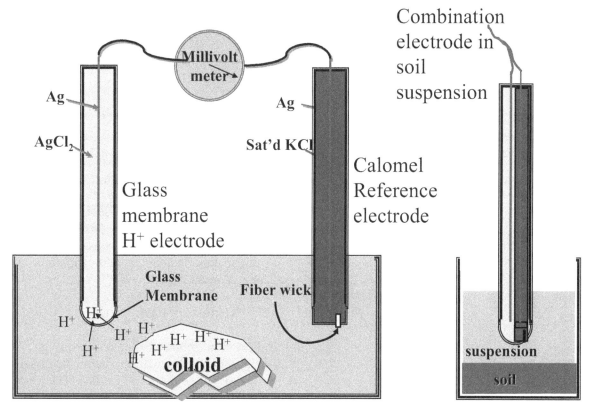

Figure 14. 2 (left) Two electrodes are necessary for potentiometric determination of pH: the glass membrane electrode (selective for H+ ions) and a calomel reference electrode. The electron 'pressure' or potential between the two electrodes dipped in the same solution is measured by a sensitive voltmeter that converts millivolts into the pH scale (i.e. a pH meter). (right) Most modern pH electrodes combine the two electrodes into a single body called a combination pH electrode.

The pH may be measured by the use of organic dyes which change color as the $[H^+]$ changes. It may also be measured electrometrically using a glass electrode and a reference electrode. The pH meter essentially measures the electromotive force produced by the difference between $[H^+]$'s inside the glass electrode and outside of it. The former method is cheaper and easier to use in the field. The latter is more accurate and usually used in the laboratory, although small, portable meters are available. We will use both methods in this exercise.

MATERIALS

- pH meter with combination pH electrode (accurate to 0.1 pH unit)
  - Soil pH Test kit (Lovibond Model 694, formerly Hellige-Truog), https://www.zoro.com/lovibond-kit-soil-ph-tester-694-694/i/G4688862/
    - $BaSO_4$ powder in small glass bottle with screen in cap for sifting.
    - Spot plate
    - Mixed pH indicator solution and color chart
    - Flat spatula
- 50 mL beakers, plastic or glass (4)
- 500 mL "waste water" beaker (plastic or glass)
- 0.01 M NaOH
- 1 M KCl solution
- CO_2-free distilled water (boil distilled water, then cool with ascarite-filled CO_2 trap on carboy).
- Lab tissue paper (e.g., Kim wipes™)
- Wash bottle with distilled water
- pH buffers (pH 4 and pH 7, color coded) in small, wide-mouth plastic bottles with screw tops.
- pH electrode keeping solution in small bottles with a hole in the cap sized to fit the electrode snuggly, thus reducing evaporation during storage. A solution of 1 M KCl can serve this purpose.
- Drinking straws
- Air dry soils, a loamy sand and a clay, both with pH < 5.5 (two soils of similar texture and similar low pH, but very different organic matter content could be used instead) for buffer demonstration.
- Student's own soil for determination of pH_{water} and pH_{KCl}.
- Balance accurate to 0.1 g

PROCEDURE   COMMENTS

Part A – Soil pH Determinations and Buffering Capacity

PROCEDURE	COMMENTS
1. Measure 5 g (to the nearest 0.1g) of air dry soil into each of two 50 mL beakers.	This may be any soil –your personal soil or one from the instructor.
2. Measure 10 mL of distilled water into one of the beakers from step 1 and stir with a glass rod. Label the beaker "H₂O."	Most soil testing labs measure pH in a 2:1 suspension of water and soil, but research workers may use either 1 M KCl or 0.01 M CaCl₂ instead of water. These salts in the pH solution protect the pH readings from undue influence by salts in the soil.
3. Measure 10 mL of 1 M KCl into the second beaker. Stir. Label "KCl."	KCl is a neutral salt, that is, it makes a solution neither more acid nor more basic.
4. Measure 5.0 g of either the sandy or clayey soil (to be assigned by instructor) into a third 50 mL beaker. Label as either S or C.	The sandy soil will have a lower CEC and hence a lower amount of reserve acidity than the clay.

5. To beaker #3 (from step 4), add the volumes of distilled water and .01 *M* NaOH indicated in the Table 14.1 (below) according to the treatment number assigned to you by the instructor.

6. To a *clean and empty* fourth beaker add the same amounts of distilled water and .01 *M* NaOH, but no soil.

The NaOH dissociates in water to $Na^+ + OH^-$. The OH^- neutralizes H^+ in the soil by forming H_2O (similar to the reaction shown in the introduction). As the added NaOH neutralizes acidity in the solution, more acidity is released from the reserve pool associated with the soil colloids. The pH rise is an indication that the reserve acidity is unable counteract the neutralization effect of the NaOH in the solution.

Table 14. 1 Treatments for "titrating" soil acidity.

Trt. No.	1	2	3	4	5	6
mMol OH^- added	0.0	0.02	0.04	0.08	0.12	0.15
	----------------------- mL to add ----------------------					
mL H_2O added	25	23	21	17	13	10
mL .01 NaOH added	0	2	4	8	12	15

7. Stir beakers #1, #2 and #3 intermittently for 30 minutes. *During this time you should do parts B, C, and D of this exercise. Only after completing part B-D should you go to step 8.*

This will allow time for a near equilibrium to be reached in the exchange of H^+ adsorbed on the colloids with Na^+ in solution.

8. After 30 minutes of equilibration take your four labeled beakers to a pH meter and determine the pH of the suspensions (as described in part B). Record your results in Table 14.2 and on the board for the class to share.

See instructions, below, for operating the pH meter. Please treat the equipment with care. The glass electrode tips are very fragile.

Part B – Calibration and Use of the pH Meter

(Note: details of procedures will vary with model of pH meter used)

9. Be sure meter is turned to "on" or to "pH". Whenever not in use it should be turned off to save the battery (if battery powered model). The electrode should not be left exposed to air for more than a few minutes. Leave it submerged in about 3 cm of 0.1 *M* KCl or a pH 4 buffer.

The meter is actually a potentiometer and measures millivolts, but converts these to pH units. The calibration of the meter should be necessary only every 10 to 20 readings. The electrode can dry out and cease to function if the tip is exposed to the air for long periods.

> PLEASE HANDLE ELECTRODES GENTLY. THE GLASS BULB IN THE TIP IS FRAGILE!

10. Set the temperature control, if present, to the temperature of the solution to be measured. If the meter has a built-in automatic temperature probe, the adjustment will be automatic.

Generally, this is the same as the temperature of the room. Not all models have a temperature control.

11. Raise the electrode(s) carefully out of their keeper solution. Place an empty "waste water" beaker under the electrodes. Rinse the electrode(s) thoroughly with several squirts of distilled water from a wash bottle. Collect the washings in the "waste water" beaker. Dab the electrode tip(s) gently in tissue paper.

Two electrodes are required to measure pH – a glass H^+ ion selective electrode and calomel reference electrode. If only one electrode is present, it should be a "combination" electrode with the reference electrode built into the glass electrode (see Figure 14.2).

> **To avoid contamination, always rinse and dab dry the electrode before lowering into a new solution.**

12. If present, set the mode control to read pH (not mV). Gently lower the electrode(s) into a small bottle of pH 4.0 buffer solution. About 2 cm of the electrode tip should be immersed.

The buffer is a solution which resists changes in its pH and so should give a stable reading. It is used as a standard to calibrate the meter.

13. If necessary, turn calibration control until the dial reads pH 4.0, or follow the instructions for automatic calibration if applicable.

Most analytical instruments (pH meters included) give only relative readings and must be calibrated with known standards.

14. Repeat steps 10-12, only this time use pH 7.0 buffer and set the calibration dial to read 7.0.

If the system is working well, it should read the pH 7 buffer correctly after having been calibrated with the pH 4.0 buffer. If the reading rises slowly (more than 30 seconds) toward pH 7, or if it does not reach above about 6.5 your electrode may need cleaning or replacement.

15. Rinse the electrode as in step 11 and return it to the keeping solution.

Some portable pH meters have a electrode cap which can hold a few drops keeper solution.

16. Choose a soil suspension that has been stirred intermittently for at least 30 minutes. Re-stir the suspension, and then lower the electrode(s) into the suspension until the glass bulb and junction wick are both immersed. Allow the reading to stabilize and record. Rinse the electrode(s) as in step 10, and return the electrode to the keeping solution.

Part C – Formation of Carbonic Acid

17. To a 50 mL beaker, add approximately 30-40 mL distilled water that has been *recently boiled and cooled* and stored with a CO_2 trap.

The boiling is necessary to drive off the CO_2 which will be absorbed by water standing in contact with the atmosphere.

pH of pure water = _____

18. Measure the pH of the distilled water using the pH meter. Record at right.

when water dissociates: $H_2O \leftrightharpoons H^+ + OH^-$

the two concentrations are equal: $[H^+] = [OH^+]$

19. Using a drinking straw, *gently* blow bubbles into the beaker of distilled water while the pH electrodes are still immersed and the meter is reading. Record change in pH.

CO_2 (in your breath) + H_2O (in beaker) forms carbonic acid, which releases H^+ ions and lowers pH: $H_2CO_3 \leftrightharpoons H^+ + HCO_3^-$

pH after blowing CO_2 = _____

Part D – Soil pH Determination Using Organic Dyes

20. Obtain pH testing kit and small sample of soil to be tested. The soil should be the same one used in Part A, step 1.

Many different types of kits are on the market. One of the most reliable and simple to use is the Hellige-Truog kit for which the procedure is given here.

21. Add 2 drops of triplex pH indicator to a depression in a spot plate.

If so much soil is added that it is not thoroughly moistened, add a bare drop of additional indicator. If there is extra indicator not absorbed by the soil, mix in a bit more soil.

22. Add, gradually, a pinch of soil. Pulverize the soil between your thumb and forefinger as you add it. Add just enough to absorb the indicator.

23. Mix thoroughly with a clean spatula, then move the soil to one side of the depression and smooth off a sloping surface with the spatula. The soil should glisten with moisture, but no free solution should be present.

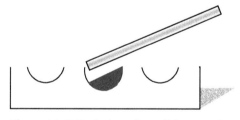

Figure 14. 3 Technique for soil in spot plate.

24. Immediately cover the moist soil with a film of $BaSO_4$ powder so that the soil is not visible. Apply powder uniformly by tapping bottle of powder fitted with a screen top. Do not remove the screen top.

The $BaSO_4$ is an insoluble white powder. It does not react in any way with the soil, but soaks up the reaction solution and allows the color to be seen against a clean white background.

25. After 1-2 minutes compare the color developed with the color standards on the chart and record the soil pH to the nearest 0.5 units on the data sheet.

The colors are best viewed in daylight.

Date _____   Name _____

Section _____   I.D. No. _____

EXERCISE 14
Soil Acidity (pH)

RESULTS AND CONCLUSIONS

Table 14.2 Values of pH for Titration of Soil with NaOH

Soil Type	millimoles NaOH added					
	0	0.02	0.04	0.08	0.12	0.15
Sandy						
Clayey						
No soil						

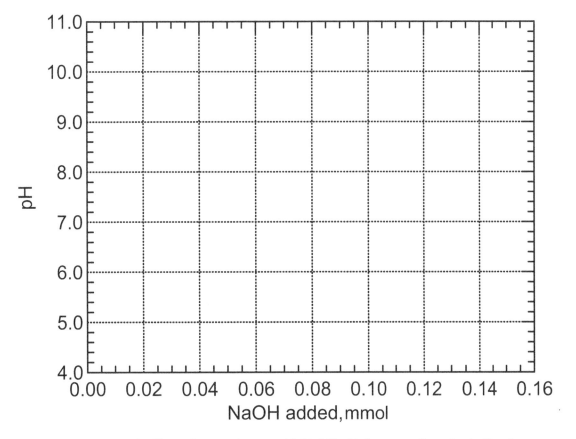

Figure 14. 4 Graph for illustrating pH changes with NaOH added to two soils and unbuffered water.

143

Determination of the pH of your soil by three methods (also add your data to Appendix G):

Soil Texture _____ (by feel or from Exercise 3)

pH in H_2O _____

pII in KCl _____

pH by color _____

QUESTIONS

1. Explain why the pH of pure water is lowered by blowing your breath into it.

2. Explain the effect of KCl on the measured soil pH using the concepts of cation exchange and reserve acidity.

3. Explain the difference between the slopes of the sandy soil and clayey soil titration curves in your graph (reverse side).

4. Which soil would need more lime to achieve a change in pH from 5.0 to 6.5? Why?

5. Using the concept of "buffering" explain why the pH in Table 14.2 and Figure 14.3 would be expected to rise much more rapidly with no soil than where soil was present as the amount of NaOH was increased.

Exercise 15
Microbial Activity Related to Decomposition and Nitrogen Transformation

OBJECTIVES

In relation to CO_2 evolution from the soil, you should be able to . . .

1. Explain how the CO_2 given off during decomposition can be captured and the amount measured.
2. Calculate the mol(e) and g of C or CO_2 given off when provided with the results of a titration of the NaOH with HCl.
3. Describe the effect of the various factors listed in Table 15.3 on the rate of CO_2 evolution.
4. Explain how the CO_2 measured is related to the rate of organic matter decomposition.

In relation to the nitrate determination, you should be able to . . .

5. Explain the purpose of the salicylic acid and the spectrophotometer.
6. Explain the reasons for any observed differences in nitrate measured in the variously treated soils.
7. Summarize the class data showing any relative differences in nitrate levels among the variously treated soils.
8. Identify what form of nitrogen was measured, what form(s) originally predominated, and what changes probably took place during incubation.

INTRODUCTION

Most of the microorganisms in the soil are heterotrophs, i.e., they derive their energy for life from the respiration of organic molecules into CO_2 and H_2O. Thus, the amount of CO_2 given off by the soil is a measure of the microbial decomposition activity taking place. Many factors will affect the rate of decomposition in the soil. The indigenous population of microbes is one such factor. The kinds and numbers of microbes found vary from soil to soil and from horizon to horizon within a soil. The soil is a complex conglomeration of micro-habitats. The environments it provides at locations only a millimeter or two apart may be radically different in terms of moisture content, acidity, nutrient availability, aeration, and temperature. Soil, therefore, normally supports a diversity of microbes.

To a large degree the kind of C-to-C bonds found in a substance will determine its rate of decomposition. The bonds in a sugar molecule are easily broken by most microbes, but the bonds between Cs in cellulose or lignin are much more difficult to break, and are attacked successfully only by a few organisms, primarily fungi. Other factors compared in this exercise are moisture, temperature, and acidity.

The C:N ratio in the material is also very important since the microbes require a definite proportion of N in their cellular tissues (proteins, etc.). Where there is not enough N, they will be unable to grow rapidly even though an easily digested energy source (e.g., sugars) is available. In this case the microbes will compete with crop plants for the soluble N in the soil solution. Where adequate N is present as part of the substance being decomposed the microbial needs are taken care of and there is no competition for the soluble soil N. Where the materials being decomposed have more nitrogen than required by the microbes there will be a release of plant available N into the soil solution and the crop will benefit. The tying up of soil nitrogen by microbes is called *Immobilization*, while the release of N from

145

organic matter is called *Ammonification* or *Mineralization*. Once mineralized, the N is usually in the NH_4^+ form. If oxygen is present, the ammonium-N is usually converted by the following reaction to the NO_3^- form in which it is most readily used by plants (and leached from soils):

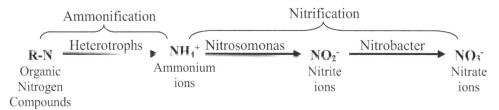

To study the above processes, you will incubate a sample of soil under various conditions and with various kinds of organic material added. The CO_2 evolved and the soluble N present as NO_3^- in the soil (written as NO_3^- - N) will be measured after an incubation period. Because of the variability in soil biology, each condition should be replicated in the class 3 times. To improve accuracy, everyone should do a blank with no soil or amendment.

MATERIALS

- safety goggles
- chemical protective gloves

For incubation and determination of CO_2 evolved:

- glass or polypropylene container (500 mL) with tight-fitting cover
- beakers, 50 mL
- fresh air-dry soil
- graduated cylinder
- balance (accurate to 0.01 g)
- $(NH_4)_2SO_4$ (crystals)
- 5 mL pipettes or 10 mL graduate cylinders
- 250 mL Erlenmeyer flasks
- K_2SO_4 (powder)
- distilled water in burettes
- activated charcoal powder

- lime powder ($CaCO_3$)
- 2.0 M NaOH (in burette), standardized
- 1 M HCl (in burette), standardized
- 1 M NaOH (in burette), standardized
- phenolphthalein indicator (0.1 g phenolphthalein in 50 mL ethanol and 50 mL H_2O)
- 1.0 M BaCl$_2$
- ground, dried alfalfa (legume)
- sawdust
- starch

For Salicylic Acid Determination of Nitrate in Soils

- Reagents for Nitrate Determination:

- Extracting solution – 0.1 $\underline{M}$ K_2SO_4 = 17.2 g K_2SO_4/1L distilled water

- Color developing solutions –

  - 5% salicylic acid (weight/volume). Place 5 g salicylic acid in an amber or foil covered bottle, add 100 mL conc. H_2SO_4 and stir until dissolved. Solution is good for 1 week if refrigerated.
  - 1.7 $\underline{M}$ NaOH – Fill a 2-liter beaker ½ full with distilled water. Add 136 g NaOH while stirring in a cold water bath until dissolved and cool. Dilute to 2L in volumetric flask with distilled water when cool.

- Standards for Nitrate Determination:
Primary standard –
1000 ppm NO_3-N = 7.218 g oven dried KNO_3/1L distilled water (dH_2O)
Secondary standards –
(a) 100 ppm NO_3-N = 100 mL primary std./1L extracting solution
(b) 10 ppm NO_3-N = 10 mL primary std./1L extracting solution

Working standards –
(b) 1 ppm NO3-N = 1 mL 100 ppm std. Diluted to 100 mL with dH2O
(c) 5 ppm NO3-N = 5 mL 100 ppm std. Diluted to 100 mL with dH2O
(d) 10 ppm NO3-N = 10 mL 100 ppm std. Diluted to 100 mL with dH2O
(e) 25 ppm NO3-N = 25 mL 100 ppm std. Diluted to 100 mL with dH2O

Use 0.25 mL of these solutions, instead of soil extract, follow steps 15-17 of the procedure to get absorbance readings for a standard curve.

- *Store all standards in refrigerator for up to 4 weeks.*

Equipment for nitrate determination:

- filter funnel
- filter paper, medium quantitative {such as VWR 94 or Whatman No. 2}
- 250 mL beaker
- 100 mL beaker
- pipette to deliver 0.25 mL accurately
- 10 mL "Repipettor" or other auto-pipettor to safely deliver concentrated acid
- 50 mL "Repipettor"
- wash bottle of distilled water
- 100 mL graduated cylinder
- spectrophotometer
- cuvettes

PROCEDURE

Incubation Set Up

1. Weigh 50 g of air-dry soil into an incubation jar (glass or polypropylene). If not air-dry, the actual moisture content should be determined. (See Appendix D.)

2. According to the number assigned to you, add one of the amendments listed at right and mix well with the soil. Label the jar. Everyone should also run a blank (#9 in Table 15.1).

3. Slowly add a pre-determined amount* of tap water to the soil, letting a little soak in at a time.
   If you are doing treatment #5, add an additional 15 mL of water. Add no water to treatment #9 (blank). Record the amount of water added: _____ mL.

4. Thoroughly clean a 50 mL beaker and fill it with *exactly* 20.00 mL of 1.00 M NaOH from a burette.

> **CAUTION: CAUSTIC STRONG ALKALI!**
> **WEAR GLOVES & GOGGLES!**

5. Very carefully place the beaker of NaOH in the *labeled* incubation jar, seating it level on the soil so it will not tip over. The jar label should include date, name, treatment.

6. Cover the jar tightly and set in a drawer or other dark place designated by your instructor, to incubate at room temperature (about 20°C), except for trts #2 and #8 which are to be kept cold (refrigerator) and hot (incubator at 30°C). During the incubation period your instructor will remove the cover for about 1 minute every few days to renew the oxygen supply inside the jar.

An incubation of 2 weeks at room temperature should allow sufficient time for microbial action, but not so long that all the NaOH is neutralized.

COMMENTS

Table 15.1 Incubation Conditions to be Compared.

Trt. No.	Soil?	Amendments(s) mixed into soil	Temperature
1	Yes	None	Room (20°C)
2	Yes	0.2 g legume	Cold (~5°C)
3	Yes	0.2 g starch	Room (20°C)
4	Yes	0.2 g sawdust	Room (20°C)
5	Yes	0.2 g legume	Room (20°C)
6	Yes	0.2 g legume + 15 mL extra H_2O	Room (20°C)
7	Yes	0.2 g starch +0.05g $(NH_4)_2SO_4$	Room (20°C)
8	Yes	0.2 g legume	Hot (~30°C)
9	No	None (blank)	Room (20°C)

The NaOH has been standardized. The molarity may differ slightly from 1.00 M. Note the actual molarity on the label. Sodium hydroxide solutions of this strength are **very caustic!** Protect your eyes and hands.

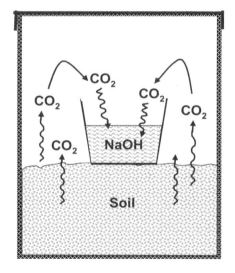

Figure 15.1 Incubation setup with small container of NaOH to absorb CO_2 given off the respiration of soil organisms.

---

* The "optimum" water content for aerobic microbial activity is commonly considered to be 60% of saturation (i.e., the water content at which 40% of the pore space is filled with air and 60% filled with water). The amount of water needed to bring 50 g of soil to this water content will vary from soil to soil and should be determined for each soil and soil/amendment combination by the procedure in Appendix D. To allow valid comparisons among treatments, all treatments (except #5) must have the same soil water condition (namely, 60% saturation as determined in Appendix D).

7. After the incubation period, find your jar and carry it carefully to your bench. Open the jar and carefully remove the beaker of NaOH. Any soil adhering to the beaker should be brushed gently back into the jar. Taking care to avoid contamination of the NaOH, clean the outside of the beaker with a paper towel. Save the jar of soil for nitrate analysis (see step 11).

    After you have removed the NaOH beaker, smell the soil remaining in the incubation jar. If you have trt. #6 with the waterlogged conditions, share your jar so others can smell the odor of H_2S and other gases produced by anaerobic decomposition under waterlogged conditions.

8. Rinse a clean Erlenmeyer flask and fill with 30 mL distilled water. Then *quantitatively* transfer the contents of the small beaker into it. Use a jet of distilled water to wash *all* of the NaOH into the flask.

During the incubation period, microorganisms decompose the organic materials in the soil. This aerobic decomposition is a respiration process by which organic carbon is oxidized to CO_2, e.g.:

$$C_6H_{12}O_6 + 6O_2 \rightarrow 6H_2O + 6CO_2$$
sugar   oxygen   water   carbon dioxide

The CO_2 thus produced diffuses into the atmosphere inside the jar and eventually is absorbed by the NaOH solution in the small beaker. *Some* of the NaOH was neutralized by the carbonic acid so formed:

$$CO_2 + H_2O \rightleftharpoons H_2CO_3 \text{ (carbonic acid)}$$

$$H_2CO_3 + 2NaOH \rightleftharpoons Na_2CO_3 + 2H_2O$$

Note: 1 mole CO_2 neutralizes 2 moles NaOH.

Determination of CO₂ Evolved during Incubation

9. To the flask of NaOH, add 15 mL of 1 $\underline{M}$ $BaCl_2$ using a graduated cylinder. Then add 6 drops of phenolphthalein indicator and swirl.

    The NaOH that has not reacted with CO_2 from the decomposition will give the solution an alkaline reaction.

10. Using the standardized HCl from a burette (marked in 0.01 ml), titrate the solution in the flask to the colorless (white) endpoint as follows. Fill the burette to the zero mark (or record the initial volume here: _____ mL). Add the HCl cautiously while swirling the flask. When the pink color begins to disappear where the HCl enters the solution, continue to add HCl drop by drop until the pink color completely disappears. (The white precipitate will remain.) Add two more drops of indicator and swirl. If the suspension remains pure white, you have reached the end point. If the pink color reappears and stays, continue to add HCl drop by drop until the pink disappears again completely. Record the final HCl volume here (_____ mL), and in Table 15.2.

The $BaCl_2$ will "fix" the amount of NaOH neutralized by CO_2 by making the reaction go completely to the right:

$$H_2CO_3 + 2NaOH \rightarrow Na_2CO_3 + 2H_2O$$

$$Na_2CO_3 + BaCl_2 \rightarrow \underline{BaCO_3} + 2Na^+ + 2Cl^-$$
White ppt.

The phenolphthalein remains pink as long as the solution is alkaline. Therefore, adding HCl will make the pink disappear as soon as all the NaOH is neutralized:

$$NaOH + HCl \rightleftharpoons NaCl + H_2O$$

The reason the pink may disappear prematurely is that the NaOH is such a strong alkali that, if not much is neutralized by the CO_2, it may destroy the organic indicator. This is why the additional indicator may be needed.

Determination of Nitrate in Soil

11. Using a volumetric flask or graduated cylinder, add 100 mL of 0.1 K_2SO_4 solution to the incubation jar, cover, and shake vigorously for 15 minutes.

Most soil nitrate is easily dissolved in water, but any absorbed to anion exchange sites would be replaced by SO_4^{-2} ions. Also, the K_2SO_4 provides a sufficiently high ionic strength to keep the soil flocculated so that the filtrate will not be too cloudy (see exercise #12) to use in a colorimetric procedure.

12. Allow the soil in the jar to settle for a few minutes. Using a filter funnel and rack, filter the extracting solution through fine filter paper into a 250 mL beaker. Be sure the filtrate is clear, not cloudy or colored. Refilter if necessary.

The nitrate is now in the solution in the beaker. The soil and filter paper can be discarded after filtration. The extractant to soil ratio is approximately 2:1 (i.e., 100 mL extractant to 50 g soil), but the soil weight must be corrected for the moisture content of the soil when it was originally placed in the jar, and in the case of trt. #6, the extra 15 mL of water added must also be included.

13. Prepare a blank by filtering about 50 mL of the K_2SO_4 extraction solution through empty filter paper. Label this as "blank" and treat it as a sample in the remaining steps.

Filter paper often contains detectable quantities of nitrate. This error can be corrected for by the use of this filtrate as a blank in the nitrate analysis.

14. Pipette 0.25 mL (250 μL) of your sample filtrate into a dry, clean 100 mL beaker.

Rinse the pipette by pipetting with distilled water several times, then with a bit of the sample solution. (Do not dispense this rinse water into your sample beaker.)

15. Deliver 1.0 mL of 5% salicylic acid/H_2SO_4 solution and swirl carefully to dissolve the precipitate which forms. Let stand until cool.

> **CAUTION: CONCENTRATED SULFURIC ACID! WEAR GLOVES & GOGGLES!**

This is best done with a fixed plunger type of pipettor in the fume hood. This solution contains concentrated sulfuric acid. A colored compound, 5-nitro-salicylate, is formed with each nitrate ion.

16. Add 23.75 mL 1.7 $\underline{M}$ NaOH and swirl gently. Allow to cool to room temperature (about 20 minutes). WEAR GOGGLES and use a large "Repipettor" or similar device set up by your instructor to deliver the NaOH without any splattering.

> **CAUTION: CAUSTIC STRONG ALKALI! WEAR GLOVES & GOGGLES!**

The NaOH raises the pH of the solution and causes the yellow color to develop and stabilize for maximum absorbance at 410 nm. The volume of the final sample solution is now 25.0 mL.

If **no** color develops with solutions known to contain nitrate, the NaOH solution may have to be made afresh.

17. The class should prepare at least one set of standards following steps 14-16 above, but using 0.25 mL each of 0 (i.e., pure K_2SO_4 extraction solution), 1, 5, 10, and 25 ppm NO_3-N standards instead of the sample solution in step 4. Visually compare the color developed with your sample extract to those developed using the standard solutions.

Your instructor will assist in the preparation of the standards, and will demonstrate the use of the spectrophotometer and the standard curve. **NEVER** POUR ANY LIQUID DIRECTLY INTO THE INSTRUMENT!

18. To set up a standard curve (Figure 15.2), be sure the spectrophotometer wavelength is set at 410 nm and measure the amount of light of this wavelength absorbed by the four solutions of known concentration.

Follow these steps to read each standard, sample, and blank with the spectrophotometer:

19. Read the absorbance at 410 nm wavelength for each sample and use the standard curve to interpolate the concentration of your samples and blanks.

Wipe a cuvette clean of any moisture, dirt, or fingerprints. Rinse it with distilled water, then rinse it with a little of the solution to be analyzed and discard. Fill with solution to the appropriate mark on the cuvette. Correctly align the tube in the spectrophotometer, close the cover, and read and record the absorbance.

CALCULATIONS

CALCULATIONS FOR CO$_2$ EVOLVED:

1.   Moles of NaOH added to beaker = L NaOH × Molarity of NaOH moles/L.
      e.g., 0.02 L NaOH × 1 mole/L = 0.02 moles NaOH in beaker
2.   1 mole of HCl will neutralize 1 mole of NaOH.
      $NaOH + HCl \rightarrow NaCl + H_2O$
      For every mole of NaOH already neutralized by absorbed CO_2, one less mole of HCl will be needed in the titration. Also note that 1 mole CO_2 neutralizes 2 moles NaOH.
3.   Therefore, moles CO_2 absorbed = (initial moles NaOH – moles HCl used) × (1 mol CO_2 / 2 moles NaOH neutralized) where moles NaOH = 0.02 L × molarity of NaOH and moles HCl used = L HCl used × molarity HCl.
4.   Moles CO_2 evolved from soil = moles CO_2 absorbed by NaOH with soil, minus moles CO_2 absorbed by NaOH in blank flask. Thus:

$$CO_2 \ evolved = \frac{1}{2}\left(\left(\begin{array}{c} moles \ NaOH \\ to \ start \end{array} - \begin{array}{c} moles \ NaOH \\ remaining \end{array} \right) - \left(\begin{array}{c} moles \ NaOH \\ to \ start \ in \\ blank \end{array} - \begin{array}{c} moles \ NaOH \\ remaining \\ in \ blank \end{array} \right) \right)$$

5.   g. $CO_2 - C$ evolved = moles CO_2 × 12 g C/mol CO_2

WORKED EXAMPLE

Data: mL HCl to titrate blank = 19 (0.019 L)
       mL HCl to titrate treatment = 15 (0.015 L)
       molarity of HCl = 1.0
       molarity of NaOH = 1.0

1. moles NaOH in beaker $= 0.020 \text{ L} \times 1.0 \text{ mole/L} = 0.02$
2. moles HCl used for blank $= 0.019 \times 1.0 = 0.019$
   moles HCl used for treatment $= 0.015 \times 1.0 = 0.015$
3. moles CO_2 absorbed by treatment NaOH $= \dfrac{0.02-0.015}{2} = \dfrac{0.005}{2} = 0.0025$

   moles CO_2 absorbed by blank NaOH $= \dfrac{0.020-0.019}{2} = \dfrac{0.0005}{2} = 0.0005$
4. moles CO_2 evolved from soil $= 0.0025 - 0.0005 = 0.0020$
5. g $CO_2 - C$ evolved per 50 g air dry soil $= 0.0020 \times 12 \text{ g C/mole } CO_2 = 0.024$

CALCULATIONS FOR NITRATE CONCENTRATION IN THE SOIL

1. The concentration of N in the nitrate form (NO_3-N) in the soil extract solution is read directly by interpolation from your standard curve on Figure 15.2. Record the concentration in ppm (same as mg/L) corresponding to the absorbance of your soil sample extract solution.

2. To express the concentration of NO_3-N on a dry-soil basis, you will need to correct for the moisture content of the soil when it was weighed into the jar, and 2) the amount of water added to the soil at the beginning of the incubation. For the first correction, you can calculate how much of the 50 g of fresh soil added to the jar was actually dry soil (not water). If your soil was air-dried prior to weighing, the amount of water is probably only 1 or 2 percent of the soil weight, and small enough to ignore. However, if the soil was initially quite moist, plug the value determined for gravimetric moisture content (see step 1 this exercise) into the equation, below.

$$weight\ of\ oven\ dry\ soil\ =\ grams\ air\ dry\ soil \times \frac{100}{100\ +\ \%\ moisture}$$

3. For the second correction, see amount recorded in step 3 of the procedure and plug this amount into the equation, below. In the case of treatment #6, be sure to also include the extra 15 mL of water added to waterlog the soil. In calculating the concentration of NO_3-N in the soil, remember that the NO_3-N in approximately 50 g of soil was dissolved in 100 mL of extractant (plus the water already in the soil). Thus, the equation below, is used to take into account this roughly 2 to 1 dilution, converting ppm (mg/L) in the extract to ppm (mg/kg) in the soil.

$$\frac{mg\ NO_3 - N}{kg\ \textbf{soil}} = \frac{mg\ NO_3 - N}{L\ \textbf{extract}} * \frac{L}{1000\ mL} * \frac{1000g}{kg} * \frac{(100mL\ extr + mL\ H2O\ added + ml\ H2O\ in\ soil)}{g\ oven\ dry\ soil}$$

WORKED EXAMPLE

1. Assume an absorbance reading of 0.185, which (according to the hypothetical standard curve) corresponded to 12 m/L NO_3-N in the extract.
2. Assume our soil had a moisture content = 10% initially. Then weight of oven dry soil = 50 × (100/(100+10)) = 50 × 0.909 = 45.5 g oven dry soil.
3. Assume that we added 6 mL of water to the 50 grams of fresh soil in the jar to bring it to optimum moisture content (see step 3 in procedure). Then, mg NO_3-N/kg dry soil (or ppm NO_3-N in soil) = 12 mg/L in extract × (100 mL extract + 6 mL water + 4.5 mL water in air dry soil)/45.5 g dry soil = 29.1 mg/kg dry soil.
4. Convert the result into kg N/ha: if the actual bulk density of the soil is not known, a rule of thumb is the surface soil to a depth of about 15 to 20 cm constitutes about 2 million kg dry mass per hectare (ha) of land. Therefore, one can multiply the result in mg/kg (mg per million mg) by 2 to give kg per 2 million kg or kg/ha of "surface soil." 29 mg N/kg soil = 58 kg N/ha of surface soil.

Exercise 15
Microbial Activity Related to
Decomposition and Nitrogen Transformation

Results and Conclusions

Table 15.1 CO_2 Evolution Data (Class data)

Treatment	Repli-cation	Vol. Start	HCl End-Pt	(mL) Used	CO_2 moles absorbed	CO_2 moles evolved	g CO_2-C evolved	Trt. avg. g CO_2 evolved
1. soil alone	1							
	2							
	3							
2. soil + legume (cold)	1							
	2							
	3							
3. soil + starch	1							
	2							
	3							
4. soil + sawdust	1							
	2							
	3							
5. soil + legume	1							
	2							
	3							
6. soil + legume + extra water	1							
	2							
	3							
7. soil + starch + $(NH_4)_2SO_4$	1							
	2							
	3							
8. soil + legume (hot)	1							
	2							
	3							
9. Soil-less blank	1							
	2							
	3							

Show calculations for one soil here:

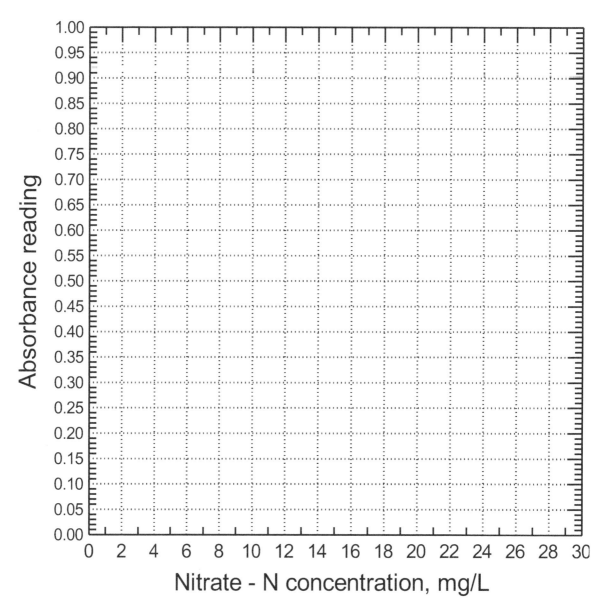

Figure 15. 2 Graph for making nitrate-N standard curve. Plot your class absorbance readings v the concentration of the nitrate standards used, then draw the "best fit" straight line through these points (or enter the data in a spreadsheet program and calculate the equation of the line by linear regression).

Date _____   Name _____

Section _____   I.D. No. _____

Table 15.2 Soil Nitrate Data

Treatment	Repli-cation	absorbance	mg/L NO$_3$-N in filtrate	mg/kg NO$_3$-N in soil	kg NO$_3$-N per hectare [*]	Trt. avg. mg/kg NO$_3$-N in soil
1. soil alone	1					
	2					
	3					
2. soil + legume (cold)	1					
	2					
	3					
3. soil + starch	1					
	2					
	3					
4. soil + sawdust	1					
	2					
	3					
5. soil + legume	1					
	2					
	3					
6. soil + legume + extra water	1					
	2					
	3					
7. soil + starch + (NH$_4$)$_2$SO$_4$	1					
	2					
	3					
8. soil + legume (hot)	1					
	2					
	3					

[*] For this calculation, assume that the layer of surface soil 15 cm thick over a hectare of land (about 2.5 acres) weighs 2.0 million kg.

Show calculations for one soil here:

155

Table 15.3 Effects of Various Factors on Rate of CO_2 Evolution and NO_3-N Concentration Measured

Decomposition conditions and treatments compared	Conclusions Regarding	
	Nitrate production	CO_2 production
Type of C-C bond Trts 3 vs. 4		
C:N ratio Trts 3 vs. 7 and Trts 4 vs. 5		
Moisture (Aeration) Trts 5 vs. 6		
High temperature Trts 5 vs. 8		
Low Temperature Trts 5 vs. 2		

Exercise 16

Buried Slide for
Observation of Soil Microorganisms

OBJECTIVES

After completing this exercise, you should be able to . . .

1. Describe the buried slide technique and the kind of information on soil microbes it can reveal.
2. Recognize and describe cells typical of soil fungi and bacteria (including actinomycetes).
3. Prepare a slide for observation of microbes under oil immersion.
4. Care for and manipulate a microscope for proper focus, resolution and lighting.
5. Describe the effect of added organic matter on the observed microorganisms.

INTRODUCTION

A handful of fertile soil is one of nature's most complex ecosystems. The unseen world beneath our feet is teeming with living things, but not only are these organisms out of sight, most of them are microscopic in size. Two early microbiologists, Rossi and Cholodny[1], discovered that many soil organisms would grow on a glass slide in contact with soil. Thus, by inserting a microscope slide into the soil and later preparing it for microscopic examination, one could learn something about how soil microbes grow and appear in their natural habitat. This is often quite different from their growth habits and appearance when cultured on media in petri dishes. The buried slide method can give us an idea of the morphology and spatial interrelationships of microbes and organic matter in the soil. The method is *not* suitable, however, for obtaining quantitative information such as the numbers of organisms in various soils. In this exercise glass slides will be buried in a soil-mix in the laboratory. The technique can also be effective in comparing natural soils when used outdoors.

MATERIALS

- soil (forest or grassland A horizon), air dry or only slightly moist and passed through a 6 mm (1/4 inch) screen.
- ground legume tissue
- $CaCO_3$ powder
- Plastic specimen cups (250 mL, 9 cm tall)
- 40% acetic acid (in pan with cover)
- microscope with oil immersion objective
- slide staining rack (½ inch wire mesh hardware cloth will do)
- water bath capable of 90°C (or a beaker of water, ring stand and burner)

- graduated cylinder
- glass microscope slides (cleaned and flamed)
- tongs or forceps for handling slides
- spatula
- stirring rod
- rose-Bengal stain, in dropper bottles: dissolve 1.0 g rose Bengal crystals + 0.03 g $CaCl_2 \cdot 2 H_2O$ in 100 ml of 70% ethanol.
- paper towels
- lens tissue
- plastic "cling" wrap
- rubber band to secure wrap on cup top

---

[1]Cholodny, N. 1930. Ober eine neue Methode zur Untersuchung der Bodenmikroflora. Arch. Mikrobiol. 1 :620-652
Rossr, G. 1936. Direct Microscopic and Bacteriological Examination of Soil. Soil Sci. 41 :53-65

Incubation Set Up

PROCEDURE

1. Working in pairs, record the empty weight of two specimen cups (to nearest 1 g). To each cup add enough air-dry soil to fill about 7 cm deep (about 200 g soil). Label the cups with your initials and section number and the letter "A" or "B." Similarly label 2 clean glass microscope slides near the end of each slide and 2 small (50 mL) clean, labeled, dry beakers

2. To cup "B:" add 0.2 g $CaCO_3$ and 1 g ground dried legume tissue. Mix well with the dry soil.

3. With a spatula or knife blade cut 2 narrow slits in the soil and insert a clean glass slide into each, leaving about 2 cm of the labeled end exposed above the soil. Press the soil carefully into contact with the slide and *gently* tap the cup on bench top several times to settle soil.

4. Using the procedure in Appendix B, determine the amount of water that will have to be added to bring each soil to 60% of saturation, a condition considered ideal for aerobic incubation.

5. Fill a graduated cylinder with the amount of water calculated to bring your soil to 60% of saturation (from Table B.1 line G). S*lowly* add this water to the soil in the cup. (This should require a volume of water roughly ¼ that of the soil in the cup.) Let the water soak in a little at a time. Do not stir the soil once it is moist as this will destroy its structure and cause it to smear.

6. Cover the cup with plastic film and secure it with a rubber band. Incubate for 1 to 3 weeks at room temperature in a dark place. Do not allow soil to dry out. After 1 week, re-weigh each cup to check that it has not lost a significant amount of water.

COMMENTS

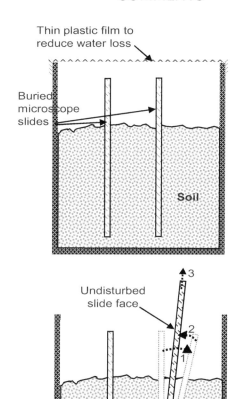

Figure 16.1 Technique for burying and retrieving microscope slides.

Thin food wrap film has pores too small for water vapor (clusters of H_2O molecules) to pass but does allow some of the smaller O_2 and CO_2 molecules to pass. *Alternatively, the cup may be covered with its plastic top, but with 3 or 4 pinholes made in it to allow some gas exchange.*

Post Incubation Examination of Microbes

7. After the incubation period, reweigh each cup, then remove one slide at a time from the soil. Do this by pressing gently to an inclined position and withdrawing in a manner such that one face is not disturbed (see Figure 16.1, lower). This side will be stained. Wipe the *other* side clean with a moist tissue or paper towel. Allow slide to dry for a few minutes.

8. Gently tap the end of each dry slide on the bench top to shake off the loose soil particles. Empty the cup into a waste container and wash the cup with water. Thank you.

> **WEAR GLOVES AND GOGGLES!**

9. Soak the slide in a covered pan of 40% acetic acid for 3 minutes. Then rinse off thoroughly.

10. In a fume hood, place the slide in a staining rack (or on a wire mesh) above a boiling water bath. Cover the slide with a small piece of single thickness paper towel and add 5 to 6 drops of rose Bengal stain (enough to thoroughly wet the towel and slide). Keep the slide wet with stain in this manner for 10 minutes, adding a drop or two of stain as necessary to prevent the towel and slide from drying out.

11. Carefully remove the paper and wash the slides in a *gentle* stream of distilled water from a squeeze bottle and allow the slide to dry.

Unless the soil dried excessively, the cup of soil should weigh close to the same weight as when the incubation began.

> Please be sure to wash and dry your cup so it will be clean for the next use.

> The acetic acid should be kept in the fume hood.

If a vent hood to remove acetic acid fumes is not available, you instructor may ask you to use this alternative procedure which uses just heat to fix the microbes on the slide: Using tongs, hold the slide, soil-side up, a few inches above a low flame for a few seconds to "fix" the microbial cells.

Do this work with the water bath in a fume hood so you can avoid breathing the acetic acid vapor. The stain will be best retained if the slides lay *level* on the rack or wire mesh. Also, avoid getting the stain on your clothes or hands, as it will not readily wash out.

12. Place the stained slide on a microscope stage. Select the lowest power objective lens and adjust the light for optimal viewing. Still using the low power lens, find an area of the slide stained pink and therefore likely to contain microorganisms. Microbial cells as well as organic matter will absorb the pink stain.

13. Now switch to the next higher power lens and manipulate the stage to move the slide to the best area to view. Then, lower the microscope stage carefully to separate it more from the lens and place a **small** drop of immersion oil on the stained region of the slide you wish to view. Then switch to the highest power lens which should be marked "OIL". Now *very slowly* raise the stage while watching closely (NOT through the eye piece) and stop when the objective lens just touches the oil. Then view through the eyepiece and focus using ONLY the *fine* –adjusting knob.

14. In the circles provided on the hand-in sheet, sketch views from each of the slides. Label the type of organisms or other features discernable. Refer to the illustration below for guidance.

Use great care in focusing the microscope to avoid touching the objective lens to soil or slide.

Be sure to use the immersion oil ONLY with the objective lens meant for this purpose (labeled "oil"). Do not allow the oil to contact any other lenses. Dried-on immersion oil can ruin expensive lenses, so carefully wipe the objective lens and stage with a special *non-scratch lens tissue* after you are finished. The oil is necessary for very high magnification with a light microscope to prevent distortions caused by the sharply differing refractive properties of air and glass (the oil has diffractive properties very similar to glass).

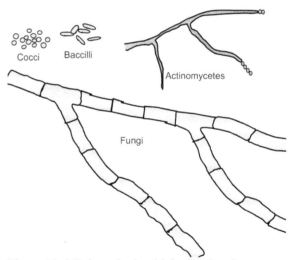

Figure 16. 2 Enlarged microbial cells showing more

The living cells will have taken in the pink stain. Look for fungal mycelia, strands of actinobacteria (actinomycete) and bacterial cells. You may also see bits of organic matter and mineral particles. Sometimes the geometric shapes of diatoms are visible. Note the spatial relationship among the organisms and the soil particles.

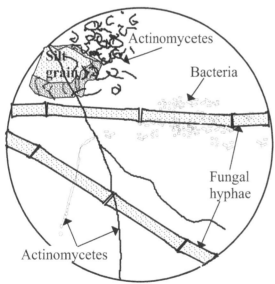

Figure 16. 1 General appearance of common micro-organisms under the microscope .

Date _____   Name _____

Section _____   I.D. No. _____

EXERCISE 16
Buried Slide for
Observation of Soil Microorganisms

Results

1. Describe your observations: _____
    _____
    _____
    _____
    _____

2. What effect, if any, could you ascribe to the soil amendments used? _____
    _____
    _____

3. Sketch 2 fields of view from the microscope slide for each treatment in the circles below.
    Label what you draw.

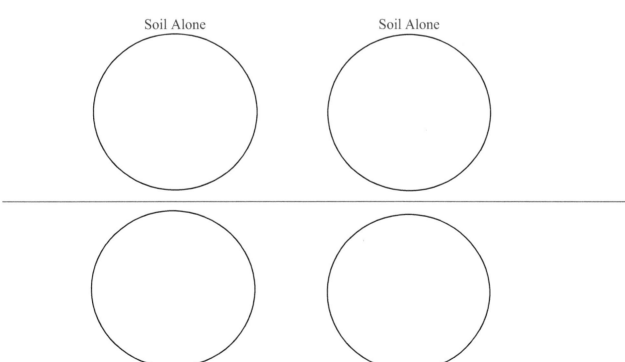

Soil Alone   Soil Alone

Soil & Amendment   Soil & Amendment

Table 16. 1 Weight data for soil incubation.

	Incubation Cup A	Incubation Cup B	
Weight of cup + two glass slides			
Weight of cup + slides + soil + amendments			
Initial weight of cup + water + soil + amendments + slides			
End of incubation weight of cup + water + soil + amendments + slides			

4. Did your soil remain near optimum water content during the incubation period? Explain

_____

_____

_____

Exercise 17

Determination of Soil Organic Matter Content

OBJECTIVES

After completing this exercise, you should be able to . . .

1. Describe the principles behind 2 methods of determining soil organic matter (OM) content and the analytical weaknesses of each.
2. Explain what takes place during the Walkley-Black wet oxidation method and the role of each reagent used.
3. Calculate both the % OM and % organic carbon in a soil sample if given data observed from the two methods in this exercise.
4. Determine the moles of electron associated with organic carbon in a soil sample if given the necessary materials and procedure.
5. Contrast the visual appearance of high- and low-organic matter soils.
6. Describe how soil organic matter is influenced by such factors as cultivation history, climate, soil texture and vertical location in the soil profile.

INTRODUCTION

How much of the soil is organic? The range of organic matter (OM) contents in soils is very wide, from over 75% in some peats and mucks (Histosols) to almost zero in some desert soils (Aridisols) and beach soils (Psamments). The amount of OM present in a soil will be the result of the difference between the rates of its production by plants and its oxidation by microbes. Among the main environmental factors that influence the accumulation of OM in soils are climate (cold soils have more OM than warm ones), water regime (wet soils accumulate more OM than drier ones), soil texture (clayey soil accumulated more OM than sandy ones), and vegetation (high net productivity and high ratio of roots to shoots favor high OM accumulation). Cropping practices, tillage, drainage and erosion are important anthropogenic factors.

In mineral soils a difference of just one percent or so in OM content often has a striking effect on soil tilth, physical properties, fertility and the web of living things that call the soil "home". Soil OM is also a major pool in which carbon is stored or from which it is released. On a global basis more carbon resides in soils than in the world's vegetation and atmosphere. In fact, managing soils to enhance their organic matter content may be an important avenue for addressing the problem of Global Warming that is being brought on largely by increased carbon dioxide in the Earth's atmosphere. It is, therefore, of practical interest to be able to accurately determine the OM content of soils. In the international effort to manage global warming, scientists are developing remote sensing methods of determining soil carbon content of soils by the spectra of infrared light reflected. Such spectral methods may allow rapid survey of this critical environmental parameter from airplanes, satellites or at least by rapid scanning on the ground. Otherwise, it is necessary to analyze the OM in soil samples by laboratory methods.

Various methods can be employed to determine soil OM levels. A crude estimate of OM content can be made on the basis of soil color, if the soils being compared are similar in other respects. Since decomposed OM or soil humus is a very complex material, it has bond lengths suitable to absorb all wavelengths of light and so is characterized by a dark brown or black color. Darker surface soils generally have more OM.

OM content can be estimated more accurately by a *wet* oxidation of OM. In the wet oxidation procedure, known as the Walkley-Black method, the OM is oxidized by a strong oxidizing agent, the dichromate ion, which changes the C^o in organic matter to C^{+4} in CO_2 gas. Only the oxidizable OM is measured. Carbon present as charcoal or graphite is unaffected. Some of the organic matter closely associated with clay minerals may also be unaffected, so a "fudge factor" is used to compensate for the estimated efficiency of the reaction.

The other method given in this lab manual chapter employs a *dry* oxidation that measures the loss of weight during ignition of a soil sample. In this method a dry soil sample is weighed before and after heating to red-hot in a crucible for a period long enough to allow all the OM to be oxidized and driven off as CO_2. Even assuming that the soil sample is totally dry before ignition, the accuracy of the dry combustion method is limited because the temperature is not precisely controlled, so the weight loss could reflect the loss of charcoal, carbonates (if the soil pH is > 7), and water of hydration in the soil minerals as well as organic matter.

Using either of these methods, one can investigate the influence of various environmental or managment factors on soil OM levels. For example, soils with similar texture, drainage and mineralogy but markedly differing organic matter contents can be compared by obtaining samples from adjacent sites with long term histories of cultivation and natural vegetation. Fence-rows v. crop fields provide one such opportunity. If you obtain (or your instructor provides you with) sufficient background information on the soils, this exercise can demonstrate how environmental factors influence soil OM.

MATERIALS FOR WALKLEY–BLACK METHOD
(Note: an alternate OM method is given in second part of this chapter)

- 250 mL beaker
- 500 mL beaker
- soil (ground in non-iron mortar to pass through 0.5 mm sieve) from the A horizon of adjacent areas of contrasting management history such as cultivated and non-cultivated areas (see exercise #6), and/or from student-selected site.
- weighing boat
- balance accurate to ± 0.01 g
- graduated cylinder *or* preferably an automatic pipetting system (e.g., "tilt a pipette" flask or "repipeter") to safely deliver 20 mL of concentrated H_2SO_4
- protective gloves and goggles
- ventilation hood
- Concentrated H_2SO_4 (**caution – extremely corrosive!**)
- 0.167 $\underline{M}$ $K_2Cr_2O_7$ (potassium dichromate) in burettes (make by dissolving 49.04 g of reagent grade, oven-dried $K_2Cr_2O_7$ in water and diluting to 1L in a volumetric flask). This solution is 1 $\underline{N}$ with respect to electrons that can be accepted by the Cr atom; i.e., 1 L of solution can accept 1 mole or 1 equivalent of electrons.
- 0.5 $\underline{M}$ ferrous sulfate solution (Dissolve 140 g of reagent grade $FeSO_4 \cdot 7H_2O$ in water, add 15 mL concentrated H_2SO_4, cool, and dilute to 1.0 L in volumetric flask. This reagent is standardized by titrating it against 10 mL of 0.167 $\underline{M}$ $K_2Cr_2O_7$ in the procedure below.)
- 0.025 $\underline{M}$ O-phenanthroline-ferrous complex indicator (available as "Ferroin")
- burettes (50 or 25 mL) for Ferrous Sulfate and Potassium Dichromate
- burette stands for two burettes
- lighted magnetic stirrer (optional)
- waste container labeled "acidified potassium dichromate"

PROCEDURE	COMMENTS

Walkley-Black Method for Organic Matter Determination

1. Weigh out 1.0 g of air-dry soil (see comments) from each, the uncultivated plot and the cultivated plot. Transfer each 1.0 g of soil to respective 500 ml-Erlenmeyer flasks. Label with your name and either "A" (uncultivated) or "B" (cultivated). Label a third flask "C" (blank) but put no soil in it.

Compare the two soils visually. Is one lighter in color? Grass sod or forest build up OM content while the tillage and erosion associated with intensive cultivation deplete OM from soils.

If a soil appears to be very high in OM (> 6%) as indicated by a dark brown to black color and lots of peaty material, then use only 0.50 g of this soil. Be sure to adjust your calculations accordingly. If too much OM were in the sample used, there would be no unreacted Cr^{6+} to titrate.

2. To the flask (use flask C first) add 10 mL $K_2Cr_2O_7$ from burette and swirl (with soil if appropriate) for 15 seconds.

The acid will help dissolve and hydrolyze the OM and the dichromate will oxidize the OM according to this reaction:

3. Carry flask C to the ventilation hood* and gently set it down. **Put on the protective gloves and goggles.** Then carefully dispense 20 mL of concentrated H_2SO_4 into your flask. Do not pour down the sides but directly into the suspension of soil and $K_2Cr_2O_7$. To measure the 20 mL of acid use a graduated cylinder *or* an automatic pipette system. *Use caution.* Do not allow acid to drip on outside of glassware. Wash your hands with water immediately if they contact acid.

$C_6H_{12}O_6$

$C°$ in sugar, representing soil OM

+

$4\ K_2Cr_2O_7$

Cr^{+6} (oxidized form)

+

$16\ H_2SO_4$

4. Swirl the flask with the acid gently for 1 minute while under a hood*. Record the time that the H_2SO_4 was added:

A_____ B_____ C_____

$\downarrow$

$6\ CO_2$

C^{+4} is oxidized from $C°$ carbon dioxide gas accounts for the bubbling.

+

$4\ Cr_2(SO_4)_3$

Cr^{3+} (reduced from Cr^{6+})

5. Carry flask C back to your bench and let stand for 30 minutes on an asbestos pad. **CAUTION: The flask may get quite hot.** Return your gloves and goggles to the hood area for other students to use.

+

$4\ K_2SO_4$

+

$22\ H_2O$

6. Repeat steps 2-5 for flask B.

---

* If these steps cannot be done behind the glass front of a ventilation hood, then protective goggles must be worn. The room should be well-ventilated.

7. Repeat steps 2-5 for flask A.

NOTE: Your instructor may suggest using the 30 min. break at this point to carry out another exercise, such as the first part of Exercise #12.

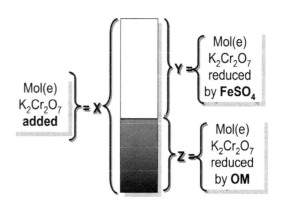

Figure 17. 1 Reaction diagram.

$Z = X - Y$ (see calculations)

mol(e) = moles of electrons in the Chromium

8. After 30 minutes have elapsed since the addition of H_2SO_4, add 200 ml distilled water to flask C. Then add 3 to 4 drops of "ferroin" indicator. Swirl.

9. Titrate against 0.5 $\underline{M}$ $FeSO_4$, from a burette. Initially the color should be dull green with chromous ion, then it should shift to a turbid blue and finally at the end point the color shifts suddenly to a dull red.* Add $FeSO_4$ drop by drop with swirling as the end point is reached. Use a sheet of white paper under the flask to aid in color detection. Record mL $FeSO_4$

at start: _____

at end: _____

10. Repeat steps 8 and 9 for flasks B and A.

11. Complete Table 10.1 showing all calculations.

12. Clean all glassware. Pour chromium-containing solutions into a labeled waste container.

The Cr^{6+} in chromate *not* reduced by soil OM is *now* reduced by $FeSO_4$ by the following reaction:

$$K_2Cr^{6+}_2O_7 + 6\ Fe^{2+}SO_4 + H_2SO_4$$

$$\downarrow$$

$$K_2SO_4 + Cr^{3+}_2(SO_4)_3 + Fe^{3+}_2(SO_4)_3$$

$$+\ 2\ Fe_2O_3 + H_2O$$

---

* These colors are difficult to see with some soils, especially if a lighted stirring table is not available. Without transmitted light the end point color is more of a steel-gray than a red. Watch for a sudden color change, then stop the titration immediately. It is good practice to titrate the blank flask (C) first since the colors are clearer in the absence of soil.

CALCULATIONS FOR ORGANIC CARBON CONCENTRATION

Org. Carbon = Mol (e) from

$$\frac{C^{4+}\,reacted}{g\,drysoil} \times \frac{12g\;C^{4+}}{mol\;C^{4+}} \times \frac{1mol\;C^{4+}}{4mol(e)} \times \frac{1g\;C\;in\;soil}{0.77g\;C\;oxidized\;by\;K_2Cr_2O_7}$$

Where

1. $g\;dry\;soil = g\;air-dry \times \dfrac{100\;g\;oven-dry\;soil}{(100 + \%H_2O)\;g\;air-dry\;soil}$

2. mol(e) from C^{4+} reacted = 0.01 mol(e) acceptable by 10 mL $K_2Cr_2O_7$ − mol(e) accepted from $FeSO_4$

    2a.
    $$mol(e)\;acceptable\;by\;10\;mL\;K_2Cr_2O_7 = \frac{10\;mL \times 0.167\;mol\;K_2Cr_2O_7}{1000\;mL\;K_2Cr_2O_7} \times \frac{6\;mol(e)}{mol\;K_2Cr_2O_7} = 0.01$$

    2b. $mol(e)\;acceptable\;from\;FeSO_4 = mL\;FeSO_4\;used \times \dfrac{mol(e)}{1000\;mL\;FeSO_4}$

    2c. $\dfrac{mol(e)}{1000\;mL\;FeSO_4} = \dfrac{10\;mL\;K_2Cr_2O_7 \times 1\;mol(e)/L\;K_2Cr_2O_7}{mL\;FeSO_4\;used\;to\;titrate\;blank}$

3. 0.77 is the fraction of the organic carbon in a typical soil that will react in this procedure to give up e's to $K_2Cr_2O_7$. The remaining 23% of the C is too resistant to react. The 0.77 factor is in widespread use, but is really only a rough estimate of the reaction efficiency and may not be valid for all soils.

4. 12 is the atomic weight of C.

5. 4 is the number of e's available from the complete oxidation of one C.

6. 10 mL is the amount of $K_2Cr_2O_7$ solution used.

CALCULATIONS FOR % ORGANIC MATTER

$$Organic\;matter = 1.72 \times organic\;C$$

Where 1.72 is the so-called "Van Bemmelen factor" which is based on the assumption that soil organic matter contains 58% C (i.e., 1.72 = 1/0.58). Though widely used by convention, this factor is not the same for all soils, or even all horizons of a given soil.

WORKED EXAMPLE

Data: $FeSO_4$ to titrate blank   =   19.5 mL

$FeSO_4$ to titrate sample =   8.0 mL

air dry soil used   –   1.0 g

moisture in air dry soil =   0.03 g/g

Step

1. $g \ oven \ dry \ soil \ = (1.0 \ g \ air \ dry \ soil) \times \dfrac{100 \ g \ oven \ dry \ soil}{103 \ g \ air \ dry \ soil} = 0.97 \ g$

2a. $\dfrac{mol(e)}{1000 \ mL \ FeSO_4} = \dfrac{10 \ mL \ K_2Cr_2O_7 \times 1 \ mol(e)/L \ K_2Cr_2O_7}{19.5 \ mL \ FeSO_4 \ to \ titrate \ blank} = 0.513$

2b. $mol(e) \ accepted \ = 8.0 \ mL \ FeSO_4 \ used \times \dfrac{0.513 \ mol(e)}{1000 \ mL \ FeSO_4} = 0.0041$

2c. $mol(e) \ reacted \ = \ 0.010 - 0.0041 = 0.0059$

$Org.\,C = \dfrac{0.0059 mol(e) \ from \ C \ reacted}{0.97g \ ovendry \ soil} \times \dfrac{12gC}{molC} \times \dfrac{1molC}{4mol(e)} \times \dfrac{1}{0.77} = 0.0237 \ g \ C/g \ soil$

Since many commercial labs traditionally report soil organic matter as a percent of dry soil we can calculate % OM as follows:

$\% \ organic \ matter \ = \ 100 \times 0.0237g \ C/g \ soil \times 1.72 \ g \ OM/g \ C \ = \ 4.08$

MATERIALS FOR LOSS ON IGNITION METHOD

Ring stand
Ceramic triangle
Crucible tongs
Burner
Ceramic crucible, 50 mL
Glass stir rod
Soils (as above)
Desiccator with dry desiccant
Balance to weigh ± 0.01 g

Determination of Soil Organic Matter Content by Loss on Ignition

PROCEDURE	COMMENTS

1. For each soil to be analyzed set up a ring stand with a ceramic triangle and burner (see figure). **Wear goggles while burner is on.** Adjust burner flame for maximum heat (a short blue flame). Turn off burner. Using tongs, place a clean ceramic crucible in the triangle and adjust height so blue flame will just touch crucible. Heat until crucible glows red hot for 2 minutes. Then turn off burner and allow crucible to cool.

2. Weigh the cool crucible to the nearest 0.01 g. Record in Table 17.2 line B.

3. Loosely place enough air-dry soil into the crucible to fill it about 1/3 full. Do not pack down the soil. Weigh to nearest 0.01 g and record in Table 17.2 line C.

4. Place the crucible with air-dry soil on a microwave oven turntable and microwave on high power for 3 minutes. Then cool it in a desiccator for a few minutes and weigh to nearest 0.01 g. Record in Table 17.2 line D.

5. Set crucible of oven dry soil over burner. Light burner and gradually heat until the ceramic glows red. Then continue to keep it red-hot for 1 to 2 hours. Stir the soil occasionally with a glass rod. Take care not to lose any of the soil material. When the dark colored organic matter is completely destroyed by ignition, most soils will become uniformly light tan or red in color.

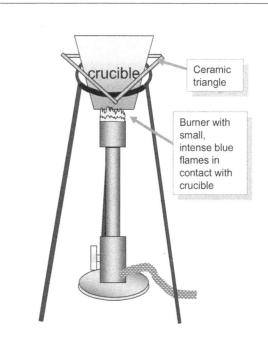

Figure 17. 2 Crucible set up for loss by ignition.

- **KEEP YOUR HAIR AND CLOTHING AWAY FROM FLAME!**
- **AVOID TOUCHING HOT OBJECTS!**
- **WEAR GOGGLES**

It is essential that the crucible be clean and that any substance that might burn off be burned off now. The intense heat (ignition) will oxidize the organic substances to water vapor and carbon dioxide.

169

6. After ignition is complete, turn off the burner and cool the crucible in a desiccator. Reweigh the cooled crucible of soil and record data (to nearest 0.01 g) in Table 17.2 line H. Calculate the percent organic matter. Compare this value to that obtained for the same soil using the Walkley-Black method if that method was also used.

The crucible now contains only the non-organic mineral portion of the soil (ash). The weight lost during ignition is that of the organic matter (and any carbonates, etc. that may have volatized).

If you used your own soil, also enter the final value for % organic matter in Table G2, Appendix G.

7. Please clean up your materials and work area. Thank you.

Date _____   Name _____

Section _____   I.D. No. _____

Exercise 17
Determination of Soil Organic Matter Content

Results and Conclusions

Table 17.1 Data for Walkley-Black Organic Matter Determination

Soil ID	Soil description (mgt. history, location, etc.)	mL FeSO$_4$			*weight of soil (g)	Organic C g/g	Organic Matter %
		start	end	used			
Blank							
A							
B							
C							

*weight of oven-dry soil (g) = g air-dry soil $\times \dfrac{100}{(100 + \% \ moisture)}$; where % moisture is determined as shown in Appendix D.

Show calculations here for one soil:

Questions

1. Why is it preferable to report in scientific journals the organic carbon (g/g) rather than % organic matter if the Walkley-Black method is used?

   _____

   _____

   _____

2. Considering your data and that of the class, was there a difference in organic carbon between cultivated and uncultivated plots of soil? Explain.

   _____

   _____

   _____

171

Table 17.2 Organic Matter Determined by Loss on Ignition

Row	Variable	Calculations	Data			
A	Soil Used	Identifying label				
B	Crucible, g	measured				
C	Crucible + air dry soil, g	measured				
D	Crucible + oven dry soil, g	measured				
E	Water content of the airdry soil, θ_m	$100 \times \dfrac{C - D}{D}$				
F	Soil, air dry, g	(C – B)				
G	Soil, oven dry, g	(D – B)				
H	Crucible + ash, g	measured				
I	Ash, g	(H – B)				
J	Loss on ignition, g	(D – H)				
K	Organic matter in soil, g/g	J/G				
L	Percent Organic Matter	$100 \times J/G$				

1. What conditions or experimental errors could give a too-high result for % OM?

2. What errors or conditions could give a too-low result for % OM?

3. What color was your soil after ignition? Relate this color to the likely minerals found in the soil.

4. If both methods were used, compare your results and explain any inconsistencies.

Exercise 18

Active Fraction Carbon and Soil Health

OBJECTIVES

After completing this exercise, you should be able to ...

1. Define the terms "active organic matter" and "passive organic matter."
2. List the soil properties most influenced by active and passive organic matter.
3. Define the relationship between soil organic carbon and soil organic matter.
4. Explain why the purple permanganate anion color becomes lighter if the soil used has more C_A in it.
5. Explain why a very weak solution of potassium permanganate gives results more related to active fraction carbon (C_A).
6. Estimate the C_A in a soil based on the degree of color "bleaching" reaction of 0.20 M potassium permanganate.
7. Interpret the soil health implications of the amount of C_A in a soil, and the proportion of total soil carbon that is in the active fraction (C_A/C_T).

INTRODUCTION

In most A-horizons (surface soils), the organic portion constitutes only 1 to 4% of the total soil dry mass. However, this small amount of soil organic matter (SOM) exerts a tremendous influence over a wide range of important soil properties. These organic matter-affected properties include the soil's capacity to hold cations (the CEC), its capacity to hold water for plants, the rate of nutrient release by microbial mineralization (especially for nitrogen, phosphorus and sulfur), the development and stabilization of aggregate structure (which in turn influences soil aeration, water infiltration and susceptibility to erosion), and several other properties. The level of organic matter in a given soil is largely a function of such inherent (and relatively unchangeable) soil characteristics as the local climate (cooler, wetter sites accumulate more SOM), the soil texture (finer soils accumulate more SOM), and the drainage class (poor drainage promotes SOM accumulation). However, the way we manage the soil also impacts the level of SOM. For example, intensive tillage, the use of periods of bare fallow and the removal of crop residues all eventually result in a lowering of the SOM level.

Because of the many soil properties and ecological functions influenced by SOM level, the measurement of SOM is considered an important part of assessing soil quality or soil health. Soil health is a concept somewhat akin to human health. It indicates the degree to which a soil is in "good condition", that is, how well the soil is able to function up to its potential. The functions referred to may depend on the purpose of the assessment, but usually include such things as the soil's productivity in producing plants, it's efficiency in cycling and purifying water, it's support for a diversity of soil biota, it's ability to decompose organic wastes added to the soil, it's ability to resist erosion, and its ability to store and cycle essential nutrients.

The organic matter content of soils is commonly reported in one of two ways; as the amount of soil organic matter (SOM) or as the amount of soil organic carbon (SOC). Most methods of analyses actually measure the amount of organic C, so a conversion factor is often applied to convert values for organic C to values for organic matter. Although not accurate for all soils, the factor traditionally used is 1.72, which assumes that soil organic matter contains about 58% C:

$$\text{SOM} = 1.72 \times \text{SOC} \qquad\qquad \text{Eq. 18.1}$$

This type of conversion may be fine for communicating with landowners, but scientifically it would be more accurate to simply report the amount of organic C without converting it to SOM.

In exercise 17 two methods are given for measuring the SOM or SOC. Both of those methods are designed to measure the total organic matter, one by determining the total amount of organic carbon (C_T), the other by the weight loss upon ignition. However, organic matter in soils is not a homogenous substance. Our understanding of soil organic matter dynamics and functions can be greatly improved if we recognize that the total organic matter in soils includes a portion (or *fraction*) that is highly humified and resistant to microbial decay, as well a fraction that is readily available as food for microorganisms (Figure 18.1).

The highly protected or resistant material is called the *passive fraction* and accounts for the bulk (75 to 95%) of the organic matter that has accumulated in most soils. It is protected from microbial attack either by its recalcitrant chemical structure (as in charcoal), by its being bound to clay surfaces, or by its physically inaccessible location inside minute pores within soil aggregates. Typically, the material in the passive organic matter fraction remains in the soil for centuries or even millennia, unless conditions are altered.

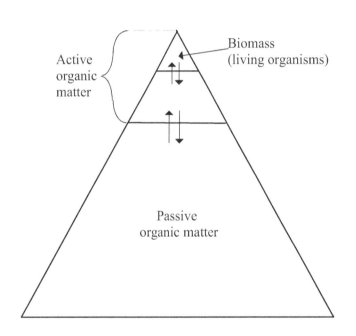

Figure 18. 1 The total organic matter in a soil includes microbially active and passive fractions, the biomass being part of the active fraction.

By way of contrast, active fraction organic matter is much more readily metabolized and is actively being transformed by microorganisms. The material in the active fraction typically lasts only a matter of a few weeks to a few years. It consists of tiny bits of partially decomposed but not well protected plant tissue, microbial cells, both dead and alive, and many kinds of biological compounds synthesized by the microorganisms (such as the polysaccharides and glycoprotein glues that hold soil particles together to form aggregates).

The two organic matter fractions play different roles in the soil. The passive organic matter is mainly responsible for the increased water holding capacity and cation exchange capacity associated with higher organic matter. The active fraction, on the other hand, accounts for the stabilization of soil aggregates, the release of nutrient by mineralization and the support of general microbial activity that may result in suppression of plant diseases, enhanced plant growth, and more efficient recycling of organic wastes. The size of the passive organic fraction is mainly a function of climate, texture and soil drainage over decades and centuries, but the level of active organic matter is quite responsive to soil management over periods of just a year or two.

Maintenance of the active fraction requires a constant supply of fresh organic materials (usually from growing plants) and soil management that minimized the losses of organic matter by oxidation and erosion. The amount of active organic matter in a soil, and its proportion of the total organic matter, is therefore considered a more sensitive indicator of soil health than total organic matter. In well managed soils, active C (by the method in this exercise, often referred to as *permanganate oxidizable carbon* or POXC) can be expected to be 2 to 3% of the total C (or 1 to 2% of the organic matter). Poorly managed, "worn out" soils may have less than half these amounts of active C. Thus, for cultivated soils, active C typically ranges from as high as 1000 mg/kg in fine textured soils in excellent condition to as little as 100 mg/kg in poorly managed sandy soils. Fortunately, a number of commercial labs are now analyzing for active C as well as total organic C.

In this exercise, you will determine the level of active organic carbon in three soils:

     i. soil A is expected to be high in active C because of a long history of perennial vegetation without tillage (e.g. a pasture, grassland or forest),

    ii. soil B is a similar soil expected to have had much of its active C depleted by years of intensive tillage and little plant residue return, and

   iii. soil C --- that's your soil. You'll find out how it stacks up.

MATERIALS

- soils (see above), dried and ground to 2mm.
- colorimeter (or spectrophotometer) capable of reading absorbance at 550 nm. For use in a field kit, a generic 550 nm pocket colorimeter is available from HACH Company, Boulder, CO
- glass cuvettes appropriate for spectrophotometer used.
- 50 mL graduated polypropylene conical centrifuge tubes (2 per sample + 3 for standard solutions)
- two graduated disposable bulb dropper pipettes (1 ml capacity, graduated in 0.10 mL)
- soil scoop that holds ~5 g of ground soil (may be calibrated for greater accuracy)
- balance with 0.01 g precision (if greater precision than scoop is desired)
- plastic cup (50 mL)
- rack to hold conical centrifuge tubes in upright position
- black heavy paper cut into 10 cm squares (for drying soil)
- lab tissues for wiping cuvette
- distilled water in a squeeze bottle
- 0.01 M ascorbic acid solution (0.176 g $C_6H_8O_6$ dissolved in 100 mL distilled water) – for cleaning built up purple/brown Mn stains on cuvettes and tubes.
- stock solution: 0.2M $KMnO_4$ in 1M $CaCl_2$ (pH 7.2). Adjust pH of $CaCl_2$ solution to 7.2 by adding a few drops of 0.1M NaOH while reading pH with a calibrated pH electrode. The pH-adjusted 0.2M $KMnO_4$ stock solution should be kept in a dark color/amber bottle (plastic for safety if used in the field) for up to 6 months. *Safety note: $KMnO_4$ in crystal form is a very strong oxidizer so wear goggles and gloves. Be prepared for heat to be generated when the $CaCl_2$ is dissolved in water.*
- standard solutions: 0.005, 0.01, and 0.02M $KMnO_4$. Add 1.25, 2.5 and 5.0 mL of stock solution to respective 50 mL volumetric flasks. Fill and empty the pipette several times with the diluted solution to be sure all the solution is delivered. Then add distilled water exactly to the 50 mL mark, cap and shake to mix. Store in dark glass or brown plastic bottles labeled Standard Soln. 0.005, 0.01, or 0.02M $KMnO_4$.

PROCEDURE[1]	COMMENTS
1. Record details about each soil in Table 18.1. Write soil ID on three clean 50 mL graduated conical centrifuge tubes.	
2. With a 1 mL graduated bulb dropper pipette, place 2.0 mL of 0.2 M $KMnO_4$ in each of the tubes. Add distilled water to the 20 mL mark to dilute the $KMnO_4$ to 0.02 M. Cap the tube and swirl to mix the solution thoroughly.	If moist soil is sampled, it must be air-dried before analysis by gently crumbling about 20 g and spreading it thinly on black paper (preferably in direct sunlight). Air-dry about 15 minutes until soil no longer looks or feels moist. Mix the crumbled soil two or three times during air-drying. Be sure all samples compared are equally dry. *Do not use moist soil, as results may be erratic.*
3. Add 2.5 g of air-dry soil to each tube and cap tightly.	The soil organic matter will react with the dilute (0.02 M) $KMnO_4$. The carbon will be oxidized (lose electrons) and the $KMnO_4$ will be reduced (gain electrons). The reduction of $KMnO_4$ destroys its purple color.
4. Shake all three tubes vigorously and continuously for 2 min, then stand them in a rack for 10 min to allow soil to settle. Protect the tube from direct sunlight. **Do observe the colors, but do *NOT* disturb or shake the tubes!** During this 10 minute waiting period we will standardize the instrument.	During the 10 min waiting period, the $CaCl_2$ in the solution will cause the soil to flocculate and therefore settle rapidly, clearing the upper portion of the solution. The color will be stable only if the tubes are NOT disturbed.
5. Fill a clean glass cuvette with distilled water. Wipe the outside with a tissue and place in the colorimeter well. Put the cover in place and "zero" the instrument. After a few seconds, it should read "0.00". Remove the cuvette.	The first step in calibrating the colorimeter is to "zero" the instrument with a solution (distilled water) that contains none of the light-absorbing compound. Directions for operation of your instrument may differ slightly from those given here.
6. With a clean pipette, transfer 0.5 mL of the 0.005 M $KMnO_4$ standard to a clean graduated tube, bring to 50 mL volume, cap and shake. Pour some of this diluted solution into a cuvette, wipe the cuvette with a tissue, insert into the colorimeter and cover. Press "read" and record absorbance in Table 18.2.	It is very important to rinse out the dropper pipette with the diluted solution from the tube to be sure all of the $KMnO_4$ remaining is transferred. Carefully avoid getting any liquid on or inside the instrument. The absorbance readings for the blank and the standards will be used to construct a *standard curve* to calibrate the instrument.

---

[1] Modified from Weil, R.R., K.R. Islam, M.A. Stine, J.B. Gruver, and S.E. Samson-Liebig. 2003. Estimating active carbon for soil quality assessment: A simplified method for lab and field use. Amer. J. of Alternative Agric. 18:3-17.

7. Repeat step 6 using first 0.5 mL of 0.01M KMnO$_4$, then 0.5 mL of 0.02M KMnO$_4$ standard solutions. Record absorbance for each diluted standard. Construct a standard curve (x-axis = abs., y-axis = conc.).

Even if your instrument has a "concentration mode" it is best to make a standard curve to check for linearity.

8. After measuring the absorbance of the standard solutions, use a clean bulb pipette to slowly withdraw 0.50 mL of clear liquid from near the top of the soil-KMnO$_4$ suspension for SOIL A. Transfer this to a clean 50 mL centrifuge tube that already contains approximately 45 mL distilled water. Mix the solution and clean out the dropper by filling and emptying the dropper at least twice with the diluted solution from the same vial. Bring to 50 mL volume with distilled water, cap, and shake. Pour enough in a cuvette to fill it about half full. Wipe the outside of the cuvette with a tissue and place in the colorimeter well. Put the cover in place and press "read". Record the absorbance for the sample in Table 18.3.

In this step, you are treating the soil sample solutions in exactly the same manner as you did for the standard solutions.

If absorbance for your soil is less than 0.05, your sample may be higher in active C than measurable by this procedure. In that case, you should repeat steps 1-8, but use only 1.0 g soil in step 3. If you do this, you will have to substitute 0.001 instead of 0.0025 "kg of soil" in the last term of equation 12.2 when doing the calculations.

9. Repeat step 8 for the remaining soil samples. Record the absorbance readings in Table 18.3.

The *loss* of absorption (bleaching of KMnO$_4$ purple color) is proportional to the amount of oxidizable C in soil. Lighter purple colors mean that most of the KMnO$_4$ reacted with soil C and therefore indicate higher amounts of active C. Darker purple colors mean that little of the KMnO$_4$ reacted with soil C and therefore indicate that the soil has little active C.

10. Using the graph axes provided in Figure 18.3, construct a standard curve from the readings recorded in steps 6-7. It should look similar to Figure 18.2. Complete Table 18.3

11. Thoroughly clean all tubes and cuvettes. A 0.01 M ascorbic acid solution may be needed to thoroughly remove all residual purple/brown stains from the cuvettes to restore their original optical transparency.

Caution: If you use ascorbic acid to clean the tubes or cuvettes, be sure to rinse them *thoroughly* as any traces of ascorbic acid will react with the KMNO$_3$ and drastically alter the results!

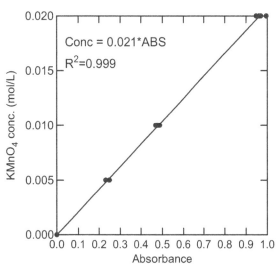

Figure 18. 2 Typical standard curve (using HACH pocket colorimeter II). Other instruments will give different absorbance values. Multiple dots are for same standard solutions used several months apart.

Calculation of mg active C / kg soil from data on mol/L KMnO₄ remaining after reaction with soil.

To estimate the amount of C oxidized, we assume that one mole of MnO_4 is reduced (3 e⁻ gained as Mn^{+7} goes to Mn^{+4}) in the oxidation of 0.75 mole of (9000 mg) of C (4 e⁻ lost as C^0 goes to C^{+4}).

$$\text{Active soil C (in mg C/kg)} = \left[\begin{array}{c} \text{Molarity of} \\ \text{KMnO}_4 \\ \text{shaken with} \\ \text{soil} \end{array} - \begin{array}{c} \text{Molarity of} \\ \text{KMnO}_4 \text{ after} \\ \text{reaction} \end{array} \right] \times \frac{9000 \text{ mg of C}}{\text{Mol KMnO}_4} \times \frac{0.02 \text{ L KMnO}_4}{0.0025 \text{ kg of soil}} \quad \text{Eq. 18.2}$$

Remember that the initial molarity of the KMnO₄ solution shaken with the soil was 0.02 Mol/L (see step 2). The molarity of KMnO₄ after reacting with the soil C is found by extrapolating your absorbance reading on the standard curve. Remember, too, that 0.0025 kg (2.5 g) of soil was shaken with 0.02 L (20 mL) of KMnO₄ solution in step 3 (unless you had a sample very high in active C and used 0.001 kg soil instead of 0.0025 kg soil).

Permanganate redox chemistry

The following half reactions show the oxidation of carbon (in the organic matter) balanced by the reduction of the manganese (Mn) in the potassium permanganate solution. Note that a mole of Mn reduced in this half reaction involves the gain of only 3 electrons while the oxidation of carbon involves the loss of 4 electrons. Therefore, a mole of Mn oxidized only ¾ mole C. This is the basis for the 9,000 mg of C in equation 18.1 (9,000 mg is ¾ of 12,000 mg, which is 1 mole of C).

Reduction half reaction:

$MnO_4^- + 2H_2O + 3e^- \rightarrow MnO_2 + 4OH^- \quad E^\circ = 0.60V$
$Mn^{+7} \qquad\qquad \rightarrow Mn^{+4}$

Oxidation half reaction:

$CH_2O + O_2 \rightarrow CO_2 + H_2O + 4e^-$
$C^0 \qquad \rightarrow C^{+4}$

Exercise 18
ACTIVE FRACTION CARBON AND SOIL HEALTH

Results and Conclusions

Table 18.1 Identification and management history of soils analyzed for active C.

Soil I.D.	Expected level of active C	Management History		Location where sampled	Textural class	Drainage class
		Vegetation or crop rotation	Tillage or disturbance			
Soil A	High					
Soil B	Low					
Soil __	Unknown					

Table 18.2   Data for standard curve. Enter your readings for standard solution here and plot in Figure 18.3.

Standard (mol/L)	Absorbance reading
0	
0.005	
0.01	
0.02	

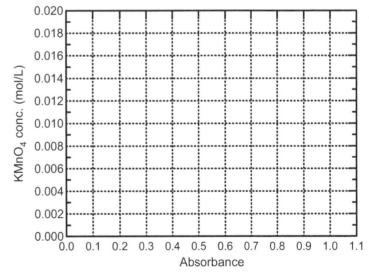

Figure 18. 3 Graph for making standard curve.

179

Table 18. 3 Data from analysis of active soil C.

Soil I.D.	Absorbance	Concentration of $KMnO_4$ after reaction, Mol/L	Active C in soil (C_A), mg C/kg[*]	Total organic C (C_T),[**] mg/kg	Ratio of active to total C, C_A/C_T[**]
Soil A					
Soil B					
Soil ____					

[*] From calculation using equation 18.2.
[**] From exercise 17, if available, assuming organic matter is 58% C: mg/kg C_T = (% Organic Matter * 10^4)/1.72.

Show your calculations of mg/kg active C here:

Questions:

1. Describe the colors of the three soil-suspensions after they had been standing in the rack for a few minutes. Could you see a difference between soil A and Soil B? Explain what this color difference tells you about the active C in these soils.

2. From the description of the history of Soils A and B (see your instructor), explain whether each soil is aggrading (gaining organic matter) or degrading (losing organic matter) over time.

3. How does the amount of active C you measured in each soil compare to the amount of total C in each soil (based on either actual measurement of total C in exercise 17, or on typical values for this type of soil provided by your instructor)?

Exercise 19
Movement of Phosphorus and Nitrogen in Soils

OBJECTIVES

After completing this exercise, you should be able to . . .

1. Describe two mechanisms by which phosphates are immobilized in soils.
2. Explain the effect of pH on P- mobility.
3. Compare the relative mobility of nitrates and phosphates in soil.
4. List the two nutrient elements most commonly implicated in water pollution from land and relate their pollution potential to the results of this exercise.
5. Make visual colorimetric comparisons of N and P concentrations.

INTRODUCTION

Nitrogen and phosphorus are usually the most limiting nutrient for plant growth in many parts of the world. Nitrogen is especially limiting in sandy soils, while phosphorus is especially limiting in highly weathered soils and calcareous soils. Many soils have very low contents of phosphorus and the little that is there is present in relatively unavailable forms. The availability of phosphorus to plants is governed by a complex set of reactions by which organic compounds and rather insoluble mineral compounds slowly release P to maintain the concentration of P in the soil solution. It is this dissolved P upon which plants depend directly for their needs.

Maintaining adequate P in solution (about 0.02 to 0.2 ppm is required for good growth of many plants) is a serious problem in many soils. The ion HPO_4^{2-} tends to form very sparingly soluble mineral

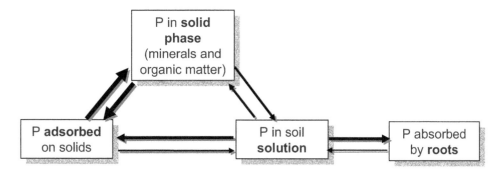

Figure 19. 1 Equilibria among the principle pools of soil P.

compounds by combining with Ca in alkaline soils. The $H_2PO_4^-$ ion tends to be held very tightly by positively charged clay surfaces in acid soils. In acid soils, iron and aluminum combine with phosphorus to also form insoluble phosphates. These reactions cause P to be very immobile in the soil. Because of the immobility of P in the soil, it is a common practice to apply P-fertilizers in a band near the seed so the young roots will reach it easily.

Nitrogen and phosphorus are also the two most important nutrients causing water pollution by eutrophication. Under most circumstances, the main pathways for N loss from land to water is via leaching of soluble N, primarily nitrate ions that do are not strongly adsorbed by soil colloids. In contrast, the main pathway for P to be lost from soils to water is as ions adsorbed on soil particles lost by erosion, or as ions dissolved in surface runoff water. If organic forms of P are plentiful, however, significant amounts of organic P may leach through the soil as well as become dissolved in runoff water. It is unlikely for much inorganic P to be leached below the rooting zone by excess rainwater and so, unlike nitrate-nitrogen, P is unlikely to contribute to pollution of groundwater.

This exercise demonstrates several factors affecting the behavior of P in soils. The first part also contrasts the mobility of P and N in soils.

MATERIALS

- Ammonium molybdate solution (Made by dissolving 15 g of reagent grade $(NH_4)_6 Mo_7O_{24} \cdot 4H_2O$ in 350 mL of warm distilled water in a 1 L volumetric flask. Filter if necessary to remove sediment. Add 350 mL of 10 $\underline{N}$ HCl to the flask *slowly*, while stirring. Cool to room temperature and bring to 1 L with distilled water. Protect from light. Store solution in dark brown glass (or aluminum foil wrapped) tightly closed bottle. Discard after 2 months.)
- Stannous chloride solution
  (*Stock solution* prepared by dissolving 10 g of $SnCl_2 \cdot 2H_2O$ in 25 mL concentrated HCl. Store up to 2 months in polyethylene bottle in refrigerator.
  Dilute solution prepared fresh within 2 hours of use by adding 1 mL of stock solution to 333 mL distilled water and mixing thoroughly.)
- $Ca(H_2PO_4)_2$ solutions (1 ppm and 10 ppm-P)
- $FeCl_3$ solution (1% by weight)
- Saturated $Ca(OH)_2$ solution
- KNO_3 solution (10 ppm-N)
- Diphenylamine solution in dropper bottles (dissolve 0.03 g diphenylamine in 25 mL conc. H_2SO_4)
- Test tubes (25 mL)
- Test tube rack
- Dropper bottles
- Spatula
- Beakers (50 mL)
- Graduated cylinder (50 mL)
- 5-gram scoop
- Clamp and stand
- Funnels and rack
- Filter paper (Whatman No. 42 or VWR 494) disks slightly smaller in diameter than the leach tube.
- Glass or clear plastic tube (approximately 15 cm long × 2 cm diameter) fitted with one-hole stopper with 4 cm long thin glass tube (a 65 mL plastic syringe without plunger can be substituted).

PROCEDURE	COMMENTS

PROCEDURE

1. Set up a leaching column as shown at right. Place a filter disk in the bottom to retain the soil. Moisten the walls of the column and the filter. Then add about 30 cm³ of loam soil and place a *clean* beaker beneath the drain tube to catch the leachate. If your soil is high in clay, you may mix it with clean sand to increase its permeability. Place a second moistened filter disk on top of the soil.

2. Mix 25 mL of 10 ppm-P and 25 mL of 10 ppm-N solutions in a 50 mL cylinder. Stir.

3. Pour 5 mL of this N-P solution into a test tube. Label as P- control. Also place 1 drop of N-P solution into a well of a porcelain spot plate. Label as N- control. These will serve as checks so that the concentrations of N and P in the leachate can be compared to those in the original solution.

4. *Slowly* add the remaining 45 mL of N-P solution to the soil in the leaching column. Discard the first 5 mL of leachate. Rinse beaker and replace. The solution should soak through the soil -- not run down the walls of the column.

> **For most loamy soils the leaching process will take about 30 minutes. Use this time to carry out steps 8-21 of this exercise.**

5. When at least 6 additional ml of leachate has been collected, pour about 5 mL of it into a *clean* test tube. Label "leachate." Also place 1 drop of leachate into a clean well of a spot plate and label "leachate."

6. Test for dissolved P in the test tube containing leachate and in the tube of N-P solution. The test for P is described in steps 10-11. Record your results in Table 19.1.

7. Test for nitrate-N in the 2 spot plate wells by adding 4 drops of diphenylamine to the solution in each well. Allow 3 minutes for the color to develop. Compare the color developed in the leachate with that in the original N-P solution. Record your observations in Table 19.1.

8. Fill 2 *clean* test tubes ¼ full with Ca (H₂PO₄)₂ solution (1 ppm P).

COMMENTS

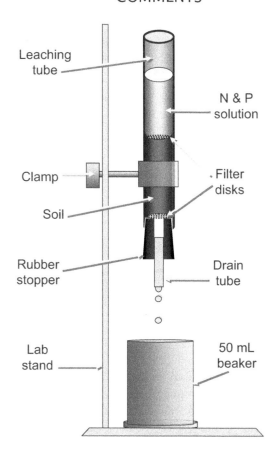

Figure 19. 2 Set up for leaching N and P solutions .

Since you will be comparing the tubes to one another, try to have both filled to the same level. If the leachate is cloudy, filter it before adding it to the test tube and spot plate.

How does the P concentration in the leachate compare to that in the original N-P solution? Explain any difference you find in Table 19.1.

The deeper the blue color, the more nitrate-N there is in solution. Did the soil allow more of the N or more of the P to leach through it? Record your answers in Table 19.1.

$Ca(H_2PO_4)_2$ is monocalcium phosphate, the form of P in single superphosphate fertilizer.

9. To one test tube add 10 drops of 1% $FeCl_3$ solution and shake. Leave the other tube to serve as a check.

The $FeCl_3$ provides ferric iron which can react with P to form insoluble iron phosphates. Red soils derive their color from abundant ferric iron.

10. Add 5 drops of ammonium molybdate solution to each test tube.

Any dissolved P present will form a complex with the molybdate.

11. Add 2 drops of stannous chloride solution to each test tube and shake. Let them stand in rack for 1 minute.

The stannous chloride reduces the P-molybdate complex to a form which has a blue color. The deeper the blue color, the more P was in solution.

12. Record your observations in Table 19.1.

What was the effect of iron on the solubility of phosphorus? Answer in Table 19.1.

13. Repeat step 8 using clean test tubes.

All glassware should be washed thoroughly with tap water and then rinsed twice with small quantities of distilled water.

14. To one test tube add 5 mL of a saturated $Ca(OH)_2$ solution. Swirl gently. To the other tube add 5 ml of distilled water.

Ca in the alkaline $Ca(OH)_2$ form will react with the dissolved HPO_4^{2-} ions from the monocalcium phosphate to form tricalcium phosphate [$Ca(PO_4)_2$] and other relatively *insoluble* compounds.

15. Set up 2 filter funnels with folded filter paper and filter the contents of each test tube, collecting the filtrates in other (clean) test tubes. Collect only approximately 5 mL of filtrate. Discard the rest.

The solution may look clear but filtration is necessary as very fine calcium phosphate precipitates may not be visible.

16. Test for dissolved P in the filtrates by repeating steps 10 and 11. Record your observations in Table 19.1.

What is the effect of free Ca^+ on the solubility of phosphorus? Record you answer in Table 19.1.

17. Add 5 gm of soils labeled 1, 2, and 3 to three separate clean glass beakers.

Soil 1 is an acid sandy soil, soil 2 is a clay soil high in iron oxides, and soil 3 is a sandy soil high in humus or a calcareous soil with high pH.

18. Add 20 ml of 1 ppm phosphate solution to each beaker and mix by swirling intermittently for 10 minutes.

19. Filter the suspensions using clean filter paper for each. Collect 5 ml of each filtrate in 3 respective test tubes.

20. To a 4th test tube add 5 ml of the 1 ppm –P solution.

This will serve as a standard against which to judge the others.

21. Test for dissolved P as in steps 10 and 11 and record your results in Table 19.1.

Do the 3 soils have different P fixing powers? Explain the differences in Table 19.1.

EXERCISE 19
Behavior of Phosphorus and Nitrogen
In the Soil

Results and Conclusions

1. List 3 soil properties which affect P- fixation.

2. Briefly describe what management practices you could use to reduce P- fixation in various types of soils.

3. What are the implications of the first part of the exercise for the timing and placement of N and P fertilizers, respectively?

4. What are the implications of this exercise for the control of nutrient pollution of ground and surface water from agricultural fields?

5. How might $FeCl_3$ be used to reduce P pollution in sewage effluents?

Table 19.1 Results and Conclusions from N and P analyses.

Step in Procedure	Results and Observations	Comments, Explanations and Conclusions
6		
7		
12		
16		
21		

Exercise 20
Test for Plant–Available Soil Phosphorus

OBJECTIVES

After completing this exercise, you should be able to . . .

1. Explain the meaning of the terms "extractable-P" and "available-P".
2. Name two extractants used to determine available P and state under what soil conditions each is most appropriate.
3. Interpret the results of an available P determination, given the ranges of concentrations considered to be low, medium, and high.
4. Determine the P content of a solution using the spectrophotometer.
5. Calculate the available P content of a soil given the spectrophotometer reading, a standard curve, and the extraction procedure.

INTRODUCTION

Analysis to assess the nutrient supplying ability soil in a particular field or location is often called *soil testing*. Soil testing enables site-specific fertilizer recommendations to be made. This is of prime importance in the efficient use of soil and fertilizer resources and the production of high-yielding, healthy plants without causing water pollution from excessive nutrients. A fertilizer recommendation made in the absence of soil testing is likely to be uneconomic and wasteful.

The total amount of a nutrient element in a soil is a poor guide to the amount of that nutrient that the soil can supply to plants. Most of the nutrient content of the soil will be in complex forms, such as rock minerals, organic matter, or insoluble precipitates. Plants are unable to utilize nutrients in such forms. Plants depend upon simple nutrient ions in solution. Soil tests therefore try to assess how much of a nutrient is likely to be released in soluble forms during a growing season. The chemical tests are designed to mimic the plant root in extracting nutrients from the soil. A good soil test is one that measures a portion of the soil's supply of a nutrient corresponding to, or correlated with, that portion which would be available to plants. Much research goes into developing appropriate soil tests and relating the results of laboratory tests to the response to fertilizers shown by plants in the field.

In this exercise you will carry out a typical soil testing procedure to determine the availability of the nutrient, phosphorus, in a soil. Phosphorus and potassium are the two fertilizer elements most commonly tested for in soil testing labs. On the basis of these tests, the likelihood of a profitable response to the application of P or K fertilizers can be predicted. Most soil tests, like the one outlined in this exercise, consist of two basic steps: the extraction step and the chemical analysis step. In the extraction step, a soil sample is shaken with a reagent – the soil test extractant—that has been formulated to dissolving those forms of the element which would be likely to be dissolved and taken up by plant roots over the course of an entire growing season.

If a very low amount of P is extracted from a soil, then plants will likely be deficient in P when grown in that soil and a good response to added P fertilizer would be expected. Conversely, a soil testing high in P would be expected to keep plants well supplied with that element and a positive response to fertilizing with additional P is unlikely.

A number of different extractants have been developed for testing soil P. In this exercise you will use one of two common extractants -- either 0.5 M NaHCO$_3$ (known as the bicarbonate or Olsen extractant) *or* a mixture of 0.05 M HCl + 0.0125 M H$_2$SO$_4$ (known as the Mehlich1 extractant). The former is most suitable for calcareous and slightly acid soils as unavailable Ca-phosphates are not much dissolved. The Mehlich1 method is most suitable for acid soils with iron- and aluminum-bound phosphates but is not suitable for calcareous soils because the acids would dissolve some Ca-phosphates that plants cannot readily use.

MATERIALS

- *Sodium bicarbonate solution: 0.5 M NaHCO$_3$ buffered at pH 8.5. Weigh 84.01 g NaHCO$_3$ (AR) into a 2 L volumetric flask. Dissolve in about 1800 mL distilled water. Adjust the pH to 8.5 using 1 M NaOH. Make up to volume. Store in plastic container with 3 drops chloroform added per 100 mL to discourage microbial growth. Check and adjust pH within 2 days of use.
- *Mehlich1 solution: 0.05 M HCl and 0.0125 M H$_2$SO$_4$. Add 1.33 mL conc. H$_2$SO$_4$ and 8.11 mL conc. HCl to 1.5 L distilled water. Dilute to 2.0 L with distilled water.
- sodium hydroxide (NaOH), 1 $\underline{M}$
- hydrochloric acid (HCl), 1 $\underline{M}$
- Ammonium paramolybdate (NH$_4$)$_6$Mo$_7$O$_{24}$ · H$_2$O: Dissolve 12.0 g of ammonium paramolybdate in 250 mL of distilled water. Dissolve 0.2908 g of potassium antimony tartrate (KSbO · C$_4$H$_4$O$_6$ · ½ H$_2$O) in 100 mL of distilled water. Add these dissolved reagents to 1 liter of 2.5 M H$_2$SO$_4$ (141 mL of concentration acid diluted to 1 liter), mix, and dilute to 2 liters. Keep cool in a dark glass bottle.
- Ascorbic acid reagent: Dissolve 1.320 g of ascorbic acid in 250 mL of the above ammonium paramolybdate solution, and mix. *This ascorbic acid reagent should be prepared as required because it does not keep more than 24 hrs.*
- activated charcoal powder specifically designated for P analysis (others may be contaminated with P)
- P-nitrophenol pH indicator (0.5% aqueous solution) in dropper bottle
- Stock phosphate solution (50 mg/L P): Dry a few grams of KH$_2$PO$_4$ (Potassium dihydrogen phosphate) in an oven at 60° C for at least one hour. Cool in desiccator. Weigh 0.2194 g dry KH$_2$PO$_4$ into a 1 L volumetric flask. Dissolve in distilled water. Add a few drops of conc. H$_2$SO$_4$ and 5 drops of toluene (to control microbes). Make up to volume with distilled water.
- Standard P solutions: Prepare standards by adding 0, 0.5, 1.0, 2.0, 5.0, 10, and 20 mL of the 50 mg/L stock solution to separate 50 mL volumetric flasks labeled 0, 0.5, 1.0, 2.0, 5.0, 10, and 20 mg/L P, respectively. Fill each flask to volume with extracting solution and cover and shake. Then proceed with step 4.
- volumetric flasks (50 mL and 25 mL)
- 120 to 150 mL disposable specimen container with screw on lid, suitable for shaking
- small disposable beaker (60 to 150 mL)
- mechanical shaker (optional)
- filter paper (Whatman 40 or 42) and funnels
- funnel rack or stand
- ½ teaspoon scoop
- pipettes (5 mL in 0.01 and 1 mL in 0.01)
- balance (± 0.01 g)
- wash bottle with distilled water
- spectrophotometer and cuvettes/tubes
- soil (air dried and passed through 2 mm sieve)
- graduated cylinder (100 mL)

---

* Only one of these is required, depending on the type of soil being tested. See text.

PROCEDURE

1. Weigh 2.5 g of air dry soil into a clean specimen container. Add ½ teaspoon of activated charcoal. Then add extracting solution (50 mL of sodium bicarbonate *or* 10 mL of Mehlich1, as specified by your instructor).

2. Tightly cover the container and shake for the required time (30 min. if sodium bicarbonate used, *or* 5 min. if Mehlich1 used).

3. Set up a filter funnel with filter paper and a clean beaker to catch the filtrate. Swirl the flask again and filter the contents. If the filtrate is not clear, re-filter with new paper and another ½ teaspoon charcoal.

4. Place a portion (aliquot) of the filtrate into a clean 25 mL volumetric flask. The size aliquot to use is 5 mL for sodium bicarbonate *or* 1 mL if Mehlich1.

5. Neutralize the aliquot as follows:
   - Add 2 drops of p-nitrophenol pH indicator to the flask and swirl.
   - *If* the aliquot with indicator is initially colorless, add 1 M NaOH dropwise with swirling until it turns yellow.
   - *If* the color of the aliquot with indicator is yellow, add 1 M HCl dropwise with swirling until color just disappears.

6. Bring the volume of the liquid in the 25 mL flask up to approximately half full with distilled water. Then pipette in 4.0 mL of the ascorbic acid reagent and swirl. Fill the flask just to the 25 mL mark with distilled water. Cover flask and shake well. (Do <u>not</u> use your finger to cover!) Allow to stand for 10 minutes.

7. Compare the blue color of your sample with that of the *highest standard* (also in 25 mL volumetric flask). *If* your sample's color is within the range of the standard colors, proceed with step 8. *If* your sample is a deeper blue, then it must be diluted before reading with the spectrophotometer: Using a clean 5 mL pipette, transfer 5 mL of the blue solution to a clean 50 mL volumetric flask and dilute up to the 50 mL mark with distilled water. Stopper and shake well. Proceed with step 8, but remember

COMMENTS

New disposable containers do not need to be washed. However, if glassware is used, it must be washed, rinsed with tap water, soaked for at least 1 hour in 1 M HCl (acid washed), and then double rinsed with distilled water. Detergents containing P should be avoided

The shaking time and proportions of soil to extracting solution must be correct for each method if the results are to be interpreted according to the guidelines given in Table 20.2.

With some soils, organic compounds may be extracted giving the extract a tea-like color. These colored compounds must be removed by the charcoal in order to avoid interference with the spectrophotometer reading.

Use a 5 mL or 1 mL pipette for accuracy. This aliquot should contain from 1 to 40 µg of P, depending on the availability of P in the soil used.

The P analysis procedure will only form the blue molybdate complex properly if the solution pH is near 7.0. The p-nitrophenol indicator is colorless in acid and yellow in alkaline solutions. Failure to neutralize the solution properly may give falsely high P readings or no reading at all.
Add the HCl cautiously if sodium bicarbonate extractant was used, since CO_2 will be produced and frothing may occur.

The molybdate forms a complex with dissolved $H_xPO_4^{-y}$ ions and this complex has a deep blue color when reduced by the ascorbic acid in the mixed reagent. The more P in the soil extract, the deeper the blue color. It takes about 20 minutes for the color to react to its full intensity, and it is stable for several hours thereafter.

The concentration of P in solution is linearly related to the absorbance or intensity of the blue color only over a certain range. It is not wise to extrapolate beyond the absorbance of the highest P standard, so, if necessary, your sample solution can be diluted by a factor of 10 to bring it within the range of the standard curve.

Indicated here if you used the 10x dilution:

to multiply your resulting concentration reading by 10.

8. Set up and calibrate the spectrophotometer as described in Appendix F. Set the wavelength for 882 nm. Construct a standard curve on Figure 20.1 from the absorbance readings corresponding to the concentration in each of the P standards. If these readings are not provided by the instructor, obtain them by carrying an aliquot of each standard solution through steps 5-9.

The standard curve is necessary to allow you to convert your absorbance readings to units of P concentration. The more P in the aliquot, the deeper the blue color formed and the more 882 nm wavelength light absorbed.

9. Rinse a spectrophotometer tube/cuvette with about 2 mL of your blue soil extract solution and discard the washings. Add more of your blue solution to make the tube/cuvette about 2/3 full. Wipe the sides of the tube/cuvette with a tissue.

Do not let the tube/cuvettes come in contact with each other, the bench or any surface that might cause abrasion or scratches.

10. Insert the tube/cuvette upright into the spectrophotometer, making sure the orientation is correct. Close the cover and read the absorbance and record it in Table 20.1.

P concentration is directly related to the absorbance of 882 nm light by the blue P-molybdate complex. If using a tube, be sure to align the mark on the tube with that on the machine. If using a square cuvette, make sure the clear sides are lined up with the light beam.

Calculation of Extractable P in Soil

$$\frac{\mu g\ P}{g\ soil} = \frac{x\ mL\ extractant}{2.5\ g\ soil} \times \frac{\mu g\ P}{mL\ extract} \qquad \text{Eq. 20.1}$$

Where x = 50 for sodium bicarbonate *or* x =10 for Mehlich1 and μg P/mL extract = mg/L interpolated from standard curve in Figure 20.1

Worked Example

Data: extractant used was sodium bicarbonate
P conc. from absorption reading and standard curve = 1.5 mg/L

$$\frac{\mu g P}{g soil} = \frac{50\ mL\ extractant}{2.5 g\ soil} \times \frac{1.5 \mu g\ P}{mL\ extract} = \frac{30 \mu g\ P}{g\ soil}\ or\ 30\ ppm\ in\ soil \qquad \text{Eq. 20.}$$

190

EXERCISE 20
Determination of Plant Available P

Results

Table 20.1. Data and results.

description of soil sampled:		
weight of soil extracted:		
extracting solution used:		
mL extracting solution used:		
aliquot analyzed (mL):		
absorbance reading for sample (indicate on Fig. 20.1)		
mg/L P in extractant (show extrapolation on Fig. 20.1)		
*μg/g P in soil (show calculations below)		

*Show calculations here:

Interpretation of Results

Table 20.2 Suggested guidelines for interpreting P soil test results. The guidelines have been developed from extensive experimental work correlating soil test P values with crop yields and P uptake.

Soil Test Result		Interpretation	
Olsen Bicarbonate	Mehlich1	P-supply	Fertilizer Response
	μg/g P in soil		
0-3	0-10	low	very likely
4-8	11-31	medium	likely
9-11	31-56	high	unlikely
11-20	56-100	very high	no response
> 20	> 100	excessive	pollution hazard

Indicate your interpretations by circling one term on each line:

| P supplying power of soil: | low | medium | high | v. high | excessive |

| Likelihood of response to P fertilization: | very likely | likely | unlikely | no response | pollution hazard |

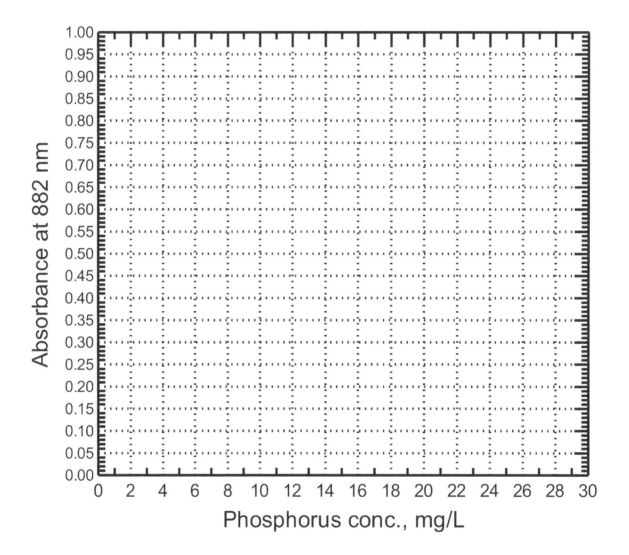

Figure 20. 1 Graph for plotting your P standard curve. Plot the absorbance readings for each of the standard P solutions and draw the best fit straight line through the data (or plot the regression equation of absorbance regressed on conc.) The plotted standard curve can then be used to estimate the P concentration in a soil sample extract solution from a sample absorbance reading.

Exercise 21
Simulated Wetland Soil Mesocosms
(Winogradsky Columns)

OBJECTIVES

After completing this exercise, you should be able to ...

1. List at least five chemical properties that change with depth and time in a homogenized water-saturated soil.
2. Describe *how* these chemical properties change with depth and time.
3. Explain *why* these chemical properties change with depth and time.
4. Describe what evidence you can see in the column for changes in microbial biochemical activity.
5. Explain the role of carbon in Winogradsky column changes.
6. Explain the role of sulfur in Winogradsky column changes.
7. Explain the role of iron in Winogradsky column changes.
8. Explain the role of light in Winogradsky column changes.
9. Interpret the color changes in a steel wire inserted in the column of saturated soil.
10. Relate your observations in the Winogradsky column to the functioning of a wetland.

INTRODUCTION

Wetlands are a very special landscape feature with characteristic types of plants, animals, microbes and soils. They provide many ecological services such as flood control, wildlife habitat and protection on water quality. Wetlands are environments that are saturated – or even inundated – with water while conditions are warm enough for microbes to be active. Wetlands are also characterized by the presence plant species adapted to growing in waterlogged soils. Finally, wetlands are, of course, also characterized by having wet soils, otherwise known as *hydric* soils.

Hydric soils are a special group of soils because they are water-saturated for so much at the time that molecular oxygen from the air is usually in very short supply or absent. In this sense, it is their lack of oxygen that makes these soil hydric, more so than just the fact that they are often very wet. For instance, if the soil is wet for period of time when temperatures are cold and microbial and plant root activity are minimal then the oxygen dissolved in the soil water will not get used up quickly and the system will remain aerobic or nearly so. But if a soil tends to be water-saturated for long periods when conditions are warm so microbes and plant roots are actively respiring, then the oxygen dissolved in the soil water will be used up very rapidly. Furthermore, because water is filling all the pores and because the rate of oxygen gas diffusion through water is about 10,000 times slower than it is through air, very little oxygen will diffuse into the soil to replace that which was used up in respiration. Therefore, under warm conditions, many soils will become devoid molecular oxygen within a day or so of the onset of waster-saturation water.

Lack of oxygen is obviously a problem for any organism which uses oxygen as its electron acceptor in the process of respiration, including plant root cells, fungi, and many types of bacteria. Under these conditions, what happens these organisms? Most of them will die, just as the humans would die if deprived of oxygen for more than a few minutes. Confronted with the existence of these conditions, certain microorganisms called facultative anaerobes have evolved the flexibility to change their metabolic chemical pathways in order to use elements other than oxygen to accept electrons. Many archaea and certain bacteria are adapted to life in an environment where oxygen is not present. Some use nitrate as their electron acceptor by reducing the nitrate ion (NO_3^-) to nitrogen gas (N_2) or to nitrous oxide (NO). The element iron (Fe) can exist oxidized and reduced states, so oxidized iron (Fe^{3+}) can accept an electron to form ferrous iron (Fe^{2+}). Manganese (Mn) can be reduced in a similar way. Carbon and sulfur can be reduced, as well, carbon is often reduced from a valence of zero or a negative valence in a compound like carbon dioxide or sugar and can be reduced to a negative valence in a compound such as methane, CH_4. Sulfate (SO_4^{-2}), an ion in which sulfur (S) has a +6 charge can be reduced to sulfide (S^{-2}), in which sulfur has -2 charge.

Oxygen most easily accepts electrons and will be used preferentially by organisms when it is present but when oxygen is depleted and cannot be replenished because pores are filled with water, the above-mentioned elements will be used sequentially, from nitrate which is the easiest to reduce to the most difficult to reduce, which is sulfate. These chemical changes have a profound influence on life and chemistry in the soil and environment. For example, when water contaminated with nitrate from septic systems or fertilizer may be stripped of potential pollutant as it moves through a wetland system on its way to a stream or river. Microorganisms in the wetland use the nitrate as an electron acceptor, reducing the N and turning the nitrate into nitrogen gases which are volatilized from the system. Beyond the importance of such ecological functions of hydric soils, these soils are especially fascinating objects of study because of the enormous diversity of microorganisms and chemical processes that occur within them. Many of these microorganisms and chemical pathways may be similar to those that existed a billion or more years ago when planet Earth did not yet have an oxygen rich atmosphere and was a very different place from what it is today.

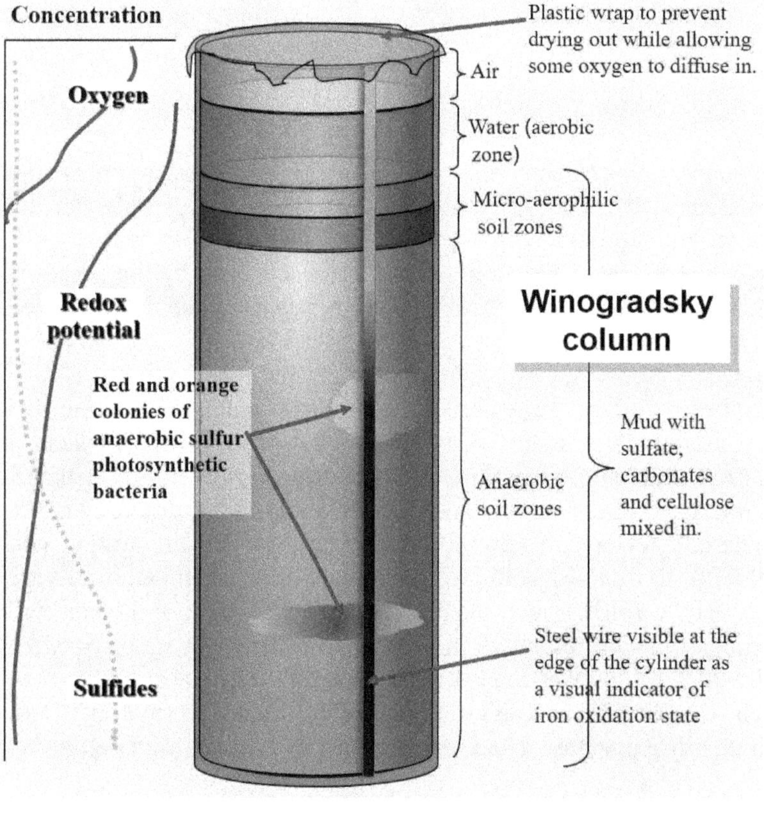

Figure 21.1 Conceptual illustration of Winogradsky column type water-saturated soil mesocosm several months after assembly. (Adapted from Weil and Brady (2017).

One way to study this kind of complex system, and even make some of these changes not only measurable but actually visible, is to create a mesocosm of a hydric soil. A mesocosm is a "cosm" or model system that is bigger than a microcosm (which might be the size of test tube) but not so large as a macrocosm (such as a field plot in a real wetland). Thus, a mesocosm is intermediate in size, usually less than 1 meter but more than a few cm across.

In this exercise we will construct a mesocosm of a wetland soil in order to observe what happens when a soil becomes inundated with water under conditions that allow for microbial growth. Our mesocosm will consist of a tall, narrow column about 25 cm tall and 5 to 10 cm across. Such a column was first used to study anaerobic microorganisms and processes in the 1880s by the pioneering Russian microbial ecologist and soil scientist, Sergei Winogradsky. To this day, such columns are often referred to as *Winogradsky columns.*

In our columns, we will manipulate and compare four environmental factors. The first is light, which allows the growth of photosynthetic bacteria and archaea and algae. We will compare mesocosms exposed to sunlight or kept in darkness. Second, we will manipulate the presence of oxidizable carbon which serves as the main energy source for most of the organisms in soils. We will do this by adding shredded plant material (cellulose as in newsprint paper). The CO_2 from calcium carbonate as well as that produced by fermentation of cellulose can then be used as an electron acceptor by methanogens (archaea) that convert the C^{+4} in CO_2 into the C^{-4} in methane (CH_4) gas. Third we will manipulate the amount of sulfur in the mesocosm. Sulfur is an element that is present in large amounts in sea water as the sulfate ion and therefore plays an important role in coastal wetlands such as tidal marshes. Sulfur can be used as an electron acceptor when it is reduced or as a source of energy when it is oxidized. Lastly, we will observe the effect of adding to the column a small amount microbial inoculant - soil from an established wetland. The purpose of this addition to ensure that a wide range anerobic microorganisms are present from the start.

Although you will thoroughly mix the ingredients so the soil in the column will initially be uniform, over a period of weeks and months vertical gradients of various chemical properties will develop due to the combination of diffusion of ions and gases up or down the column and the production or consumption of specific chemicals by certain microorganisms that thrive only under the conditions found in specific layers. In this way the ecosystem will become stratified (vertically differentiated) within the column. The resulting zones can be seen with the naked eye because of variations in the colors of the microbes and the inorganic compounds they produce. In this lab activity, you will set up four Winogradsky column mesocosms using the same natural non-hydric soil to illustrate different types of microbial metabolism in a colorful way. At the end of the incubation period, you will disassemble the column, sample the soil from the different layers and measure various characteristics.

MATERIALS

- Bulk soil collected from the topsoil (A horizons) of one or more pedons of interest. Collect 2 L of bulk soil per column to provide about 1.2 L of sieved soil per column. Collect enough of one soil to make four columns, or multiples of four (4, 8, 12) columns. Crumble the collected soil, if necessary, allow it to partially air-dry until easily sieved through large mesh (~4 mm). After sieving, completely air-dry the soil at room temperature under fan air circulation.
- Coarse mesh (4 mm) sieve (for sieving soil, above)
- Fresh soil from a saturated wetland or sediment from a pond. Stir to make a slurry and refrigerate in covered container for up to 2 weeks. Collect enough to add 100 mL of this wetland soil slurry as an anaerobic organism inoculum to every fourth column.
- Calcium sulfate 10 g per column treated
- Finely shredded nonglossy newspaper, 10 g per column treated. Other dry, ground plant material will also work.
- Columns (closed at one end, open at the other, approximately 22 -30 cm tall x 6 - 8 cm across). One option is to cut the top off of a 1.5 Liter Polyethylene Square Beverage Bottle (e.g. https://www.usplastic.com/catalog/item.aspx?itemid=124924 for about $1 each) to make a square column about 22 cm tall and 8 cm wide. Note that while round bottles are satisfactory, the straight flat sides of a square bottle facilitate observation and photography without reflections. Multiples of four (4, 8, 12, or 16) columns should be used in a class (at least one for each treatment), but each pair of students needs to make only one.
- Water. If municipal tap water is used, it should be allowed to degas chlorine for 24 hours in a wide mouth open container.

- Balance capable of weighing in 10 g to 0.01 g
- Large (2 to 4 quart) bowl for mixing
- A large wooden kitchen spoon or spatula to mix soil and water into a smooth slurry.
- Piece of aluminum foil sized to wrap certain columns to prevent light penetration.
- Piece of plastic wrap to cover the column top to be held in place with a rubber band.
- Rubber bands to hold in place the plastic wrap cover and aluminum foil, if present.
- Permanent marker
- Ruler marked in cm (to 30 cm)
- A stiff straight uncoated steel wire cut 1 cm less than the height of the column to be used. The wire staff from a survey flag works best, but you can cut a straight piece of wire coat hanger. Be sure to use steel wool or sandpaper to remove any coating on the wire so shiny steel is exposed.
- Stainless steel long (640 mm) handled 75 mL (3 oz) ladle (64 mm diameter) (e.g. https://www.amazon.com/meekoo-Stainless-Pouring-Kitchen-Cooking/dp/B0811NW9VL/ref=psdc_289765_t2_B001VZAWQU?th=1) for scooping layers of mud from completed column.
- pH meter and electrode (combination glass electrode with calomel reference electrode) and calibration buffers. See the instrument and calibration buffers used for Exercise 14.
- EC meter and probe. Inexpensive pocket EC meters are available that read in Siemens or ppm.
- 100 mL beakers (5 per mesocosm)
- Optional: platinum electrode and Ag-AgCl reference electrode for measuring Eh (redox potential). Different electrodes may require various calibration standards and storage solutions. Measuring Eh in soil solutions can be complicated and subject to drift and other effects.

Mesocosm setup

PROCEDURE

1. Be sure you are starting with a clean, clear, straight-sided plastic bottle at least 25 cm tall. To make an open-top column carefully cut the top off where the bottle begins to narrow.

2. Label your column near the top with the date, your name, the soil used, and the treatment ID from table 21.1. If you are working alone, you should make five columns, one with each of the set of amendments/conditions listed. If you are working in a class, your instructor may assign a particular treatment to you while ensuring that a set of all five mesocosm conditions are available for comparison.

3. Using a permanent marker, make a lines on your column to indicate 20 cm and 22 cm from the bottom.

4. Place this soil into a large (4-liter size) bowl and add water slowly, a few mL at a time, with stirring. Add the water very slowly, allowing each addition to thoroughly soak in before stirring and adding more water. Try to avoid lumps. Continue until you have made a thick, muddy slurry that can just barely be poured.

5. For mesocosms labeled as WC, WCS, WCSI, or WCSIL to be amended with carbon (C), add 10 g of dry, finely-shredded newspaper or ground dried leaves.
   For the mesocosms labeled as WCS WCSI, or WCSIL to be amended with sulfur (S) add 10 g of calcium sulfate (gypsum) powder.
   For mesocosms labeled as WCSIL to be amended with inoculum (L) consisting of fresh wetland soil, add 100 mL of saturated wetland soil slurry.

   Stir your soil slurry with a wooden spoon or stirring stick to uniformly mix in the selected amendment(s).

COMMENTS

Avoid bottles with ridges or curved sides. In particular, remove any wrappers from your bottle if is a used drink container. Hint: To begin the cut, try poking a small horizontal slit in the bottle with a sharp pointed knife, then use scissors to cut the top off evenly. USE CARE TO AVOID INJURY FROM THE KNIFE OR SCISSORS

Table 21.1 Labels for mesocosm treatments. Note that all five system are to be kept inundated and saturated with water.

Environmental factors (amendments) applied	Trt ID
No amendments	W
Carbon	WC
Carbon + Sulfate	WCS
Carbon + Sulfate + Inoculum	WCSI
Carbon + Sulfate + Inoculum + Light	WCSIL

You will need enough air-dry, sieved (< 4mm) soil to fill the column 20 cm deep (about 1200 cm^3 of sieved soil).

Generally, the more clay in your soil, the more time and effort it will take to make a uniform slurry. Consider this a great opportunity to observe how soil and water interact. Notice how the slightly moist soil may be crumbly. As the soil gains moisture, it may become malleable and plastic and then sticky. Finally, with enough water absorbed, the soil will begin to behave like a thick viscous liquid.

Table 21.2 Amendments to add to each mesocosm treatment.

Trt label	Add
W	nothing
WC	10 g shredded newspaper
WCS	10 g shredded paper + 10 g calcium sulfate
WCSI	10 g shredded paper + 10 g calcium sulfate + 100 mL fresh wetland soil slurry
WCSIL	10 g shredded paper + 10 g calcium sulfate + 100 mL fresh wetland soil slurry

6. Pour this slurry into the column until the slurry is 20 cm deep, leaving 3 to 4 cm headspace at the top. Stir out any visible air bubbles using a long handled wooden spoon or stick. Then let the soil settle or 15 minutes.

After the soil slurry has settled, there may be a layer of water on top of the soil. If this layer of water is less than 2 cm thick, slowly add enough water to make a layer 2 cm thick on top of the soil

7. Obtain one straight piece of uncoated steel wire that is 1 cm shorter than the cutoff bottle. Insert this wire along the inside edge of the bottle so that it is visible along its entire length.

You may have to remove the wire and try a few times to get it right up against the edge of the column, so it is visible.

8. Finally, cover the open top of the column with a single layer of plastic "Saran" wrap and hold it in place with a rubber band.

9. For all mesocosms not labeled as WCSIL, wrap the entire column from the water line down with aluminum foil to prevent light penetration from the sides. Hold the foil in place with two or three rubber bands.

10. Incubate the mesocosms standing upright where the temperature will remain above 20°C (70°F) to encourage microbial activity. Take care not to spill any water or shake the mesocosms. The mesocosm without aluminum foil covering (abled WCSIL) should also be labeled with ☼ on one side and incubated with that side exposed to strong light (but not direct sunlight).

Periodic Observations

11. Observe and photograph the mesocosms at least four somewhat evenly-spaced times over a period of 8 to 12 weeks (for example, after 2, 5, 8 and11 weeks of incubation). To observe the WCSIL mesocosm, turn it so you are observing the side that was facing the light and marked with ☼. For the aluminum foil wrapped mesocosms, carefully remove the rubber bands and aluminum foil to allow observation of the full length of the soil incubated in the dark.

Check for any visible changes in colors or consistency of the soil that indicate the development of distinct layers or zones. Remove the plastic wrap covering briefly and waft the air towards your nose to detect any odors.

Once constructed, the Winogradsky column mesocosms can be kept for months to years. The microbial communities can slowly change making them interesting to continually observe over time. Be sure to keep the mesocosms covered plastic wrap and maintain the 2 cm layer of water on top.

Tip: For best photography, place you mesocosm in an area of bright light and wipe the sides clean with a cloth. If your column has flat sides, take the photo perpendicular to one of the flat sides. Position the bottle and light source in such a way as to avoid seeing glare and reflections on the side of the bottle. If you have access to a camera with filters, the use of a polarizing lens filter can

Record a summary of what you observed (colors, shapes, odors) in the appropriate blank mesocosm column in Figure 21.4.

12. Observe and record in Figure 21.4 the colors along the length of the steel wire.

13. After making your observations, photograph the most interesting side of the mesocosm. Save these photos with a file name indicating the date and the mesocosm treatment.

14. Add de-chlorinated water if needed to maintain a 2 cm thick layer of water on the top of the mesocosm. Replace the plastic wrap cover to prevent the mesocosm from drying out.

15. At the end of the incubation period, after making the above observations, you will take apart the columns and sample the muddy soil as described below.

eliminate glare and show the colors in the soil more clearly.

The patterns and colors that slowly emerge in each mesocosm depend on its soil, amendments, and incubation conditions. Three major zones may become distinguishable: an aerobic zone, in which O_2 diffuses through the overlying water and a few mm into the soil; a microaerophilic zone where oxygen is not completely depleted and nitrates, sulfates, and oxidized iron are present; and a reduced zone near the bottom where ammonium, sulfide, and reduced iron are evident. Each zone is habitat for specific microorganisms. Algae and cyanobacteria (prokaryotic photoautotrophs) may be present in the aerobic zone near the top. In the anaerobic zone, denitrifiers and sulfate reducers may produce nitrogen gasses and hydrogen sulfide. Chemoautotrophs may dominate the foil-wrapped dark mesocosms, while in mesocosms receiving light anaerobic photoautotrophs may live. This zone also supports methanogens and fermenters (alcohol producers).

Mesocosm Take-Down, Sampling and Measurements

16. On the date of the last observation, before disturbing the mesocosm, use a marker pen to circle and label any features that you can see where the column of soil has changed over time. These will be areas you will want to identify and include when you collect samples. Take a new set of photos that include your markings.

17. Based on Figure 21.2, use a ruler to mark the upper and lower boundaries of layers A – E. If a boundary runs right through a feature of interest, you may want to adjust the boundary depths up or down a little so that different visible features are captured in different sampled layers.

18. Once you are ready to disassemble and sample the mesocosm, first pull the steel wire up and out of the column. Observe and record in Table 21.3, the colors along the length of the wire. Wipe the different colors with a paper towel. Record whether they wipe off or not.

19. Label five clean, graduated 100 mL beakers with the mesocosm treatment code (see Table 21.1) and layer (A-E) as shown in Figure 21.2.

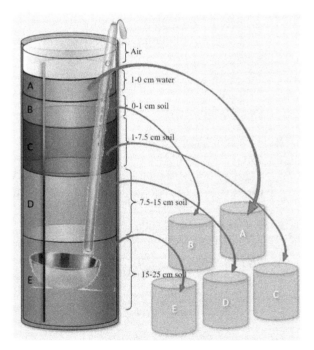

Figure 21.2 Scheme for transferring samples from five layers of mesocosm soil into labeled beakers for analysis.

199

20. Next, slowly, and carefully, without disturbing the muddy soil, pour off and collect some of the overlying water layer into beaker A so that the 100 mL beaker is about one third full.

21. Next, slowly, and carefully, without disturbing the muddy soil, pour off and collect some of the overlying water layer into beaker A so that the 100 mL beaker is about one third full.

22. Use a long-handled ladle (as used for soup) to carefully dig up mud from the top 0-2.5 cm layer and place about 30 mL of it into a second labeled beaker (B). With minimal disturbance to the layer below, remove the remainder of the 0-1 cm layer and discard the material in a waste container.

23. Then ladle out a sample of the muddy soil from the 1-7.5 cm layer into a third beaker (C). Again, with minimal disturbance to the layer below, remove the remainder of the 1=7.5cm layer and discard the material in a waste container.

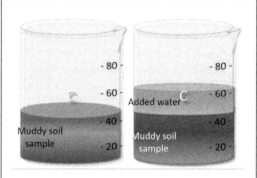

Figure 21.3 Illustration of sampling, dilution

24. Repeat step 24 for the last two layers (D) and (E). You should end up with a total of 1 beaker of water and 4 beakers of muddy soil from each mesocosm examined. The soil samples you have collected should be saturated with water, containing about equal amounts of soil solids and water.

25. Once more, record in Table 21.3 the colors of the muddy soil in each beaker.

26. To each sample add an additional distilled water equal to 50% of the sample volume, as shown in Figure 21.3. Stir each beaker gently three or four times to mix and let the soil settle for 5 minutes.

27. For samples A-E measure the pH and EC using the appropriate sensors. Immerse each sensor in the supernatant water, not the settled soil (see Figure 21.4, right). Use Table 21.3 to record the measured pH and EC values in the appropriate columns for each layer of your mesocosm.

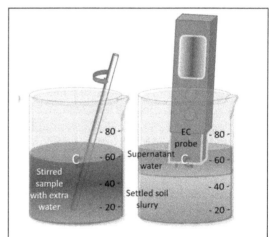

Figure 21.4 Illustration of gently stirring the added water with the sampled soil from mesocosm layer C and measurement of EC in the sample using a pocket EC meter. Note that **the pH and EC sensors should be immersed in the supernatant water, NOT in the settled soil** slurry.

28. Finally, bring each beaker slowly toward your nose and record the type and strength of odor.

29. Complete all 25 rows of data in Table 21.3 using the data that you and your classmates have collected.

EXERCISE 21

Simulated Wetland Soil Mesocosms (Winogradsky Columns)

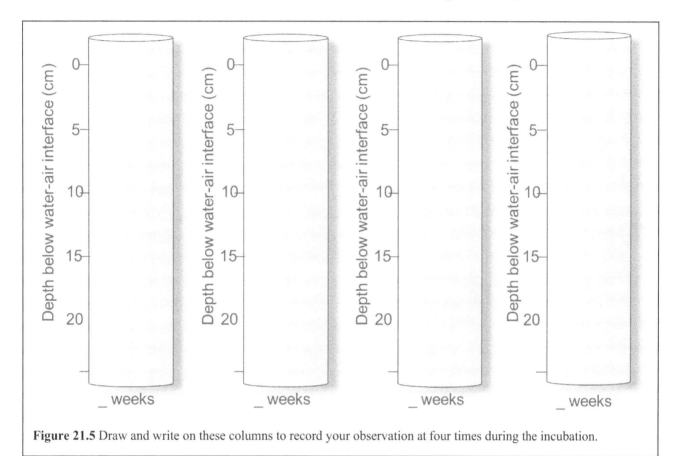

Figure 21.5 Draw and write on these columns to record your observation at four times during the incubation.

Questions

1. Using the data in Table 21.3 that you and your classmates collected from all five types of mesocosms, explain how the different mesocosm treatments differed? In what ways were they similar? Explain the differences in the data.

201

2. Describe and explain changes that occurred over time. When did you first observe specific features? Explain here and draw in Figure 21.5.

3. Winogradsky columns form oxygen concentration gradients. Predict the distribution of oxygen throughout the column. Consider the entire column: the soil, the water, and the air. Draw a graph to show this.

4. Winogradsky columns form sulfide - sulfate concentration gradients as sulfate is reduced to sulfide or sulfide is oxidized to sulfate. In the columns that contain added gypsum (calcium sulfate), predict how sulfides and sulfates will be distributed throughout the column. Consider the entire column: the sediment, the water, and the air. Show this using a graph.

5. In which of the various layers and mesocosm treatments would you be likely to find photosynthetic organisms such as cyanobacteria and algae? Explain why. Describe evidence, if any, that you observed that suggest the presence of such organisms.

Table 21.3 Evaluation data for soil and water layers in mesocosms at end of incubation period. Circle which mesocosm (W, WC, WCS, WCSI, WCSIL) was made and evaluated by you (as opposed to by your classmates). *All five* mesocosms evaluated in the table should use the same soil. Identify the soil used here: _____ _____

Meso-cosm ID	Layer	Depth cm	Odor		Colors in soil[c]	Steel wire color[d]	pH	EC dS/m	Eh[e] mV
			Type[a]	Strength[b]					
W	A	1-0[e]							
W	B	0-1							
W	C	1-7.5							
W	D	7.5-15							
W	E	15-22							
WC	A	1-0[d]							
WC	B	0-1							
WC	C	1-7.5							
WC	D	7.5-15							
WC	E	15-22							
WCS	A	1-0[d]							
WCS	B	0-1							
WCS	C	1-7.5							
WCS	D	7.5-15							
WCS	E	15-22							
WCSI	A	1-0[d]							
WCSI	B	0-1							
WCSI	C	1-7.5							
WCSI	D	7.5-15							
WCSI	E	15-22							
WCSIL	A	1-0[d]							
WCSIL	B	0-1							
WCSIL	C	1-7.5							
WCSIL	D	7.5-15							
WCSIL	E	15-22							

[a] Earthy (E); Metallic (M); Rotten egg odor from sulfides (S); other: _____

[b] **strong (2)** = smells 20cm away from nose, **weak (1)** = smells only if nose almost touching soil; **absent (0)**

[b] Munsell codes for matrix and other colors. See Exercise 03.

[c] rusty-red/orange (R), black/blue (B), Gray-metallic (G)

[d] 1-0 cm refers to the layer of water just above the soil.

[e] Optional if equipment is available

Appendix A
Obtaining a Representative Soil Sample for Analysis

While chemical and physical analyses are always subject to some variation, by far the greatest potential source of error in most soil analysis projects is the *sampling* of the soil, not the lab analysis. Most lab tests use only a teaspoonful or less of soil. This tiny amount of soil is supposed to represent the thousands or millions of kilograms of soil in a plot, backyard, farm field or other site! Since soil fertility or other chemical properties may vary greatly from spot to spot, even within a small site, it is imperative that great care be taken to ensure that the sample of soil used for the soil analysis is truly representative of the entire area in question.

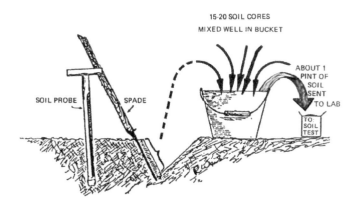

Figure A.1 Obtaining a soil sample with a spade or coring device.

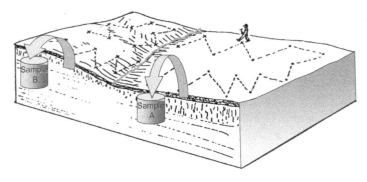

Figure A.2 Collecting soil cores from many random locations in a field.

A sample obtained from just one location in a field or garden may result in management recommendations that are inappropriate for the field or garden as a whole. A proper, representative sample should be a composite of small sub-samples taken from 15-20 locations and mixed well. About ¼ liter of this mixed soil is usually enough to be kept for analysis, the remainder being discarded in the field.

Each of the sub-samples that went into the composite mixture should be a uniform slice of soil (Figure A.1) from the surface down to whatever depth is being studied. It is important that each subsample include the same exact depth of soil. For example, for a sample taken to guide fertility management, the sample depth should correspond to the depth that fertilizer is apt to be mixed into the soil (10 cm for lawns and pastures; plow depth or spading depth in field or gardens). The boundaries of natural horizons in the soil profile (such as A, E and B horizons) should also be considered in choosing a soil sampling depth.

A separate composite sample should be obtained from each area that is obviously different on the basis of soil conditions, and/or past management, provided each area sampled separately could also be managed or studied separately. Note that the field shown in Figure A.2 has been divided into two sampling areas, one on the slope and one on the level ground. By the same token, a homeowner would obtain separate composite samples from such different areas as the front lawn, the back lawn, a flower bed, and the vegetable garden.

It is advantageous to use a high-quality soil probe that has a cutting edge designed to cut an uncompressed cylindrical core of soil (Figure A.3). If the depth of each core is carefully measured and the number of cores collected is carefully counted, the total weight of the combined cores (before subsampling and discarding the bulk of the sample), along with a determination of the water content, can be used to calculate the bulk density of the soil as it was in the field. This value of bulk denisty will allow the analytical results to be converted from a mass fraction (e.g. μg/g) to a mass per volume or mass per area (e.g. g/m^3 or kg/ha).

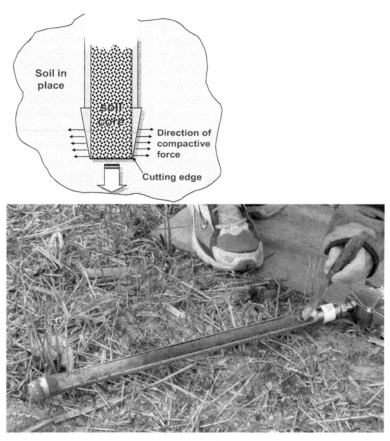

Figure A.3 (*upper*) Cross-section of a soil probe cutting tip designed to avoid compaction of the soil sample core. (*bottom*) An open-sided soil probe used for obtaining composite soil samples consisting of many uniform, non-compacted soil cores. The core shown will be cut into two 15 cm long cores, representing the 0 to 15 cm and 15 to 30 cm depths.

Appendix B

Water Needed to Bring Soil to 60% of Saturation for Aerobic Incubation

PROCEDURE

1. As you follow this procedure, enter your data in Table B.1. Rows *A* and *B* in Table B.1 are to be filled in with data from exercise 15.
2. Weigh a clean small beaker. Enter the weight in row *C*.
3. Add a scoop (about 10 g) of the soil in question to the beaker. The soil should be in the same condition (e.g. air "dry") and packed in the same manner as it will be when used for the experiment.
4. Weigh the beaker + soil. Enter in row *D*.
5. Then add water drop-wise, using a dropping pipette (or "eye- dropper"). Let each drop soak in before adding then next drop.
6. Stop adding water as soon as the soil becomes saturated. The soil is saturated when the next drop of water does not soak in and the soil glistens with water. Do *not* add more water than this.
7. Weigh the beaker of saturated soil. Enter weight in row *E*.
8. Record all weights in Table B.1 and calculate the amount of water needed to bring 1 g of the soil in question to 60% saturation.

Table B.1 Determination of amount of water needed to bring soil to 60% saturation.

Line	Parameter		Soil ID___	Soil ID___
A	Empty incubation container, g			
B	Incubation container + "dry" soil[*] and amendments[**], g			
C	Clean small beaker, g			
D	Beaker + "dry" soil, g			
E	Beaker + saturated soil, g			
F	Water needed to bring 1 g "dry" soil to 60% saturation, mL:	$F = \dfrac{E-D}{D-C} \times 0.60$		
G	Water to bring amount of soil used for incubation to 60% saturation, mL:	$G = F \times (B-A)$		

[*] Negligible water is assumed to exist in the "dry" soil; however this procedure and calculation will also work if the initial soil is somewhat moist.
[**] Determine amount of water needed for each soil treatment seperately if the amounts of soil differ or if the soil is amended with materials that may absorb more or less water than the soil itself.

Appendix C
Available Water Holding Capacity Based On Soil Texture

Table C.1 Maximum Amounts of Available Water Held by Soils of Various Textures[*]

Texture	Available Water		Texture	Available Water	
	inches H_2O / inch soil	cm H_2O / cm soil		inches H_2O / inch soil	cm H_2O / cm soil
Sand	0.04	0.04	Sandy Loam	0.12	0.12
Loamy Sand	0.07	0.07	Loam	0.13	0.13
Sandy Clay Loam	0.10	0.10	Silty Clay Loam	0.14	0.14
Sandy Clay	0.10	0.10	Clay Loam	0.14	0.14
Silty Clay	0.11	0.11	Silt Loam	0.18	0.18
Clay	0.11	0.11	Silt	0.18	0.18

[*]These estimates are for temperate region soils with primarily layer-silicate type clays. Soils high in organic matter will usually hold somewhat more moisture than indicated here.

Table C.2 Categories for Interpretation of Available Water Holding Capacities

Category	Available Water in Root Zone[*]	
	inches	cm
Very Low	< 2	< 5
Low	2-4	5-10
Medium	4-6	10-15
High	> 6	> 15

[*]Rooting depth for corn is considered 36" (90 cm). Approximate rooting depths for some other crops grown on uniform medium texture well drained soils are as follows (in cm): alfalfa—150; beans—50; carrots—50; cotton—100; deciduous orchards—100; grass—50; potatoes—40; soybeans—60; sunflower—80; tomatoes—70; wheat—100.

Worked Example

Soil Depth	Texture	Available Moisture (cm)
0-20 cm	Silt Loam	$\dfrac{0.18\ cm.^*\ H_2O}{cm\ soil} \times 20\ cm\ soil = 3.6\ cm\ H_2O$
20-60 cm	Silty Clay Loam	$\dfrac{0.14\ cm\ H_2O}{cm\ soil} \times 30\ cm\ soil = 4.2\ cm\ H_2O$
60-120 cm	Sandy Clay	$\dfrac{0.10\ cm\ H_2O}{cm\ soil} \times 30\ cm\ soil^{**} = 3.0\ cm\ H_2O$

*from Table C.1
**Only the 60-90 cm depth is considered to be within the root zone of corn. Other root zone depths may be appropriate for other plants.

Total available moisture in 90 cm depth of soil $= 3.6 + 4.2 + 3.0 = 10.8$ cm H_2O. This is in the medium category (see Table C.2).

Appendix D
Determination of Soil Moisture Content (θ_m)

PROCEDURE	COMMENTS
1. Weigh a clean, dry, <u>labeled</u> container. Record the empty (tare) weight to 0.01 g. If you will sample soil in the field, be sure that the container can be closed with a moisture tight seal. Include the cover, if any, in your tare weight.	**Important:** If you will be drying the soil in a microwave oven be sure to use a microwaveable container made of polypropylene, Pyrex glass or other microwave-transparent material. This container should be about twice as tall as wide, and should be large enough so that it is only 1/3 full with 25 g of soil. If you will use a conventional oven, be sure to use a container that can withstand at least 110 °C, such as metal or Pyrex glass.
2. Place approximately 25 g (20 cm^3) of soil loosely into the tared container. If sampling in the field, immediately seal the container. Record the container label and soil sample description. Weigh the container with soil as soon as possible. Record the weight of "container + fresh soil" to 0.01 g.	Work quickly as the soil may rapidly lose moisture once disturbed. For a sealed container, speed is not so critical because moisture evaporating from the soil will condense on the inside of the container and will be included in the weight recorded.
3. Place the open container of soil in an oven to dry. For a **microwave** **oven**, set the control to "high" (about 850 Watts output) for 5 minutes, and then stir each sample and microwave for one or two additional 3 minute doses. Weigh the sample. Repeat microwaving and stirring for additional 3 minute exposures until weight is constant. Be sure not to lose any soil on the stirring rod. Go to step 4. For a **conventional** **oven**, set the temperature for 65 °C for 24 h, followed by 105 °C for 2 h.[1]	If the container has a cover, be sure to remove the cover and place it next to or under the container so the soil and inside of the cover can dry. If you have more than one container, be sure that each cover stays with its own container. The times given at left are only a guide. When using a microwave oven, the time needed will depend on initial sample wetness and total weight of samples in the oven. Use fewer and shorter microwave exposures for less soil.
4. Remove the dried sample from the oven and place in a desiccator to cool to room temperature. Then re-weigh the container of soil, including the cover, if any. Record to 0.01 g as "container + dry soil".	The sample must be cooled before obtaining the final weight because a warm sample will create updrafts that interfere with accurate weighing. The desiccator is needed because a dry soil left in humid air will absorb moisture and not remain dry. You can demonstrate this by weighing an oven dry soil sample on a balance capable of resolving 0.0001 g. The balance reading will continuously increase as the soil absorbs moisture from the air.

---

[1] Some procedures call for 24 to 48 h at 105 ° C to oven-dry soil. However, at such a high temperature, if much organic matter is present in the sample, a significant amount of mass may be lost due to oxidation of the organic matter. This loss would appear as water loss and would lead to over estimation of the moisture content.

5. Calculate the moisture content of the original soil sample as follows:

$$\text{Soil water content by weight } (\theta_m) = \frac{(\text{container} + \text{fresh soil}) - (\text{container} + \text{dry soil})}{(\text{container} + \text{dry soil}) - \text{container}}$$

6. Once the soil water content by weight (θ_m) has been determined as in steps 1-5, above, then a **moisture correction factor** (MCF) can be calculated as the g moist soil per g dry soil:

$$MCF = (100 + \% \text{ soil water content}) / (100)$$

7. It is customary to express analytical results in terms of concentrations per unit dry soil. If the soil sample weighed out is not actually oven dry (that is, it contains some water), then it is necessary to multiple the analytical result by a moisture correction factor in order to express the result in terms of dry soil.

For example, consider an analytical result for carbon (C) in soil of 10.0 g of C in a 125 g sample of moist soil. The C concentration in the moist sample is 10/125 =0.080 g/g. However, if the moist soil was at 25% water content (θ_m), the 125 g sample would have consisted of 25 g water + 100 g dry soil. Remember that for soil, the percent water content is the g water / 100 g dry soil. The MCF for this sample would be 1.25 [(100 + 25)/100]. The C concentration in the *dry* soil could therefore be calculated using this MCF as follows:

$$\frac{0.080 \text{ g C}}{\text{g moist soil}} \; x \; \underbrace{\frac{1.250 \text{ g moist soil}}{\text{g dry soil}}}_{MCF} = \frac{0.100 \text{ g C}}{\text{g dry soil}}$$

Appendix E
Using Moles and Moles of Charge

One gram of hydrogen consists of 6.23×10^{23} atoms. This incredibly large number (something like a trillion trillion!) is known as Avogadro's Number and is the basis for the units of measurement by which chemists express the quantities of substances participating in a reaction. It is also the basis for the terms atomic weight, molecular weight and equivalent weight.

The *atomic weight* of an element is the weight (in grams) of 6.23×10^{23} atoms of that element. Similarly, the *molecular weight* of a substance (i.e., 1 mole of the substance) is the weight (in grams) of 6.23×10^{23} molecules of that substance. In addition to a mole of atoms or molecules, we may also speak of a mole of charges or a mole of electrons when describing reactions, such as cation exchange or oxidation-reduction reactions. The following provides some examples of this usage for the element calcium:

$$
\begin{aligned}
\text{atomic wt. of } Ca^{2+} \quad &= 40 \text{ g} \\
1 \text{ mole of } Ca^{2+} \quad &= 40 \text{ g} \\
1 \text{ mole of } charge \text{ from } Ca^{2+} \quad &= 40/2 = 20 \text{ g}
\end{aligned}
$$

An important concept to remember about cation exchange reactions is that 1 mole of *charge* from one substance is equivalent to, or will replace, 1 mole of *charge* from any other substance. A mole of positive charge is written: 1 mol(+).

Consider the reaction of hydrochloric acid with calcium carbonate:

$$ 2\,HCl + CaCO_3 \rightarrow CaCl_2 + H_2O + CO_2 $$

In the above reaction, 2 moles of H react with (are replaced by) 1 mole of Ca^{2+}. However, in terms of charges, 2 mol(+) from H are replaced by 2 mol(+) from Ca. This is true because each mole of Ca^{2+} provide 2 charges, so 1 mol(+) from Ca = ½ the molecular weight of Ca. Table A.1 gives some examples of the relationship between atomic or molecular weight and the weight of the substance that provides 1 mole of charges or 1 mole of electrons.

Table E.1 Relationship between formula weight and weight of a mole of charges.

Substance	Molecular or Atomic Wt. (g)	Valence		Wt. (g) of substance to provide 1 mole of + or − charge
H^+	1	1		1
K^+	39	1		39
Cl^-	35.5	1		35.5
Ca^{2+}	40	2		40/2 = 20
Al^{3+}	27	3		27/3 = 9
C^{4+}	12	4		12/4 = 3
CO_3^{2-}	60	2	$[Ca^{2+} + (CO_3)^{2-}]$	60/2 = 30
$FeSO_4$	152	2	$[Fe^{2+} + (SO_4)^{2+}]$	152/2 = 76
$K_2Cr_2O_7$	294	2	$[K_2^{2+} + (Cr_2O_7)^{2-}]$	294/2 = 147

According to the information given in Table E.1, the following reactions or replacements are balanced. Be sure that you understand why this is so in each case.

$$1 \text{ mol(+) } Ca^{2+} \leftrightarrows 1 \text{ mol(+) } H^+$$
$$1 \text{ mol(+) } Ca^{2+} \leftrightarrows 1 \text{ mol(+) } Al^{3+}$$
$$1 \text{ mol } Ca^{2+} \leftrightarrows 2 \text{ mol } H^+$$
$$3 \text{ ions } Ca^{2+} \leftrightarrows 2 \text{ ions } Al^{3+}$$

From Exercise 13:
$$2 \text{ mol } (C_{25}H_{30}N_3^+) \leftrightarrows 1 \text{ mol } Ca^{2+} \quad)$$

From Exercise 15:
$$1 \text{ mol(+) } CO_3^{2-} \leftrightarrows 1 \text{ mol(+) } C$$
$$40 \text{ g } Ca^{2+} \leftrightarrows 2 \text{ g } H^+$$
$$20 \text{ mg } Ca^{2+} \leftrightarrows 1 \text{ mg } H^+$$

From Exercise 17:
$$1 \text{ mol(-) } K_2Cr_2O_7 \leftrightarrows 1 \text{ mol(-) } C$$
$$147 \text{ g } K_2Cr_2O_7 \leftrightarrows 3 \text{ g } C$$
$$1 \text{ mol(-) } K_2Cr_2O_7 \leftrightarrows 1 \text{ mol(-) } CO_3^{2-}$$
$$1 \text{ mol(-) } K_2Cr_2O_7 \leftrightarrows 30 \text{ g } CO_3^{2-}$$

Using mol(+) to Express Charge Concentration or Cation Exchange Capacity (CEC) of Soils

The CEC of soil is expressed in terms of moles of charge per unit mass of soil. The Soil Science Society of America recommends the "Le Systems International d'Unites" (SI) be used to express CEC and other soil properties. In the SI system, CEC is expressed as moles of charge per kilogram. For small quantities, it may be more convenient to use units 1/1000 as large, namely millimol/kg. Although the traditional unit "milliequivalent" (m.e.) is not used in this system, to achieve values numerically the same as those in the traditional "m.e./100g" units, the SI unit "centimole/kilogram" (cmol/kg) is often used.

Thus, a soil may have a CEC of 8 centimoles of charge for every kg of dry soil. This is actually $0.08 \times 6.02 \times 10^{23}$ charges per kg of soil. One kilogram of this soil can hold 8 centimoles (+) of cations – it doesn't matter what cation species are involved. It could hold 8 cmol(+) of Al^{3+}, or 8 cmol(+) of Mg^{2+}, or 8 cmol(+) of Ca^{2+}, or 8 cmol(+) of K^+, or some combination such as 2 cmol(+) from each of these cations.

If 1 kg soil held 8 cmol(+) of Ca^{2+}, it would have 8×200 or 1600 mg of exchangeable Ca^{2+} per kg of soil. If the soil were "saturated" with Al^{3+} on the other hand, the 8 cmol(+) of Al^{3+} would represent $8 \times 90 = 720$ mg of exchangeable Al^{3+} per kg of soil. Therefore, in a cation exchange reaction 720 mg of Al^{3+} could replace 1600 mg of Ca^{2+}.

To review these concepts, be sure you understand why each of the following quantities is equivalent:

$$
\begin{aligned}
40 \text{ mg } Ca^{2+} \quad &= 0.001 \text{ mol } (Ca^{2+}) \\
&= 1 \text{ mmol } (Ca^{2+}) \\
&= 0.1 \text{ cmol } (Ca^{2+}) \\
&= 0.2 \text{ cmol } (1/2 \ Ca^{2+}) \\
&= 0.2 \text{ cmol(+)}
\end{aligned}
$$

Appendix F
Using the Spectrophotometer

The spectrophotometer is an instrument that measures the absorbance and transmittance of light through a solution. A colored ion in solution will absorb certain wavelengths of light more strongly than others. Using a system of filters or gratings, the wavelength of light in a spectrophotometer may be adjusted to correspond to that which is best absorbed by the substance in question.

The more concentrated the substance is in solution, the more light will be absorbed and the less will be transmitted. The relationship between absorption of light and concentration is described by Beer's Law.

$$I_t = I_o e^{-kcd}$$

where: I_o is the incident radiation
I_t is the transmitted radiation
k is a constant
c is the concentration
d is the path-length of light through the solution.

Thus,
$$\log I_t = \log I_o - kcd$$

and $\quad c = -K \log_{10} \dfrac{I_t}{I_o}$

where K is a constant for all solutions measured for the type of cuvette and instrument.

Definitions:
$$\dfrac{I_t}{I_o} = \text{transmittance}$$

and

$$-\log_{10} \dfrac{I_t}{I_o} = \text{absorbance}$$

Therefore, we see that concentration is directly related to the $-\log_{10}$ of the percent (%) transmittance. Over the range of concentrations for which Beer's law holds true, a graph of concentrations vs. the log of % transmittance should be a straight line. Logarithmic graph paper can be used instead of calculating the log of the transmittance. If regular graph paper is used, the plot of absorbance vs. concentration will yield a straight line since absorbance = the negative log of transmittance. Most spectrophotometers can give readings of absorbance.

These relationships are used to construct a standard curve. A series of solutions of known concentrations are run on the spectrophotometer and the resulting % transmittance or absorbance readings are graphed vs. the known concentrations. The % transmittance or absorbance measured for an unknown solution can then be converted into a concentration by extrapolating from the standard curve.

PROCEDURE

1. Set the wavelength to the desired wavelength of light (e.g., the Gentian violet dye in Exercise 15 absorbs strongly at 580 nm. The blue molybdate-phosphate complex absorbs strongly at 640 nm and the nitrate-salicylic acid complex absorbs best at 410 nm.).
2. Be sure that the instrument is turned on and has warned up.
3. With the cuvette holder empty (no light can be transmitted), adjust the low-end calibration until the % transmittance reads 0.
4. Insert a blank cuvette (distilled water or "zero" standard in a clean cuvette) into the cuvette holder. Many cuvettes have a mark indicating how they should be oriented in the holder. Close the cover and set the high-end calibration to get a reading of 100% transmittance or zero absorbance. Open the cover and remove the blank cuvette.
5. Insert your sample cuvette. This should be wiped clean with a soft towel or tissue before inserting. Close the cover and read the % transmittance or absorbance reading. Record.
6. Repeat steps 3 and 4 each day or before each new batch of samples are read.
7. Using readings from a series of 3 to 6 solutions of known concentrations, construct a standard curve. This "curve" may be either a plot on graph paper or a linear regression equation determined using a statistical calculator or a computer spreadsheet program.
8. From the standard curve or it regression equation, extrapolate the concentrations corresponding to the readings from your unknown samples. Some spectrophotometers can do the math internally and can be set to read out concentrations directly; however, to avoid errors, it is best to construct your own stanc

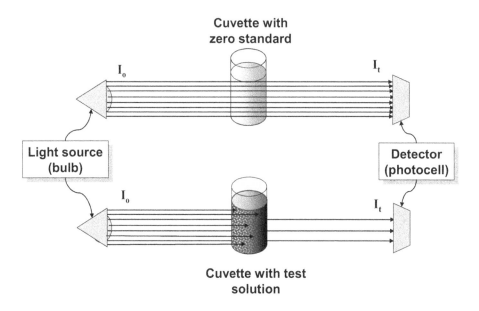

Figure F.1 Principle of the spectrophotometer.

Appendix G
Soil Characterization Project

1. Introduction.

- This cumulative project should result in your generation of practical information about a soil that is important to you. Choose an area to sample that is of interest to you personally, such as your home garden, a pasture near your home, a lawn you are caring for, or an environmental site you are studying. The only restriction is that the soil be *a natural mineral soil*, not an organic mulch or synthetic potting medium. The reason for this restriction is that many of the analyses you will perform are not designed to work with organic or soilless media such as peat or perlite mixes. As you will use the soil sample you obtain in numerous laboratory exercises throughout the semester, it will be worth your while to give some serious thought to the selection of the site and the method you will use to obtain the sample. At the end of the course, you will write a report that summarizes your characterization of this soil and draws conclusions from the data and compares it to class data, if available.
- Record relevant information about the site from which you obtained the soil sample by filling in Table G1 and making a sketch map of the site, showing the boundaries of the area represented by your sample and the relative locations of such features as roads, paths, buildings and trees.
- Tabulate your results in Table G2. Retain this table with your lab book so that they are convenient for recording the results throughout the semester. For each property measured, record the exercise No. from which you obtained the data and the units (if applicable). Also add a comment on how the data should be interpreted: Is this an unusually low or high value? Does the result indicate a need for management action or suggest an environmental problem?

2. Methods of soil sample collection.

- See Appendix A in this lab manual and Chapter 16 in Brady and Weil (2008) or Weil and Brady (2015) for information on properly obtaining a soil sample. Samples are usually taken from the surface of the mineral soil to a predetermined depth (usually 10 to 20 cm), however you may sample deeper soil layers from the wall of an excavation. Discuss with your instructor how and from what depth you should obtain your soil.
- It is best to obtain 15-20 soil cores from throughout the area sampled, then mix these cores thoroughly in a bucket, and finally place about 1 cupful a subsample into a plastic (or plastic lined) sample bag. Be sure to label the bag with the date, your name, and the sampled location and depth. This type of "composite sample" approximates an average of the area being studied. For this class, it may be acceptable to take fewer cores than normal (6-10), particularly if you are sampling with a spade or shovel in an area in which you do not want to leave many holes. If the ground is frozen, cores may be obtained with the help of a heavy rubber mallet.
- The best tool with which to obtain a soil sample is a soil probe that cuts a thin cylindrical core of soil that is slightly smaller in diameter than the inside of the probe. A spade or large knife can also be used. See your instructor if you need help obtaining a soil probe or spade for a short-term loan.
- Drying the soil sample will take about <u>2 days</u>, so plan ahead.
- Gently crumble the soil with your fingers and spread it out in a thin layer on some newspaper.
- Allow to dry and stir once a day. Do not heat or place in direct sunlight.
- A gentle breeze from a fan will speed the drying process so it may be complete overnight.
- Place the <u>dried</u> sample in a ziplock sandwich bag with your name and sample date and location. Bring this into the lab for processing. You will need it for many of the lab exercises. It must be ground for most lab determinations. See your instructor about how to grind and sieve your soil.
- Remember to fill in all of the items in Table G1 when you collect your soil sample, and bring the completed table into class with the soil sample.

Date _____   Name _____

Section _____   I.D. No. _____

Appendix G
My Soil and Its Properties

KEEP THIS FORM IN A SAFE PLACE AS YOU ACCUMULATE DATA TO FILL IT IN.

Table G1. General information on soil sample.

Date Sampled	
Sample Depth (cm)	
Location of site	
Site Description	
1. Current Land Use	
2. Vegetation	
3. Past Land Use	

Sketch Map of Site Sampled:

N

Table G2. Soil properties and their meaning for my personal soil.

Property	Ex. No.	Result	Units	Interpretive Comments*
Textural class name (by feel)			---	
Textural class name (by hydrometer)				
% Sand (by feel)				
% Clay (by feel)				
% Sand (hydrometer)				
% Silt (hydrometer)				
% Clay (hydrometer)				
Color (moist)			----	
Agg. Stability rating			----	
Water content at -5 kPa Ψ_m				
Total organic matter or total organic carbon				
Active organic carbon (POXC)				
pH_{water}			---	
pH_{KCl}				
CEC				
Plant-available P				
Soil survey map unit designation			----	
Soil Taxonomy classification			----	

* Comment on the meaning of the result or indicate how "good" the value is for your intended uses --and why.

CPSIA information can be obtained
at www.ICGtesting.com
Printed in the USA
LVHW010323150721
692686LV00002B/3